UNMASKING
MASCULINITY

Critical studies in men and masculinities

Jeff Hearn and David H.J. Morgan (editors)
Men, masculinites and social theory

David Jackson
Unmasking masculinity
A critical autobiography

David H.J. Morgan
Discovering men (forthcoming)

UNMASKING MASCULINITY

A critical autobiography

DAVID JACKSON

London
UNWIN HYMAN
Boston   Sydney   Wellington

© David Jackson 1990

This book is copyright under the Berne Convention. No
reproduction without permission. All rights reserved.

Published by the Academic Division of

Unwin Hyman Ltd
15/17 Broadwick Street, London W1V 1FP, UK

Unwin Hyman Inc.
955 Massachusetts Avenue, Cambridge, MA 02139, USA

Allen & Unwin (Australia) Ltd,
8 Napier Street, North Sydney, NSW 2060, Australia

Allen & Unwin (New Zealand) Ltd in association with the
Port Nicholson Press Ltd,
Compusales Building, 75 Ghuznee Street, Wellington 1, New Zealand

First published in 1990

British Library Cataloguing in Publication Data

Jackson, David
    Unmasking masculinity : a critical autobiography. – (Men,
    masculinities and social theory).
    1. Masculinity   II. Series
    692.5

    ISBN 0-04-445553-4
    ISBN 0-04-445552-6 pbk

Library of Congress Cataloging in Publication Data

Jackson, David.
    Unmasking masculinity : a critical autobiography / David Jackson.
        p. cm.
    Includes bibliographical references and index.
    ISBN 0-04-445553-4 : $49.95 (U.S.). – ISBN 0-04-445552-6 (pbk.) $14.95
    (U.S.)
    1. Jackson, David.   2. Men–United States–Biography.
    3. Men–United States–Psychology.   4. Masculinity
    (Psychology)–United States.   I. Title.
    HQ1090.3.J33 1990
    305.31′092–dc20   90–12525
                                         CIP

Typeset in 10 on 12 Bembo
Printed by Billing and Son, London and Worcester.

Contents

Series Editor's Preface

Gender is one of the most pervasive and taken-for-granted features of our lives. It figures strongly in the make-up of all societies. Yet it is easy to see that gender may also create problems – in terms of power, oppression, inequality, identity and self-doubt.

The growth of modern feminism and the associated development of women's studies have brought a deep questioning of women's social position. At the same time feminism and women's studies have provided continuing critical analyses of men and masculinities. In a rather different way the rise of gay liberation and gay scholarship has shown that previously accepted notions of sexuality and gender are no longer just 'natural'. This has led to a recognition that the dominant forms of men and masculinities are themselves not merely 'natural' and unchangeable. In addition, inspired particularly by important research in women's studies and the need for a positive response to feminism, some men have in recent years turned their attention to the critical study of men. These various focuses on men are clearly very different from the traditional concern with men that has characterized the social sciences, where in the worst cases men have been equated with people in general. Thus men and masculinities are not seen as unproblematic, but as social constructions which need to be explored, analysed, and indeed in certain respects, such as the use of violence, changed.

This series aims to promote critical studies, by women and men, on men and masculinities. It brings together scholarship that deals in detail with the social and political construction of particular aspects of men and masculinities. This will include studies of the changing forms of men and masculinities, as well as broader historical and comparative studies. Furthermore, because men have been dominant in the writing of social science and production of malestream theory, one area of special interest for critical assessment is the relationship of men and masculinities to social science itself. This applies to both the content and 'result' of previous social research, and to the understanding of social theory in all its various guises – epistemology, ideology, methodology, and so forth.

Each volume in the series will approach its specific topic in the light of feminist theory and practice, and where relevant, gay liberation and gay scholarship. The task of the series is thus the critique of men and masculinities, and not the critique of feminism by men. As such the series is pro-feminist and gay-affirmative. However, this critical stance does not mean that men are simply to be seen or understood negatively. On the contrary, an important part of an accurate study of men and masculinity is an appreciation of the positive features of men's lives, and especially the variety of men's lived experiences. The series includes a range of disciplines – sociology, history, politics, psychoanalysis, cultural studies – as well as encouraging interdisciplinarity where appropriate. Overall, the attempt will be made to produce a series of studies of men and masculinities that are anti-sexist and anti-patriarchal in orientation.

Finally, while this series is primarily an academic development, it will also at times necessarily draw on practical initiatives outside academia. Likewise, it will attempt to speak to changing patterns of men's practice both within and beyond academic study. Just as one of the most exciting aspects of feminism is the strong interrelation of theory and practice, so too must the critical study of men and masculinities and change in men's practice against patriarchy develop in a close association.

Jeff Hearn, 1990

Acknowledgements

I would like to express my thanks and my sense of being indebted to all those people who sustained, motivated and challenged me while writing this book.

It was only through their continuing support, encouragement and often detailed re-reading that I was able to keep going.

So a warm thanks to:

Brenda Mould, Jeff Hearn, John Brown, Norman Todd, Mike Luck, Zbyszek Luczynski, Mike Wilkinson, Robin Cowpertwait, Linda Wickens, Alan Dewar, Mike English, David Morgan, Chris Bristow, Paula Allman, Antonio Melechi, Peter Clough, Shirley Faulkner, Richard Johnson, Graham Dawson, Anne Ousbey and the Italian Consulate for Education, Nottingham.

The *Rover* story, 'The Tough of the Track', is reproduced by kind permission of D. C. Thomson & Co. Ltd.

CHAPTER 1

Introduction

The starting point of critical elaboration is the consciousness of what one really is, and is 'knowing thyself' as a product of the historical process to date which has deposited in you an infinity of traces, without leaving an inventory.

(Antonio Gramsci)[1]

We live at a time when many women are turning away from men for a variety of reasons: structural reasons (economic inequalities), physical survival reasons (violence to women) and personal reasons (emotional neglect). After twenty years of the second wave of the women's movement many women are fed up with waiting for men to come clean about what's been going on in their lives, and what prevents them from moving towards some kind of inner and outer change.

It's now fifteen years since Sheila Rowbotham threw out the challenge to conventional masculinity to start remaking itself by joining in the mutual investigation of gender identity: 'At the same time I sensed something very complicated going on in the heads of men who were about my age. It's for them to write about this. I wish they would very soon.'[2]

The problem is that most men don't feel safe in publicly dealing with Sheila Rowbotham's 'something very complicated'. They feel a complicated mixture of envy, baffled rage and regret at the sight of women turning their backs on them. Also, that process of exposure involves the fear of a loss of identity along with the loss of power, in that they would have to give up their public faces of boldness and strength. Many men hold themselves together through these public presentations of self: through the appearance of correctness and certainty they often forge masterful, controlling selves that help them to maintain a privileged set of divisions and relations. As a result many turn their backs on all that contradictory messiness that threatens to break up their unruffled masks of confidence.

[1]

However, it is this pretence of rational, masterful authority that stops any movement towards change in men. The illusion of mastery is sustained through many men learning to manage a split in their daily lives: the division between their working relations and a whole range of unsettling emotions that they try to keep buttoned up but which leak out in personal relations, usually at home. It is only by recognizing these disturbing inconsistencies (and wanting to do something about them) between public actions/relations and everyday feelings, pains and desires that help men to start opening up their lives.

Many men I know feel numbed and helpless in the face of the need for change. They either suggest that they are inadequate because of individual weakness ('My life is just a can of worms. I daren't open the lid'), or that they are stuck with a fixed, biologically determined personality, that is compulsively driven by wave after wave of urges and needs ('I want to fuck. I need to fuck. I've always needed and wanted to fuck').[3]

That's why if we are to stand a chance of getting more men to change we have to start by challenging and deconstructing the isolating individualism and the apparently fixed and unified identity of men like those above. The seemingly 'natural' and 'normal' behaviour of men who are addicted to pursuing drives, needs, targets, chequered flags has to be challenged by a critical interrogation that reveals that behaviour as being much more damaging than our taken for granted images might have suggested (to others and themselves), contradictory and problematic, and socially and historically shaped.

This gradual opening up of men's everyday behaviour for critical scrutiny is dependent upon the removal of competitive individualism and resignation. It is when men's lives are seen as partly made up of common, collective features that have been produced by social forces, as well as specially singular and unique personal histories, that those lives can become open to political choice and change. It is at the point where 'natural' urges and instincts are converted into explicitly visible options and choices that a growing sense of active, human agency can be developed. Before this recognition there is just the forlorn shrug of the shoulders, muttering, 'I was dealt a rotten hand of cards. All I can do is go on playing them'. But afterwards there can be a more purposeful movement towards, 'Now I can see how my masculinity was made within certain, social frameworks and power relations and I'm now involved in a personal and political struggle to change those frameworks and relations'. Indeed, it is possible to argue, like Bob Connell does, that one of the most important ways of breaking out of the estrangement and dehumanization of a male, oppressor role is by actively reconstructing your identity through the naming and taking of oppositional choices that cut back against the grain of what feels most 'natural': 'What is human is precisely the process of constructing oneself by choices that transcend given circumstances.'[4]

In more precise detail, what going beyond the 'given' and the 'natural' in men's lives means is a process of critical understanding, linked to changing relations and actions. This process connects up the web of social, cultural and psychological forces that go into the making of masculinities, at different historical moments and in different regions and places. That includes a developing, conscious awareness of the daily, institutional practices and routines of the family, school, church, peer group, clubs, workplaces, interwoven with psychoanalytic perspectives, and cultural and ideological struggles over the meaning of masculinity, like in the media (such as boys' comics, boys' toys etc.)

This autobiography sees itself as a part of that process of critical understanding. Its potential for personal and social change is that it can play a part in the undermining of those assumptions of what it is to be a 'real' man in this culture.

What is now needed is for more men to come out of hiding and to start excavating, in public, the sedimented layers of their own particular and diverse life histories. Men urgently need to delve much more deeply into the contradictory construction of their masculine identities. And into the hidden networks of male power that are so effectively concealed in those constructions. Hopefully, other men can learn from these newly mapped terrains. They can recognize the similar features of certain parts of the landscape, and also notice the differences in particular parts of the journey, especially in terms of race, class, sexual orientation, religion, disablement and age. Specific and detailed accounts such as these, or (in Gramsci's terms) 'critical inventories', are needed to counter essentialist categories, like man as the natural hunter and aggressive predator, so commonly found in dominant, heterosexual culture.

However, to write effective, critical autobiography is a complex task. Working within the established legacies and conventions of

[3]

traditional, male autobiography makes it very difficult to escape
entirely from the known format – the familiar narrative patterning,
the definition of what is important and meaningful in men's lives
etc. Stories of energetic activity in the public domain, tales of
playful, boyhood 'scrapes', sporting success, fights, the first sexual
encounter – all of these familiar features can't just be uncritically
accepted, however exuberant and convincing their telling is. The
triumphs of male personality can't just be celebrated. All of these
features have to be scrutinized through the critical lens of anti-sexist
values and an awareness of how gender identity is put together for
the account to become useful to other men. That often means trying
to dissociate the condition of maleness from the cultural construction of masculinity by explicitly pointing out the taken-for-granted
benefits and privileges that exist in a gender-blind and power-blind
world. Along with this goes an attempt to expose 'male as norm'
assumptions that often appear to give some men an established right
to grab the limelight and take up a centre stage position.

As Ros Coward[5] suggests, if autobiographies are to question
rather than endorse dominant ideologies, then personal histories
cannot just be unanalytically confessional but they have to be
integrated into a critical frame that excites and provokes an engaged
questioning in the reader. The aim here in 'Unmasking Masculinity'
is to try and move towards a new 'genre that would fuse theoretical
and confessional writing'[6] – a form that would keep open a dynamic
negotiation between the specific incidents, atmospheres and events
of a personal history and a critical analysis that would investigate conventional assumptions about masculinity. The constructive
tension in this negotiation would often come from the changing
relations between the interpretative framework and the personal
stories themselves. It would come from the framework, at times,
dictating the selection and quality of the personal history events, to
other occasions where the power of the personal stories, through
their charged ability to engross the reader emotionally, might
generate and define the terms of an analysis that wouldn't iron
out the independent complexities of the stories.

This book, then, represents a first, tentative step towards such a
new form of autobiography that has learned from what has gone
before but also tries to tread its own distinctive path as well.
The process of unmasking comes from the questioning of the
seeming inevitability of traditional masculinity, by combining the

idiosyncrasies of my personal testimony with a critical commentary that emphasizes the collective and relational features of such a life history.

Some of the key, distinctive features of the new form are explained below.

Autobiography as critical inquiry

Refusing the search for the true self

This book rejects the familiar, quest format for autobiography – 'in search of the true self' – because that implies a naive acceptance of autobiography as unmediated experience, or self-expression. What lies at the centre of the questing for the authentic self is the illusion of transparency. But transparent recall to reveal a neutral, fixed, absolutely truthful past does not exist.

What we have instead is a blurring of the boundaries between truth and fiction. Autobiography is much more like fictional reconstruction, loosely based on life-history events. So when I'm investigating my past, all the personal memories I have to work from are hints, glimpses, snatched conversations, shreds of unreliable information that have been reworked in the light of the present/past dialogue (see p.7), and the changing cultural codes and images which I feel both a part of and increasingly outside.

Often the sharp details of life-history events have faded, have had other stories plastered over them, or been too neatly rehearsed over the years. Instead, what I'm left with is a shadowy emotional structure, made up of atmospheres that often imply social relations, a hazy sense of power differentials, an elusive flavour that marks that particular moment. To re-create that emotional structure I have to invent other factual details and backgrounds that seem to fit into my selective reconstruction of that emotional structure.

Also more deliberate personal and family-history investigation can help here. Oral-history testimonies from sisters, brothers, aunts, uncles, parents, grandparents can often produce unusual perspectives, different viewpoints that can awaken other ways of looking at life-history episodes and relationships about which you thought you knew all there was to know. My sisters' testimonies have certainly done that for me.

[5]

Life-history deconstructions in other forms are also very useful, like Jo Spence's visual investigation of her family photograph album 'to identify the process by which I had been "put together"'. In *Visual Autobiography: Beyond the Family Album*[7] she sets out to explore the silences and gaps implied by the selection of pictures of herself in the album.

To do this she looks beyond the literal surface of the faces to the conventional class- and gender-related fictions, codes and frameworks through which those faces have been selectively arranged and interpreted. She critically decodes the arranged 'looks' on her face through the years, ranging from Shirley Temple, through Petula Clark to an 'Easy Rider' image of herself in rebellious dark glasses. She also shows how other suppressed images, that challenge the happy, harmonious face of family life, can be used to oppose traditional visual rhetoric.

The myth of unified identity

This book also challenges the myth of unified identity and self. The quest narrative also implies an authentic core or essence at the heart of identity. All the seeker has to do is to strip away the onion-skin layers of deception and the authentic self will be revealed. The difficulties in this approach lie in the assumption that there is a stable, coherent identity, or a kernel of 'I'-ness just waiting to be uncovered.

Instead this book works inconsistently within the oppositional image of decentred, fragmentary 'I's that are constantly shifting over time and in different contexts and interactions. This notion of multiple identities, formed within different discursive frameworks, seems to have advantages and disadvantages. It usefully escapes the trap of essentialist views of the self, and makes those acts of building selves much more contradictory and open to change.

But fragmentariness can also dissolve into isolated, individual acts rather than build up collective strength. Perhaps we need a more dialectical view that tries to bring together an awareness of multiple identities with a recognition that some versions of the self seem to be more significant than others. Perhaps they seem more important because they offer a greater continuity and coherence to us at times of flux. This can mean inviting us to embrace the illusory safety of a temporary 'real me', while, at the same time, being in the midst of other transitional selves that are continuously coming into conflict with the 'real me'?

Rethinking the relationship between past and present

we ourselves are shaped by the past, but are also continually reworking the past which shapes us.[8]

In the process of writing this book I've tried to problematize the relationship between past and present, very much in the spirit of the above quotation.

What this means for me is that the significance of past events isn't immutably set for all time, but is constantly being selectively edited and refocused in terms of my present-day world-view and dominant view of myself. I have been very powerfully influenced by the socio-economic structures and the frameworks of thought and interpretation that I grew up in, but all the time I am in the process of reworking those legacies in the light of changing relations, experiences, new perspectives in the present moment of time.

These approaches inform my references to the remembering process in the book. I've tried to remain loyal to this dialogue between past and present in the way I've tied together a mixture of adult retrospective viewpoints and other attempts to get under the skin of what it might have felt like to be there as a young boy in 1947. That's why I've occasionally used clumsy phrases like: 'Looking back now from a very different vantage point I can reconstruct one brief moment of my life as. . .'

Challenging chronological, linear sequence

An awareness of identity as much more diverse, precarious and contradictory also implies a need to dismantle the illusion of chronological, linear sequence in the telling that goes with an imaginary unity in the self.

Unmasking Masculinity sets out to challenge the fake, hierarchical order that conventional, linear, male autobiography offers for the organization of our lives. Instead of being squeezed into the tight, uni-directional focus of an ascending, step-by-step goal, striving towards an ultimate, male achievement, my way of telling is structured much more around the idea that narrative time 'springs forth in the plural unity of future, past and present'[9].

What that means in practice is an attempt to arrange each chapter, thematically, so that there is an interweaving of time references to different periods of my life. Generally, that interweaving cuts across a rigidly chronological ordering of my autobiographical raw material but there are exceptions. For example, in Chapter 6 on sexuality I use a strictly linear approach to indicate the historical origins and also the linked continuity of my present sexual identities.

In another chapter we have a much more scrambled approach to time references in my life. In Chapter 5 on my relations with my father the interlinking of the themes – men in families and the relationships between fathers and sons – could only be suggested by moving back and forth, between generations, in a totally non-chronological way. To show, in detail, how this works look at the first half of that chapter:

(a) Toy fort episode : 1947–8.
(b) My grandfather's problems as an Italian immigrant : 1895–1930.
(c) Death of my father : 1972.
(d) Crying after arguments with my father : 1953–4.
(e) Christmas party at Torquay fire station : 1946–7.
(f) Present-moment contrast between me writing upstairs and builders working outside : 1989.

Acknowledging diversity in my approach to different chapters

I haven't tried to impose a unified consistency of approach on each chapter. Instead, each chapter generates its own method of telling, and its own particular relationship between the personal stories and the critical comments.

In some chapters, like 'Relations with my father', I have started from an initial, muddled way of feeling and allowed that to generate the continuing structure of the chapter. In others, like Chapter 9 on everyday violence, I have started the other way round, from critical categories that I've tried to use in understanding my autobiographical stories.

In others, like Chapter 7, 'Critical language autobiography', I have begun the chapter in the direct experience of using language in 1988–9 and gradually worked backwards towards an analysis of how I came, historically, to develop my language habits and relations, by trying to set them within the clashes between various discursive frameworks of understanding.

The problem of voice in critical autobiography

Always I have found the tension between different authorial voices an unsolved dilemma. In most of the chapters there is an uneasy transition between an autobiographical voice that seems to be 'telling it the way it was' and a critical/theoretical voice that feels ponderous in comparison. Perhaps in other parts, like that describing playing rugby and gaining my school colours in Chapter 10, I manage to move towards a position where the experience and the commentary begin to merge, but occasionally the mismatch in tone and voice is clearly there.

This tension in the book between different voices and styles is partly historically constructed. I grew up intellectually, as an English teacher, within a liberal-humanist framework of interpretation. I made a large emotional investment in the identity offered by that framework's field of 'personal growth'. That way of looking at the world – its uncritical acceptance of the primacy of personal experience, individual self-expression, and a search for an authentic, personal response – influenced me deeply.

I came to assume that honesty and emotional fidelity to my lived experience was everything. All I had to do was locate my 'true voice'. The result of those assumptions was to build in me a destructive split between self and society, between spontaneous feeling and critical thinking. In some ways, the effort to dissolve that split in me is at the heart of this book.

The historical legacies of that education in 'personal growth' were to make me feel more comfortable when I'm dealing with the deceptively 'direct experience' of my life stories. Usually I feel confident within a conventionally literary, autobiographical voice. Where it becomes awkward is when I shift into my critical commentary voice, in mid-paragraph. Some of that awkwardness for me is that that alternative voice comes out of a totally different, interpretative framework (derived from sociology, politics, critical theory etc.) that I've been grappling with over the last fifteen years or so.

Within this relatively new framework I feel much more insecure at times and this insecurity has often been deepened by the strain of writing against my emotional grain, without the supportive

[9]

network of being in continuing conversation with an audience who might understand what I was struggling to say. When I'm positioned in this political and critical terrain I feel slightly unsafe around the languages, styles and voices of social science and politics. I feel that I'm much more exposed in this space, measuring myself up against the 'correct' right-on-ness of Heavy Lefties, or defending myself against a prestigious academic community. That is why, at times of maximum insecurity (around difficult, unfamiliar ideas), I have a tendency to hide away behind the relative safety of established interpretation, borrowed voices and quotation. Superficially, this borrowed language of critical analysis and quotation might look a bit pushy. But it is actually very defensive. The quotations and borrowed voices work like lifejackets in a choppy sea, offering points of reassurance in a strangely disorientating arena. This need for reassurance also works at an emotional level; in the chapters like 'Family' and 'Sexuality' – where I still feel all at sea about some of the attachments and conflicts – I often reach for a distancing language when the emotional confrontation is too immediately painful or confusing.

However, these features of my autobiographical voices only become faults when seen against the strong temptation to present the text as a smooth, seamless flow, the product of a unified, consistent, single voice. Viewed in this way, the fissures and cracks in the writing need to be concealed and faked out as minor interruptions to the seamless flow. But there's another way of looking at all this.

Once the text is seen as an attempt at critical deconstruction, then the sense of disjointedness in the writing doesn't disappear but can be seen as a more positive collision between the wider social structures trying to become more visible and the life stories. Through this stylistic jarring or collision, the reader is sometimes provoked to want to reflect critically on the deceptive familiarity of her/his life stories (see Chapter 12 for a longer exploration of this point).

That's when the bumpy and uneven process of reading this book becomes a part of the critical intentions of the text. The making of my masculinity was never a conflict-free, seamless construction. My sense of myself as 'masculine' was only ever maintained as a social fiction through huge tension and strain. Keeping faith, as a writer, to that emotional strain has produced a very bumpy read but I don't want to apologize for that. The bumpiness stops being seen as an irritating fault and becomes more of an approach to set up a critical dialogue with the reader. It begins to be a technique of breaking the reader out of a settled, habituated relationship to her/his past, and a way of opening up a greater range of possible interpretations of these supposedly 'spontaneous' life experiences.

Refusing a split between the personal and the social

There is a common criticism, heard in many Left groups, of this kind of autobiographical project. Some say it's too self-indulgent, too introspective, too individualized. Or there is the dismissive sneer of 'lifestyle politics', that reductively fits this kind of autobiography into the polarities of economic/class politics or navel-gazing.

This dualistic way of thinking is so wasteful because it wrenches apart the interlocking between self and society that is at the heart of this book. Patterns of feeling, attachments, sensual pleasures, 'the burden of pain and desire' can't be kept separate from the invisible network of social structures. Rather they dovetail into each other at every point. As Russell Jacoby comments: 'The prevailing subjectivity is no oasis in a barren and dehumanised society; rather it is structured down to its core by the very society it fantasises it left behind'[10].

This book doesn't want to wallow in the individualized recollections of the personal-memoir kind of writing, or search for the true self in the inner recesses of the personal psyche. Instead it wants to attack critically the dichotomies, divisions, separate categories that split the personal from the social. It sees as an urgent part of this process of redefinition the attempt to cut through the warping dualisms of subjectivity/objectivity, personal/social, masculine/feminine etc.

Political agency in critical autobiography

Another important priority within this book is the emphasis placed on active, political agency. I have taken pains not to represent myself as a passive and powerless dummy. The dominant code of manliness wasn't just submissively accepted and reproduced in me, in a mechanical way.

I want to suggest that in every person's life history, even in the most repressive circumstances like the strictly regulated, authoritarian ethos of the boarding school I went to between 1952 and 1959, there are always daily acts of contestation, hidden ambivalences, cultural clashes and resistances going on, if you are prepared to spend time burrowing beneath the deceptively settled surface.

I want to guard against reducing my active resilience to what was going on around me, in a possibly over-determined, monolithic view of the collision between a dominating and subordinated culture. Clearly I was viciously constrained and positioned (to some degree) by that dominating culture, as is described in Chapter 9 on everyday violence in an all-boys' secondary school in the 1950s. But as I recognize in the chapter, the living dynamic that I experienced in that school was 'much more complex with inconsistencies, challenges and contradictions on both sides' (pupils and the teachers).

Acknowledging the structural
In all of this detail on particular, personal histories in the book, there is a tendency to lose sight of the underlying structural relations of power and subordination. As a result, there is a need to acknowledge the continuing force of the structural in shaping people's lives, while still hanging on to active, political agency.

But there is also a need to go on expanding our familiar definitions of what makes up the structures of domination and exploitation in society today. Although appreciating how gender and class relations interlock at every stage, this book's primary emphasis on gender relations of inequality implies a recognition that we have over-stressed the industrial mode of production at the expense of the domestic mode, and often go on using the imagery of production to conceal the relations of the reproductive mode.

By this I mean that the structure of gender inequality between women and men is tied in to the power relations within the domestic mode (the site of the family and the connected social segregation between the unequal spheres of the public and the private). Acknowledging that has forced me into understanding the importance of the invisible structures at work within the domestic arena, and has helped me to move away from an over-concentration on class relations in the workplace, in a crude, economic sense.

These invisible, reproductive structures work to secure men's domination over women. They do this through 'a complex of relationships in which men secure the sexual, child-rearing and labour services of women'[11] that benefit men every day of their lives. The complex reality of male power (including my own) involves, as Lynne Segal suggests, the gendered division of labour, 'institutions of authority (political, judicial, educational and medical) and, finally, family arrangements, tied in with patterns of desire and the expression and control of sexuality'.[12]

What are the personal roots of this autobiography?

The tension between the power I felt in the world of work (being a successful Secondary English teacher who edited textbooks, gave talks up and down the country, and wrote a stream of articles and books on English teaching and education) and a constant sense of wobbliness and precariousness in my emotional life, finally came to a head in my forties.

My awareness of the dislocation between what I said I believed in and my frequently destructive actions (often using and manipulating women for my own ends) gradually provoked a critical stocktaking and re-ordering that was a part of a more general life crisis.

My previously shaky attempts to achieve a confirming performance, as a man precarious within his conventional masculinity, eventually collapsed into physical breakdown. I found I couldn't sustain the old image of myself as a Hero Innovator, pioneering new approaches to Secondary English teaching, speaking evangelically at conferences about 'quality of feeling', and then allowing myself to casually drift into the occasional, conference affair. The force of the internal contradiction, and the mixture of feeling temporarily high with an intense distress, afterwards, finally cracked the old image right across.

These disjunctures were incredibly painful. And they all seemed interrelated in some strange way. I gave up my job as Head of English, and refused the invitation to become a Senior teacher. A long-term relationship broke up and then gradually repaired itself. I moved house three times, and underwent major heart surgery. I was in hospital for sixteen weeks.

It was an incredibly traumatizing time for me and my partner. What I learnt from it was that I couldn't go on imposing my conscious will on my feelings and bodily experience, and that I had to learn, however painfully, how to bring my feelings and my head together again.

Most of the time, after being in hospital, was spent having to avoid a confrontation with the really painful issues that I felt ashamed of and traumatized about and therefore wanted to keep buried. But slowly I got glimpses of what these issues were about. Erratically, these glimpses began to activate a process of critical reflection on the mouldering patterns of behaviour and entrenched assumptions associated with conventional masculinity. I began to awaken to other ways of relating and being in the world. I slowly and painfully learnt to come off pushing myself towards performance targets and deadlines. And gradually, with the developing wish to move in the world in a different way, came a critical consciousness of how I had been used and named by a twisted, exploitative, heterosexual culture. Alongside that, and more difficult to admit, came a dawning recognition of how much I had myself leaned on, used and been serviced by women.

Finally I stopped guilt-tripping and blaming myself and decided to do something about it. I began to see the differences between pathologizing my condition and staying where I was, and becoming a part of the creative effort to grapple for inner and outer change, redefining what seemed most 'natural' for a compulsively heterosexual man like me to do.

This book has emerged out of a six-year struggle to place myself in the world in a different way. It has played its part in helping me to re-name myself, not as an alternative hero, but as a more loving and fallible man who is now more aware of the defensive lies at the heart of a deformed culture of manliness and wants to do something about it.

No doubt the reader will find her/his own way around the book, skipping, jumping on, going back to read a particular chapter again. A strictly sequential read, from front to back, might not be the most pleasurable way of fitting your own personal style of reading to the special way the book has been put together. Certainly, there isn't one, single, best way to read this book. But perhaps a few words are needed about the varied, reading options provided by the opening chapters. I bring this up because there are at least three main ways of beginning or getting into the book.

Firstly, if you want to start straight off with reading about my early, childhood experiences in the family, then it might be best to begin with the 'Family' and 'Relations with my father' chapters and then work through towards the 'Sporting activities and masculinities' chapter.

These first two chapters provide a detailed setting for my life history. The stories are put into a chronological framework needed to understand my personal history and family background. Then, later, it might be the right time to flick back to the start of the book to have a look at the missed chapters.

Secondly, if you're more interested in how I came to write such a book, and the book's relation to my more recent past and present circumstances, then perhaps you need to start with Chapter 3, 'Falling apart'. This chapter gives an account of the emotional crisis about my masculine identity that activated this process of life history reconstruction.

You might like to read this chapter alongside two other parts of the book; my personal comment about the origins of this autobiography (pages 13–14), and then perhaps a quick glimpse into the section on 'What critical life history work has meant to me and how did I get to this present position?', (pages 253–9). These overlapping pieces might help you to understand the critical relationship between the *then* and the *now*, in re-creating a version of my past life.

Thirdly, if your main focus as a reader is on why I put my life story together in this particular form, style, voice – then it might be a good idea to begin with Chapter 2, 'Other forms of critical autobiography'. This deals with the varied potentialities and challenges of the 'life-comprehension form', and shows the diverse choices which were open to me as I defined my own autobiographical framework and organization. Throughout the book there is a rough attempt to focus on my 'pre-adult' life, up to the age of twenty. Of course, there are many exceptions to this as I shuttle backward and forward between my present position in 1990 and earlier times in my life. But, generally, the spotlight is thrown onto the formative experiences of my first twenty years.

Notes

1   Q. Hoare and G. Nowell-Smith (eds) (1971) *Antonio Gramsci: Selections from the Prison Notebooks*, London, Lawrence & Wishart.
2   S. Rowbotham (1973) *Woman's consciousness, man's world*, Harmondsworth, Penguin.

3   See the discussion on 'the male sexual drive discourse', in W. Hollway, 'Gender difference and the production of subjectivity', included in J. Henriques *et al.* (1984) *Changing the Subject*, London, Methuen.

4   R. W. Connell (1987) *Gender and Power*, Cambridge, Polity.

5   R. Coward (1984) 'Cautionary tales' (on feminist autobiographies), in *New Socialist*, July/August.

6   E. Wilson (1988) 'Tell it like it is: women and confessional writing', in S. Radstone (ed.) *Sweet dreams*, London, Lawrence & Wishart.

7   J. Spence (1986) *Putting myself in the picture*, London, Camden Press.

8   C. Hill (1974) *Change and Continuity in Seventeenth-Century England*, London, Weidenfeld & Nicolson; quoted in *Making Histories* (1982), London, Hutchinson/Centre for Contemporary Cultural Studies.

9   P. Ricoeur (1981) 'Narrative time', in W. Mitchell (ed.) *On Narrative*, Chicago, University of Chicago Press.

10   R. Jacoby (1976) *Social Amnesia*, Brighton, Harvester.

11   The argument here is indebted to A. Brittan (1989) *Masculinity and Power*, Oxford, Basil Blackwell.

12   L. Segal (1990) *Slow motion: Changing masculinities. Changing men*, London, Virago.

CHAPTER 2

Other forms of critical autobiography

In writing this book my decision to try out a critical autobiographical form wasn't just plucked out of thin air. It gradually emerged out of a growing familiarity with many different strands of life story, political essay and other forms of autobiography read over many years. It is these varied potentialities that have opened my eyes to the inner subtleties and challenges of the form. They have also helped me in a slow process of awakening to the possibility of new connections, relationships and cross-overs between conventionally separate features within the form.

What I want to do in this chapter is to present a highly selective review of some of the major autobiographical influences on me while writing this book. I also want to invite the reader to travel some of the tortuous pathways that I've moved down to arrive at this present position where I'm approaching the writing of a critical autobiography in this particular kind of way.

Probably the most useful place to start, within an anti-patriarchal focus, is to begin this review with a critique of traditional, male autobiography. More specifically I'd like to draw out some general points from a reading of three traditional, men's autobiographies:[1] *The Autobiography* by Geoff Boycott, a sporting autobiography; *Going Solo* by Roald Dahl, a children's writer's autobiography; and *Personally Speaking* by David Owen, a political autobiography.

On one level this offers me a point of critical departure as a writer in defining the focus of what I want to do in opposition to the well-worn conventions of that kind of male autobiography.

A critical exploration of traditional male autobiography

The face a man turns to the world. . .typically embodies his strength.

(Patricia Spacks)[2]

The second part of Roald Dahl's autobiography, *Going Solo*, is crammed with vigorous and dramatic events. It concerns his first job working for Shell in East Africa, and then flying as a fighter pilot in the Second World War. He has adventures with black and green mambas, sees the cook's wife saved from a lion, crash-lands in the Western Desert, and is involved in many dog-fights in the desperate aerial war against the Germans in 1941.

What these events leave out is any deep sense of the person that these things happened to. Dahl, Boycott and Owen all seem content to put on a brave, confident face to meet the questions of the world around them. Indeed, what seems most important to all of them is 'the imperative of affirmation',[3] of holding themselves together at all costs, of keeping their spirits up by limiting their focus on energetic activity in the public domain.

Estelle Jelinek[4] is surely right when she suggests that the majority of autobiographies, both male and female, have more to do with fictional deception and concealment than with their assumed qualities of confessional self-disclosure. Certainly most male autobiography is about rewriting a life in terms of the need to keep up a public, brave face. This is achieved, in Dahl, Boycott and Owen, at the expense of domestic and personal details, and any emotional account of distress, hate, love, fear and uncertainty.

An example of this is to be found in Boycott's *The Autobiography*, where this projected image of confident success in cricket is dependent on his ability to shut out all emotional crisis and personal difficulty from his public life as 'Mr Runs', as he and his ghost writer call him. In the midst of a running battle between Boycott as captain of Yorkshire and the Yorkshire cricket committee who are trying to get rid of him, Boycott suddenly reveals another shock – his mother has cancer.

The following morning I set off for Birmingham and Yorkshire's next match against Warwickshire – but not before I received another shock which shook me rigid. My mum confessed that she was having trouble with a lump under her arm and admitted when I questioned her that it had been there for at least a year. 'I didn't want to worry you, you've enough problems of your own', she said. I'm no doctor but I had heard and read about cancer. I suppose it's the first thing that comes into your mind. It was clearly worrying mum, which was why she hadn't said anything. I bundled her off to a doctor and she came back telling me that he was sending her off for tests. Driving down to Birmingham I was totally preoccupied with worries about my mum and the latest madness at Yorkshire. I got a speeding ticket and I don't think I gave a damn. The meeting with the committee was ringing in my ears. 'Talk to them, take them on one side', said Brennan. 'I don't care if you never score another hundred for England, it's Yorkshire that concerns me', said Ryan. I scored a century against Warwickshire, which meant that I might achieve my hundred first-class century in a Test match, which had never been done before. And amazingly, the next Test was at Headingley.

Boycott doesn't allow his worries about his mother (real enough as they are) to undermine his commitment to his rising arc of progress and winning glory in the public world. Instead of trying to let the reader into his present state of feeling, it's as if he keeps the world of pain and distress at bay through concentrating his attention on the cricketing details. He is able to split apart his personal and public worlds so that rigid boundaries are maintained between them. Although he is emotionally preoccupied, he is able to seal off his personal life from his life as Mr Runs, when he needs to. As a result he is able to report matter-of-factly his clocking up of yet another century on his way to another *Boy's Own* peak of fame and glory.

These gaps and inadequacies have repercussions in the sphere of gender relations. Conventional male autobiography imposes a definition[5] of what is purposeful and meaningful in life on to women, and more vulnerable masculinities. It does this through building an impression of imaginary unity, of a professional life that develops like a sky rocket. From a usually spluttering start it ascends in a curving loop to burst, in the performance climax, into a flowering cluster of exclamatory stars. Anything that deflects from this rising trajectory – the daily round of domestic happenings, emotional crises, close friendships, the everyday complexities of initimate relationships – are ruthlessly cut back, or ignored, as if they never existed. So here Boycott's life story is closely targeted on achievement goals like his hundred, first-class centuries. The implied definition of a meaningful life is realized through the whole movement of his autobiography – the upward striving towards public glory. Everything else is marginalized by comparison.

Similarly in David Owen's autobiography, after the usual playfully innocent childhood (the 'scruffy urchin' adventures and scrapes) his life story is cast into the narrative mould of preparing the reader for the later public achievement – his rise to fame as Foreign Secretary in the last Labour government and Leader of the SDP and joint Leader of the Alliance. What 'personally speaking' means to him is giving his account of the behind-the-scenes manoeuvrings of international crises like those in Rhodesia, Iran and the Falklands. For him, life purpose is very much taking up a centre stage position in world affairs. In contrast, people who aren't directly a part of these world stage negotiations are subordinated.

A sense of how one should approach writing about people and their lives comes through these male autobiographies like David Owen's. People are divided up into 'significant people', almost always men, and the others who are usually around for decorative purposes, almost always women. A striking example of this is shown at the moment where he enters the social circle of a London restaurant called The Bistro:

> There was always a most interesting collection of people there, most of them reguiars, and all knowing each other: Milton Shulman, the well-known *Evening Standard* drama critic; Peter Jenkins, industrial and later political correspondent, first on the *Guardian*, now on the *Independent*; a fashion photographer, Claude Virgin; an MP, Sir Clive Bossom; people from the theatre; diplomats; the novelist Alan Williams; and always some unusually attractive girls.

The men are entitled to their names and careers because of their public fame. The women are reduced to an anonymous backdrop

[20]

of 'attractive' scenery, whose only purpose is to embellish and possibly service the men.

The only suitable narrative shape for these male life stories that obsessively aim for the fulfilment of a single goal in a successful career or in public life is a chronological, linear form. Whereas women's lives and stories are more scattered, fragmentary, diverse, men's lives and stories are strictly funnelled into the uni-directional focus of the progressive pursuit of success, achievement and performance. In all these autobiographies there is an illusion of objectivity and detachment aimed for, instead of an attempt to make personal sense out of the often uncomfortable, daily flux of people's lives. It's as if a predetermined, interpretative framework (the sky-rocket narrative) is imposed on these men's lives to make the construct bearable, rather than allowing life in all its fears to suggest a more contradictory, sometimes painful and illuminating narrative.

The early hardships of Boycott's life, and the minor setbacks in all three (having to wear glasses in Boycott's case, crash-landing in the Western Desert in Dahl's case) are all justified by later worldly triumphs (Dahl shooting down his first German plane over Greece and surviving the Battle of Athens and Boycott's sporting feats achieved through an aggressive determination to win). The linear development of David Owen's life story is suggested by the titles of his first three chapters:

1. Forebears, Childhood, School.
2. Cambridge, Medical School, The Labour Party.
3. Into Parliament and Minister for the Navy.

There is a bolstering male, autobiographical, literary tradition that lends authority to the conventional contours of these narratives, dwelling on childhood as a time of playful innocence (crunching boiled sweets to irritate his grandfather in Owen's case, and putting a dead mouse into a sweet jar in Dahl's first autobiography, *Boy*), through a few early setbacks where lessons are learned, and then a victorious culmination through which the point and meaning of a lifetime are discovered.

What all three autobiographies have in common is the isolated individualism of all three writers. In different ways they set about constructing fictions of the lonely male hero achieving success or affirmation through energy, determination or willpower. They all take for granted that the benefits they enjoy all come from their own individual efforts rather than the invisible advantages of being male within a male-dominant society. In doing this they ignore the alternative possibilities of more collective and relational identities.[6]

At times in their autobiographies each of the writers takes on a totally uncritical, 'the world is my oyster' approach to the openings offered by their lives. Boycott is told by Neville Cardus, 'With your skill you can do whatever you like', and Dahl, in the middle of his flying training, brims over with an unlimited sense of new possibilities, tinged with self-critical irony: 'We ourselves were bursting with energy and exuberance and perhaps a touch of self-importance as well because now we were intrepid flying men and devils of the sky.'

The inherited privileges of being white, middle-class and a dominant, heterosexual male (although Boycott is a more complex, case) seem to blind all three men to the social forces that have partly shaped their lives. Certainly masculinity, as one of these social forces, is never made critically explicit as an object of inquiry.[7] All we get instead are the hidden, unquestioned norms of male superiority and privilege. This unconscious superiority is most clearly seen in the false universality (i.e. male experience = human experience) of all three men's accounts of their lives. They all want to pass their life experiences off as being able to speak, confidently and representatively, for the general condition of being human by using an objective, distanced manner of telling. They assumed that they were so special that they had a natural right to speak for others. But it's only when this false universality is exposed and demystified that the reader can see that tone of established universality as an integral part of that system of male power that silences women's perspectives, and other, more contradictory male ones.

'Colloquial, excited, immediate': the life history approach to people's lives

The main challenge to the hegemony of masculine myths of objectivity and rational detachment located in some of their autobiographies came from life-history work in all its forms.[8] First-hand engagement in the immediate, here-and-now, from

the edited selections of tape-recorded oral history life stories to
the more considered written life-history accounts, acted as a way
of breaking apart the falsely monolithic objectivity of those male
myths. I encountered that delighted shock of revaluing the personal
in three main areas of life-history work; feminist, gay and in the
anti-sexist men's movement.

Feminist life history work

> I no longer clung to that bleak pretence of objectivity routinely
> required of PhD candidates. . .My language had to reflect
> the experience itself: colloquial, excited, immediate. . .I was
> writing at last out of direct emotional involvement. I began
> to write the way I talk and feel.
>
> (Kate Millett)[9]

Initially, this emphasis on directness and immediacy of experience
was a part of women reclaiming the meaning of their lives through
life-history work. It was also there to combat the dominant, male-
defined version of what counted as a significant life. And to expose
how men's 'objective' truths worked as a way of swallowing up,
ignoring or silencing women's perspectives.

There was a new kind of dignity and self-respect (both in class
and gender terms) connected to these neglected viewpoints that
called into question the unruffled authority of these objective
accounts. The self-respect was associated with a vigorous, often
vernacular movement of women's voices talking confidently in
a relaxed and safe context. Like the voice of Maggie Fuller from
Dutiful Daughters[10] talking about her mother's advice for dealing
with periods:

> She gets me into this room, and I'll never forget it, and she
> said to me, 'When you're like that', she said, 'you just keep
> away from men'. I think now it's an awful thing she done;
> then I don't know what I thought. She got a bairn's nappy
> and showed me how to put it on! (Laughs). And do you know
> what I used when I was like that? When I saw a man I used to
> run like hell – I did!

and Marjorie Reeves from *Fenwomen*[11] on domestic service:

There weren't nothing else, only service, you see. And I loathed the idea of going to work for someone. Because in those days, you wore caps and aprons and I always felt there was something in me that I couldn't do it – I couldn't bear to be a maid to somebody. Open the door, 'Yes Ma'am'. Oh no. Even broad work (working in the fields, like potato-picking) was a freedom, compared to that.

However, that initial stress on the experiential ('the personal is political') could only take us some of the way. The need for an autobiographical mode that would take us beyond individual experience to look at 'the forces which shape our lives – make us what we are and where we live what it is'[12] was also being articulated. Without some kind of critical understanding of those social forces interacting with the personal stories, the autobiographical form could become isolated and limited.

The feminist treatment of life histories developed in response to these anxieties. A new kind of relationship was needed between the personal and the social/historical elements. Judith Okeley showed one, possible way forward by setting parts of her own life history within an ethnographic, interpretative framework. In her 'Privileged, schooled and finished: boarding education for girls'[13] she breaks from the linear, chronological expectations of a traditional telling by using feminist, thematic categories as a means of critical understanding. Her own personal account of going to a girls' boarding school is seen through the critical lens of a gendered analysis of her 'separation from urban life, from economic production and members of other social classes, from parents and home, and the separation by gender'. The analysis is sharply done and constantly illuminating but there are unresolved tensions between her life stories and the analytical structure that she fits them into. Are the life-history details there to neatly slot into, and illustrate, the predetermined structure, or could the analytical structure be built up through the engagement with and complexity of the life stories?

An example of what I'm talking about is found in the section on 'Containment and powerlessness' in girls' boarding schools.

Just as space, so was time subjected to a changeless grid. An electric bell rang at half-hour intervals, or more often.

There was no unorganised time for doing what we wanted or going where we wanted, even at weekends. No way to decide for ourselves the next move. After lessons our prep was supervised: often seventy silent girls sat in one long room. We had no private studies. One of the very few times when the girls were not within sight of an adult was 'after lights out' in the dormitory. The punishment for talking or being found out of bed was therefore the severest. We defied the invasions of our privacy which surveillance implied by hiding in the lavatory or bathroom. I would climb onto the roof at night. A former inmate confessed that she even went for moonlit walks in the grounds. The constraints on space and time were further compounded by the rules imposing silence during the ten or so hours between lights out and the morning bell.

The strangulation of independent initiative is precisely detailed. The reader is invited to understand these details, not as a uniquely individual life story, but as the common, social features of girls' boarding schools in Britain at a particular time, that might have relevance for other places, times and contexts. But there is also an unease in committing herself to her own personal story. Generally she hides herself within the collective 'we'/'the girls did this' way of telling. The point at which she switches into a direct reference to her own search for a breathing space is conspicuous in its brevity: 'I would climb onto the roof at night!'

Judith Okely's distrust of the representativeness and reliability[14] of the life-history approach prevents her from achieving a state where theoretical commentary and life stories can co-exist in a much more reciprocal form. The critical issues aren't gradually built up through her emotional investment in her own personal history. As a result, the full vitality and complexity of her own autobiography is edited down into the representative details that are needed by the critical structure. These tensions are very much at the heart of a movement towards life-history work that investigates the relations between the personal and the social. And I am entangled in them myself as I work my way through the different chapters of my autobiography. That's why I draw attention to them, here, as continuing dilemmas that I face within my own writing, with no easy solutions.

Another collection of autobiographical essays that tried to move beyond the prison of individual experience is *Truth, Dare or Promise: Girls Growing Up in the Fifties*,[15] edited by Liz Heron. All the contributions are worth reading but I'd like to concentrate my focus on just one essay 'Dreams from an ordinary childhood' by Valerie Walkerdine.

There is an attempt by both the editor and the individual writers to set their personal accounts within the specific, historical movements of growing up in the 1950s. With the new access to 'orange juice and the codliver oil, the malt supplement and the free school milk' all these women grew up as 'subjects of the post-war social policies and legislation directly affecting children'. But what is unique to Valerie Walkerdine's essay is her simultaneous interest in the inner and outer worlds of her childhood. (In fact it's more of a personal psycho-history, than an account that stays rooted to the external world.) She's engaged in the 'burden of pain and desire that formed us' as well as postwar reconstruction.

She deals with the importance of fantasy, dream and desire in her own development as a 'clever working-class girl from Derby'. She analyses the psychic damage, as well as the social results, of a scholarship girl's journey from the safety and ordinariness of her family memories in Derby, to the expanded possibilities of living in London. The damage came in the form of a deep sense of loss, of anxiety, and 'insecurities of imagined failure and rejection'. The chances offered her through passing the eleven-plus and going to a new grammar school went, hand in hand, with great personal costs: 'They held out a dream. Come, they told me. It is yours. You are chosen. They didn't tell me, however, that for years I would no longer feel any sense of belonging, nor any sense of safety.'

As a scholarship boy myself I immediately recognized that edgy sense of displacement, never feeling at home in the family or the community, and always haunted by the anxiety that the authorities would eventually find you out as an impersonator and boot you back into the class that you came from.

Gay life history

'It's not just homosexuality', he was saying. 'It's really a question of secrets. I know it must be a shock to you so much of my life I've had to keep secrets from you. I mean,

I know all kids keep secrets from their parents. But usually those secrets don't make up such a huge part of their lives.'
                    (David Leavitt)[16]

Gay life history spoke to me because of my personal pain of trying to unbury selves kept well disguised over a lifetime. The emotional schizophrenia of having to survive in a 'normal', heterosexual world, while feeling an increasing tenderness and warmth for other men is well documented in Noel Greig's 'Codes of conduct'.[17] Instead of presenting a brave, stoical face to the world he confronts his fears about making his private desires public. And it was this that I found I could tune into so closely.

In 'Codes of conduct' Noel Greig refuses an easy assimilation into the dominant, buddy-boy culture by 'naming the fears' and exposing 'the secret selves at war inside my skin'. Through particular incidents in his own life, he shows 'the struggle between the two versions of "me"'; on one side the pressure to join in with the dominant, heterosexist, male norms – the pretence of 'making it big, authoritative, [and] swear[ing] more than most'. And on the other, he could 'identify his own desires' and place himself in the world through his own efforts. In doing this he explodes the illusion of a stable, coherent sense of self by his owning up to the possible, multiple identities within his own history.

What makes this kind of life history distinctive, when contrasted to traditional male autobiography, is its unsettling intimacy. It comes through to the reader with the emotional urgency of having to face up to the confusions and contradictions inside, of the pain of camouflage and deceit, and the frustrated energy of wanting to take the lid off one's life and be able to breathe again.

A more political version of gay life history is to be found in Michael Silverstein's '*The history of a short, unsuccessful academic career (with a postscript update)*'.[18] The implications of his own personal struggle as a closeted gay, and his description of his movement, within his working life, from striving to be a 'brain' in academic life through to giving up his job and becoming a political activist, are broadened out to include a political critique of 'his full rebellion against manhood'.

He leaves out of his critique an explicit recognition that it is hierarchical, heterosexual masculinity, as the dominant form of varied masculinities, that imposes its stifling and brutalizing agenda onto women and other men. But what he suggests is that it is 'man's learned drive for interpersonal dominance' that constitutes the 'psychic engine required for capitalist society to function'. He goes on to say that

> those with real power, ruling class white males, in order to perpetuate the existing social structure and thus ensure their continued control, use their control of the educational, communications, entertainment, and religious institutions to create men who seek a positive self-image in their power over others.

In close detail he shows how the 'blind alley of an academic career' was chosen, initially, as an attempt to escape the conventional demands of manhood. But he quickly learns that academic life is as competitively cut-and-thrust, mainly through word battles, as the world he has left behind. It's only later through his encounter with the gay liberation movement that he is encouraged to 'come out' and link his personal struggle with other oppressed people.

Again, the emotional urgency of this life-history account grows out of the pressure of invisible minorities, like gays, who, finding themselves reductively defined by present society, set out to 'redefine and recreate themselves'.

In a fascinating 'postscript' Michael Silverstein dissociates himself from the self-preoccupation of the 'growth movement'. He recognizes that the 'emphasis on sensitivity and awareness rests on economic privilege', and decides that 'the people who identify with the "human growth movement" seldom are willing to face the reality of their privileges'.

Life histories from the anti-sexist men's movement
This concern with writing from the inside, rather than hiding the personal in a more distanced, rational approach, is sustained in life histories from the anti-sexist men's movement.

Instead of the pretence of a boldly confident, public face we get the voice of uncertainty. This is often expressed in borrowings from what might seem like a more female tradition of discontinuous literary forms like notebooks, diaries, letters, journals and fragmentary, 'snapshot' childhood episodes.[19]

In the pioneering writing of the anti-sexist men's movement in the early 1970s (in collections like *Unbecoming Men, A Book of Readings: For Men Against Sexism* and *Men and Masculinity*)[20] the main stress is on the direct experience of men who felt out of step with robustly heterosexual masculinity. The characteristic tone of hesitancy and an awareness of physical inadequacy is to be found in 'Out in right field', one of the very short 'snapshots' of childhood pieces included in *Unbecoming Men*.

The witty, personal detail of the anonymous writer's failure as a baseball player entices the reader to get into the narrative. It's a writing that deliberately cuts back against the traditional hair-chestedness of manhood. When reading it I hooked into it at the moments where he is pressurized to despise his own unmanliness, like in the dancing classes where 'dances like the Virginia Reel and square dancing, which were a group thing, I usually enjoyed a lot. A lot, that is, until it became clear from the actions of the rest of the guys in dance class that I was the only one having a good time. After that even that type of dancing was awful.'

This same sense of failure as a conventional boy is dealt with by Julius Lester in his piece called 'Being a boy' included in *Men and Masculinity*. But here the considerably more polished performance of self-parody probably is derived from an established literary tradition of the little man as witty buffoon. Indeed the humour, although brilliantly hilarious in parts – like where his fear of asking a girl to dance is described: 'I would push my way to the other side of the room where the girls sat like a hanging jury' – acts more like a protective device than an illuminating form. The hidden pain of some of these moments is kept well under control through the consistently wry, self-mocking tone.

What is being contained and kept at bay in Julius Lester's account is made clearly visible in David Steinberg's *Father-Journal: Five Years of Awakening to Fatherhood*.[21] Set firmly within the Californian growth movement of the early 1970s, it nevertheless confronts masculinity as an explicit object of critical inquiry.

The booklet takes the shape of intimate, often awkward musings about his developing relationships with his son (Dylan) and his wife (Susan) over a period of five years. What I was able to tap into was the dynamic process of trying to make sense out of something that is immediately pressing in his life. Just read the journal entry for 21 August 1971, for example:

[29]

I have spent most of my time running, avoiding, shutting things out. This is the energy I have used to 'accomplish things'. It is the need to keep busy: if I stop who knows what will come popping out. It is the need to keep myself under control.

Now, as having a baby tears apart my ability to control my life, I begin to explore the possibility of letting go. I learn a little about following instead of leading, about slowing down, about listening, about responding to what's going on around me and inside me.

I'm excited by this new exploring, but I'm also reluctant to let go of the old sense of accomplishment that requires more speed, more control. I'm afraid that if I let go of that driving energy I will become mediocre, common, uninteresting, unlovable. I'm afraid that if I don't push myself I'll never do anything.

I found this piece reached out to me on two levels. It not only challenges the received notion of masculinity as a driving force, identifying itself through strenuous achievement, but it also owns up to the present contradictions that the writer is going through in attempting to change himself. Does 'letting go' mean a loss of his previous strength of purpose? How can he come to terms with his fears about losing control as a man?

It's through convincing me of the present reality of his blockages that I can accept his more generalized comments about masculinity as an object of investigation.

In another booklet about the problems and pleasures of fathering (*Birth and Afterbirth: A Materialist Account*),[22] Jeff Hearn chose a more dialectical form of writing. Something of the complex interweaving of different strands to be found in his approach to the subject is suggested by his description of the story he tells: 'Experience creates work creates politics creates theory: theory changes politics changes work changes experience.' In the preface there is an owning up to inconsistency and contradiction in the process of writing as a way of exploring 'the crucial relationship between experience, work, politics and theory', rather than 'the stating of a static position'.

He starts with the actual experiences of birth and involvement in child care presented in all their intense emotion and discomfiture.

[30]

The moment of the birth of his third child is caught on the move, in a form of instant glimpses and scribblings, like the shadowy movement of thoughts inside a head: 'Very slippery things, these babies. A girl. Quick wrap up. Given to Jay [the mother] to hold and a quick feed. Then the afterbirth, which was thrown away. Jay asked for it back to see it. Like a big red sponge, quite nice really.'

Jeff Hearn also has the courage to admit 'unmanly' things in public. He tries to remain loyal to the way he felt at the time. Like at the homecoming of Jay with his third child:

> Inside the house Jay was confident and joyful. I just broke up. I just sobbed and sobbed and sobbed for a long time. . .Even now over a year after I'm not completely sure what all the crying was about. . .It was almost as if I was being involuntarily shifted in myself, and in my relationship to my children, to Jay, and to my other genders. . .The change is difficult to describe accurately and briefly. In myself I feel more effeminate, in touch with a side of myself I had been aware of before but neglected as dangerous or irrelevant.

When I'm reading that I feel that those insights were won at some considerable personal cost to the author. In a society that values tight-lipped stoicism over emotional openness, it took some courage to be honest about the sobbing, and to write a line like, 'In myself I feel more effeminate. . .'.

Learning from these disconcerting moments of experience, he goes on to reflect critically on the implications of what he's just lived through. He begins to pin down the critical issues through using the politics of reproduction as an interpretative system. He sees that men benefit in all kinds of ways through the unequal, material relations between men and women, in the neglected areas of 'sexuality, contraception, abortion, ante-natal services, birth, post-natal provision, day care, nurseries, childwork, family structures, substitute care and early education.' And this leads him on to concrete proposals for social action:

> This is why all the various attempts to change the quality and form of nurseries and day care must be carried forward and expanded – in nursery centres, combining education

and care; in comprehensive day care projects, for pre-school children and older children after school and in school holidays; in feminist playgroups, single parent playgroups and childsharing schemes; in communal and cooperative living arrangements.

Jeff Hearn ends with a theoretical commentary on the general issues related to birth and childcare. Widening the ripples out from his initial experiences, he is able to redefine conventional Marxism's emphasis on commodity production to the changed issues and social relations of reproductive labour. He ties his immediate experiences of birth and caring for his own children to the formulation of an anti-patriarchal theory:

> Patriarchy can thus be seen as the patriarchal or feudal mode of reproduction. The products of women's reproductive labour are appropriated directly and unusually by the state, in the case of mothers being deemed 'unfit' by the courts, or they are appropriated indirectly, but quite routinely by individual men in individual families, as husbands and fathers routinely receiving privileges from others without recompense for them.

Collective forms of autobiography

> . . .the past is a collective experience.
>
> (Ronald Fraser)[23]

In Search of a Past is one of the two books (*Landscape for a Good Woman* is the other, see pages 40–2) that have most influenced me in the process of writing this. The influence is an elusive and oblique one, but a significant stirring up of possibilities, nevertheless.

The book's central importance for me is that it offers an implied critique of an essentialist concept of the self. It doesn't search for an authentic core of being but shows the complexities of building alternative selves from the total range of social relations experienced in childhood. Ronald Fraser's relationships with the servants of the manor house in which he grew up were, in retrospect, at least as

[32]

important to him as his parents, so he re-creates a collective form of autobiography that generalizes on his lifetime's experiences as well as hanging on to their uniqueness. Fraser puts it like this: 'What could be more exhilarating than to start from one's lived experience and, by the art of writing, recreate it for the reader as a general experience, without for all that losing its bitter taste of singularity?'

The book is composed of a multi-layered threading together of different narratives, that disrupt conventional time sequences and linear expectations. There are five main elements:

(a)   The writer's therapy sessions with a psychoanalyst, involving his struggle to release himself from the tyranny of his child-hood, or as he puts it, 'the gloomy mausoleums of your childhood'.

(b)   The carefully rewritten, selected tape-recorded interviews with the servants of the manor house (produced ten years earlier). The servants are Ilse the nanny, Bert the gardener, Carvell the groom, Eileen the parlour-maid, and Doris the nurserymaid.

(c)   The writer's personal history, and critical commentary upon it.

(d)   Short, italicized exchanges between the now senile father and his son (the writer) 'when sons become the father of their fathers'. These exchanges describe a journey back to the manor house on the way to a nursing home where the father dies, just before the end of the book.

(e)   The personal testimony of Colin, the writer's brother, cor-roborating and redefining the writer's uncertain memories, especially during the Second World War.

Ronald Fraser's analysis of these diverse and often bewildering layers of childhood experience, his own and other people's, exists on both a social and emotional level. The social analysis is built up through the interaction between the servants' oral histories and his own memories. The recognition of 'two worlds living under one roof' is gained through the arresting clarity of Bert the gardener's memories of the gentry: 'Lucky devils, you thought, galloping about and enjoying themselves, while you've got to slog all day in the garden. And when they come home they throw their horses to the groom and walk off, knowing everything's ready for them, hot baths, food'; and: 'All the gentry'd be sitting in their cars having their lunch and a nip of whisky while us poor buggers who'd been doing the beating would be under a tree with a sandwich trying to keep out of the rain.'

The personal antagonisms of class difference come clearly through these taped interviews and join up with the writer's own social-class commentary on his privileged childhood:

> Today I went straight to the heart of the matter: on the one hand, objectively a member of a privileged class I was, on the other, unable subjectively to fill the role into which I was born. This split, I said, was foreshadowed in my parents. My father incarnated the values of his class and time and, sometimes forcibly, confronted me with them as the only ones open to me; my mother, perhaps because she was American, rejected many of the manifestations of those values and held open the door to possible alternatives. Between the two – the ought and the want – I shuttled uneasily, a traitor to both. 'And to myself', I added.

At an emotional level he moves towards an inner reconciliation between unresolved conflicts. The breakthrough comes at the stage where he identifies his emotional blockage, sandwiched between the need to be securely looked after and yet freed, at the same time. This blockage came through the conflict of having two mothers (Ilse, the nanny, and his actual American mother), 'the one [who] tied me down and the other [who] refused to release me'.

He gradually comes to terms with his own personal history through bringing together social reality and individual experience. (He even challenges the authority of his analyst in 'refusing the social' in interpreting the writer's early images, dreams and feelings.) The separate narratives come together at the point where the writer's father dies, the therapy sessions result in the writer achieving a resolution of his inner conflicts, and the writer sees a way out of the dilemma of 'How can I write about the past without an "I" to focus with?'

It is through the process of emotionally growing up and also gaining a critical understanding of his own social condition that Ronald Fraser is able to find an appropriate way of writing his autobiography, and to declare, simultaneously: 'I am a man, nearly fifty, where a minute ago I was a child'.

The relations between social reality and individual experience are approached from an entirely different perspective in some Eastern European autobiographical writing. Indeed, in this case, the tables are turned and the claims of individual experience are denied completely. For example, personal experience is thoroughly historicized in Czeslaw Milosz's *Native Realm*.[24] Instead of the growth of the individual psyche informing the shaping priorities of their autobiographies, writers like Milosz only select those personal details that are collectively and historically significant in that they throw light on the historical development of a whole country within the twentieth century.

In his introduction to *Native Realm* he comments that:

> A three year-old's love for his aunt or jealousy towards his father take up so much room in autobiographical writings because everything else, for instance the history of a country or a national group, is treated as something 'normal' and, therefore, of little interest to the narrator. But another method is possible. Instead of thrusting the individual into the foreground, one can focus attention on the background, looking upon oneself as a sociological phenomenon. Inner experience, as it is preserved in the memory, will then be evaluated in the perspective of the changes one's milieu has undergone.

The foregrounding of the historically significant personal detail is used very much as a selection principle in Milosz's autobiography. Indeed his book sometimes reads like a succession of cinematic, newsreel images, charting the unfolding movement of twentieth-century history, like these images captured in words from the Polish-Russian War (1918–20):

> Like a continuous roll of pictures, new landscapes ceaselessly unfolded in front of us. Nights were spent in barns on the hay or around bonfires in the forest. The flash of hatchets chopping up kindling, a teapot hanging on a stick over the fire, wind blowing in the pines.

and:

The highway was a swarm of interlocking wagonshafts, eyes of terrified horses, manes, mouths open in a scream, whips raised. Along the ditch by the side of the road, a soldier without a cap or gun was slipping past, bareback astride a colt and lashing it with a switch. Further ahead, the outskirts of a town opened out. July heat, wooden houses in the sun, and not a trace of life. In the middle of the street stood a huge tank, and my remembrance of this sight is so intense that I feel as if I could reach out and touch every rivet.

Conventional 'barriers between the individual and the social' are blown up on one level, but there is also a deep distrust of unconscious structures. Milosz doesn't seem to recognize that a person's inner life is also shaped by social forces. Valerie Walkerdine's 'burden of pain and desire that formed us' is nowhere to be seen. All we have instead is the anxious evasion of a male writer who feels more secure dealing with public, historical perspectives: 'I mistrust the probings into the unconscious that are so honoured in our day. I am not competent in this area and am even afraid of it'.

Joseph Brodsky is similarly concerned, in his autobiographical essay, 'Less than one',[25] with the social and historical forces that shape identity. Here he defines himself negatively, against the institutional routines of an oppressively centralized state control. It is in his refusals to accept what is most normal and seemingly natural that he begins to forge an alternative sense of self. He despises the 'omnipresent images (of Lenin) which plagued almost every textbook, every class wall, postage stamps, money, and what not'. His acts of 'decolonising the mind' through 'switching off', 'lying' and 'walking out' are carefully recorded and analysed. All these rebellious acts are ways of fighting back against the 'trimming of the self' – a passive surrendering to the 'mental straitjacket of obedience' to the state. In the essay Brodsky is particularly aware of how the institutional practices of schooling and the army produce this mental conformity: 'Four years in the army (into which men were drafted at the age of nineteen) completed the process of total surrender to the state. Obedience would become both first and second nature.'

The other major point to make about both Milosz's and Brodsky's autobiographical explorations is that their particular approaches are closely tied in to the politics of region or location. Understanding 'how a place on the map is also a place in history'[26] has led

both writers to emphasize a historical awareness of their personal
connection, as Eastern Europeans, to some of the most significant
struggles and transformations of the twentieth century. And that
experience has taught both of them to see through the myth of the
uniquely talented individual when put against the witnessing of 'a
great deal of what Europe prefers to forget'.

> Autobiographies of black women, each of which is necessarily
> personal and unique, constitute a running commentary on
> the collective experience of black women in the United
> States. They are inescapably grounded in the experience of
> slavery and the literary tradition of the slave narratives. Their
> common denominator, which establishes their integrity as a
> sub-genre, derives not from the general categories of race
> or sex, but from the historical experience of being black
> and female in a specific society at a specific moment over
> succeeding generations.
>
> (Elizabeth Fox-Genovese)[27]

Black, Afro-American women's autobiographies are usually public, collective assertions as well as specific, personal histories.
'Me-ism gives way to our-ism'[28] through the historical legacies
of racism, sexism and slavery. Speaking from the intensity of
her own personal experiences, a writer like Maya Angelou will
simultaneously speak for that group of people who are struggling
within that double oppression.

An example of this is to be found in the second part of her
autobiography, *Gather Together in My Name*.[29] After several disastrous episodes the writer moves to her grandmother's house in
Stamps, Arkansas. Maya Angelou makes it very clear that she is
moving back in historical time as well as into an inherited plantation
consciousness with its slavery narratives shaping the present social
relations.

> The South I returned to, however, was flesh-real and swollen-
> belly poor. Stamps, Arkansas, a small hamlet, had subsisted
> for hundreds of years on the returns from cotton plantations,
> and until World War 1, a creaking lumbermill. The town
> was halved by railroad tracks, the swift Red River and racial

prejudice. Whites lived on the town's small rise (it couldn't be called a hill), while blacks lived in what had been known since slavery as 'the Quarters'.

Even though she has lived in California, she is partly placed by these racial legacies and divisions. But the first thing she learns is about black solidarity, gathered together against oppression. Her fatherless child is accepted by the black community: 'I was surprised not to be asked to confess my evil ways and repent. Instead, I was seen in the sad light which had been shared and was to be shared by black girls in every state in the country. I was young, yes, unmarried, yes – but I was a mother, and that placed me nearer the people.'

It is that broad sharing of a common condition, while still holding on to an individual perspective, that makes black women's autobiographies so distinctive.

Later on in her stay at Stamps there is a recognition[30] scene, a common scene that has the ghosts of many other, almost similar scenes lurking just below the surface. By 'recognition' I mean coming to consciousness, where the writer is made aware of the political and social significance of her own blackness.

The scene centres on Maya Angelou's sortie into white territory, to collect a knitting pattern from the General Merchandise Store in the white town. On one level there is a uniquely personal twist to the story. Maya is stuffed full of San Francisco expectations (having lived there for some time) and tries to apply them to Stamps. She wants to prove her city sophistication to both black and white women, in contrast to their backwoods provincialism.

On another level, there are the common features of a racially defined history. First in Maya Angelou there is the familiar tension between black pride and self-hatred. The occasional questioning of her own self-image (she prepares for her trip into the white town by checking her hair 'which was straightened to within an inch of its life and greased to desperation') is linked to the importance of sticking up for herself and other black people.

When she gets to the store she is confronted by one of the saleswomen. They find that they can't pass each other in the narrow corridor of the store. Maya Angelou is ordered to stand still so that the white woman can get by. But this habitual mistress/slave tone brings out an angry defiance in Maya: 'Couldn't she see from my still-white though dusty gloves, my starched clothes, that I wasn't a servant to be ordered around?'

So Maya Angelou turns the tables on the white woman and commands her to stand still while she goes around her. Outraged by this 'sassy' behaviour the two white saleswomen revert to the old certainties of white power bred in the region's plantation history. Maya Angelou, the person, becomes invisible to them. Now all they see is a black slave becoming uppity.

It's at this stage of the episode that the writing deliberately broadens its context.

> [The white saleswoman's] head eased up and she looked across centuries at me. 'How do you pronounce your name, gal? Speak up.'
>
> In that moment I became rootless, nameless, pastless. The two white blurs buoyed before me.

The legacies of black history are invoked through the 'looking across centuries'. Maya's complex individuality is eroded and she is locked within the racist ideologies of the white–over–black binary system. At the same time as she becomes 'nameless' to the two white women, so the white women get reduced to 'two white blurs'.

Because of the threat of being defined by a white, racist society, she is forced into literally and symbolically naming herself. Her sticking up for herself in front of the white woman is very much an attempt to hold on to her own sense of dignity and self-respect: 'If you have occasion to use my name, which I seriously doubt, I advise you to address me as Miss Johnson.'

In defining herself through her own words she is redressing her own personal hurt but also speaking for an emerging readership[31] of black women who are coming to consciousness in the second half of the twentieth century through involvement in the black and women's movements.

These public as well as personal aspects of black, Afro-American women's autobiographies helped me in understanding the collective possibilities of writing in this form. For 'the account of the black woman's self cannot be divorced from the history of that self or the history of the people among whom it took shape'.[32]

Critical autobiography as part of the politics of subjectivity

Autobiography is often seen as individual self-expression. The assumption is that the self is fixed, coherent and innate, genetically determined, and all autobiography has to do is to go on a journey of discovery to find the true self. But these liberal-humanist assumptions are in the process of being contested by recent, feminist autobiographical work that is informed by post-structuralism, history, psychoanalysis, sociology and literary studies.

From these new perspectives the post-structuralist concept of 'subjectivity' replaces the essential, authentic self. In redefining approaches to the self, personal identity is now seen as culturally and socially shaped, constantly shifting according to changing historical conditions and the dominant frameworks of understanding and interpretation it is formed within (like class and gender). Instead of a single, unchanging self waiting to be unburied, post-structuralism decentres the traditional self and introduces the possibility of multiple selves, much more fragmented and contradictory in make-up, being socially formed within changing conditions, relations and frameworks.[33]

The contrast between liberal-humanist versions of autobiography that conceal the historical and social conditions of their own emergence, and a feminist, post-structuralist version that makes publicly explicit its own processes of construction in a critically demystifying way, is clearly pointed up in the autobiographical work of Carolyn Steedman, *Landscape for a Good Woman*.[34]

The social production of her own subjectivity is systematically laid bare by Carolyn Steedman's analysis of the interrelationships between the cultural, historical and psychological forces that shaped her. The economic analysis isn't isolated from the overall politics of subjectivity within the book. Indeed, the book's complex development of the autobiographical form is based on an appreciation of the limitations of a traditional class and gendered interpretation of two women's lives (herself and her mother). The originality of her approach is that she connects Valerie Walkerdine's 'burden of pain and desire' with the felt experience of class damage. In her own words she faces up to the contradictions of the 'conceptual and psychological baggage that people carry with them, and the disruption that the irrational and the unconscious make in its running.'

[40]

At one level Carolyn Steedman investigates the relationship between her mother and herself, 'the ways in which her mother's sense of childhood shaped the contours of the author's own childhood'.[35] To be able to do this, she has to subvert the male-defined frameworks of interpretation and literary conventions (seen in the work of Richard Hoggart and Jeremy Seabrook[36] as attributing 'a background of uniformity and passivity' to the lives of working-class women). She is able to challenge these accounts and reclaim the meaning of her mother's and her own linked life through the secret, unofficial stories of unfulfilled desire (like her mother's longing for the New Look skirt) and class exclusion.

The reader isn't given a straight, life-history narrative but fragments from the marginal lives of her father, mother and herself. Instead of a conventional, autobiographical account the writer chooses what she calls a 'case-study' approach. In her own words this means 'the ebb and flow of memory, the structure of dreams, the stories that people tell to explain themselves to others'.

Like Joseph Brodsky, both mother and daughter identify themselves negatively through their refusal to obey the official, male-defined rules of being a mother and daughter. The mother refuses to be a conventional mother as her way of hanging on to her own sense of personal grievance, of being 'refused her rightful place in the world'. Later, in response to that non-mothering, the writer refuses the conventional obligations of being a daughter: 'at twenty-seven, I wrote to my mother and said that I didn't want to see her for a while because she upset me so much'. That unrevealed history of pain and distress is left dangling in the air.

What really excited me about this book was the subtle way it demonstrated, through the specific moments of a personal history, the intricate web of social forces that had produced the writer's gendered identity. If this reworking of the past meant a critical reworking of traditional approaches to femininity, motherhood and class, then why couldn't I, in a very different way, attempt to remake my past in terms of exposing masculinity as an explicit object of critical inquiry through tracing the development of my own gendered identity?

But in trying to do so I would have to learn from Laura Marcus's[37] critique of the *Landscape for a Good Woman*, that it 'does not explicitly interrogate the notion of "identity"'. Certainly, for all its achievements, there is something left unsaid at the heart of its process of reworking. Perhaps that lies in the lack of conscious awareness about her present (1986 – the date of the book's publication) forms of subjectivity actively shaping and informing her rereading of the past? The book's central focus is on the dialectical relationship between her mother and herself. What might be missing in that focus is some kind of attempt to make that other dialectical process – the relationship between those present and past subjectivities – more open and visible so that the reader can join in that interpretative act?

The only male autobiography I know that makes the writer's own construction of masculinity an explicit object of critical scrutiny is *It Will Make a Man of You: Notes on National Service, Masculinity and Autobiography* by David Morgan.[38] As he says himself, it is an autobiographical project that uses the critical methods of sociological inquiry.

His approach to the subject is influenced by feminist post-structuralism. He deliberately sets out to problematize the auto-biographical process: challenging the false unity of a stable, fixed, authorial identity, rejecting linear narrative, shattering the illusion of total recall, exploring the dialectic between past and present.

The origins of the project are to be found in the writer's belief in the necessary integration between the personal and the social. The idea grew out of a discussion after a conference on 'masculinity and history' when the writer was gently challenged for not including himself, personally, in his account. Although he recognizes that it is difficult for men to find an appropriate voice (voices?) for their experiences, he believes it is crucial for sociology to 'represent an imaginative and critical engagement between personal experience and the analysis of social structures and processes'.

The writer interrogates a period of two years (doing national service from 1955 to 1957) from his past by viewing it through the critical lens of an awareness of gender identity. The shift from a passive acceptance of the past to the active interrogation of 'autobiographical themes' is well put: 'I cease to become a passive recipient of memories which, miraculously, order themselves into some linear sequence but shift to being an oral historian, interested in issues of masculinity, interviewing myself.'

[42]

Morgan sketches in a historical background to the period of national service. He then goes on to analyse 'sources and methods', talking about using photographs, stories, folk myths as ways of understanding his own personal and social construction, and trying to sort out puzzling phenomena.

The central focus of the book is on the common themes and features within this experience that played a part in shaping his own and others' masculinities. Implicitly, great emphasis is laid on the shaping power of institutional routines in this construction of masculinity, like the 'everyday routines of parades, inspections, saluting and regimentation'. In this way military goals and values, hardships and deprivation, the force of total institutions, all-male environments, and group solidarity are dealt with.

The sharpest analysis is found within the discussion of group solidarity. What hooked up very closely to my own autobiographical attempt was the way apparently trivial and isolated features, like smoking, swearing, drinking and sport, could be viewed as significant, social practices that contributed to forming gender identity in men and boys.

On one level, David Morgan seems more comfortable when he's engaged in social analysis rather than telling his own personal stories. Indeed, despite the three, exemplary stories he uses in the 'Sources and methods' section, his own personal investment in the autobiographical evidence he is sifting is generally muffled. This is most clearly seen in his state of emotional ambivalence in response to the issue of group solidarity.

At the heart of the making of his gendered subjectivity is a contradictory tension between belonging and not belonging which could have been shared more comprehensively with his readers. He acknowledges this in the description of one of his selves: 'It was, and is, a self that was attracted by some of the camaraderie and friendship and which wanted to belong and to be accepted while, simultaneously, being repelled by some of the harshness of language and behaviour'; and in: 'Fear of exclusion from the group became perhaps an even more powerful force than wishing to join it and to be accepted.'

What I wonder about are a series of unanswered questions about the writer's Methodist upbringing and his need to belong. What are the psychoanalytical and social origins of the writer's desire to seek oneness and fusion in the male club? Where does the pain

[43]

of exclusion come from? What is the writer's personal investment in the selective editing of what is crucial and what is trivial in his reworking of the past in those two years – 1955–7?

In a sense these questions are unfair. David Morgan might reply that they aren't a part of the deliberately limited terrain of his sociological inquiry. But in another sense they are questions that ought to be a part of any fully realized, critical autobiography. Men have always been strong on theoretical inquiry. In a way I'm asking myself and other men whether we can work from 'the burden of pain and desire' to link up with a social analysis. Can sociology, psychoanalysis, post-structuralism, history and literary studies illuminate in such an interlocking way that the urgency of the writer's personal stories contributes to the process of making visible how a particular, gendered identity was formed?

These are some of the questions and influences that still pursue me in the process of awakening to the varied potentialities of the autobiographical form, as I continue writing this book.

Notes

1 G. Boycott (1987) *The Autobiography*, London, Macmillan; David Owen (1987) *Personally Speaking*, London, Weidenfeld & Nicolson; Roald Dahl (1986) *Going Solo*, London, Cape.

2 P. Spacks (1976) *Imagining a Self*, Cambridge, Mass., Harvard University Press.

3 E. Wilson (1988) 'Tell It Like It Is: women and confessional writing', in S. Radstone (ed.) *Sweet Dreams: Sexuality, Gender and Popular Fiction*, London Lawrence & Wishart.

4 E. Jelinek (1980) *Women's Autobiography*, Bloomington, Ind., Indiana University Press.

5 See S. Juhasz (1980) 'Towards a theory of form in feminist autobiography', Jelinek, op. cit. She says, 'Autobiography as a literary genre has traditionally been one of those masculine institutions: by and about men, it has established for us all many of our notions about what people are like, what lives are like (especially what constitutes important and meaningful lives), and how one writes about people and their lives.'

6 See S. S. Friedman (1988) 'Women's autobiographical selves: theory and practice', in S. Benstock (ed.) *The Private Self*, London, University of North Carolina Press and Routledge.

7 See M. Kimmel (1987) 'Rethinking "masculinity": new directions in research', in M. Kimmel (ed.) *Changing men*, London, Sage. He says,

'But rarely, if ever, do we study men as men; rarely do we make masculinity the object of inquiry as we examine men's lives.'

8 'Across academic disciplines and national boundaries scholars have increasingly found value in inspecting "a life". In psychology's new concern with "narratives" and "story telling" (Sarbin, 1986), in the psychoanalytic concern with "narrative truth" (Spence, 1982), in the anthropologists' interest in "lives" (Langness and Frank, 1981), in the growth of oral history even by non-academic groups (Thompson, 1978), and in literature's fascination with the "biological text" (Olney, 1980), a concern with life histories is enjoying something of a renaissance.' Taken from K. Plummer (1988) 'Herbert Blumer and the life history tradition: critique, emergence, practice', unpublished paper presented at the Interactionist Research conference, 'A tribute. . .Herbert Blumer and the study of social action', May 1988, University of Windsor, Windsor, Ontario.

9 K. Millett (1973) *The Prostitution Papers*, London, Paladin. Quoted in Wilson, op. cit.

10 J. McCrindle and S. Rowbotham (1977) *Dutiful Daughters*, London, Allen Lane; Penguin edn 1979.

11 M. Chamberlain (1975) *Fenwomen*, London, Virago.

12 J. White (1981) 'Beyond autobiography', in R. Samuel (ed.) *People's History and Socialist theory*, London, Routledge & Kegan Paul.

13 J. Okely (1987) 'Privileged, schooled and finished: boarding education for girls' in G. Weiner and M. Arnot (eds) *Gender Under Scrutiny: New Enquiries in Education*, London, Hutchinson Education/Open University.

14 See Plummer, op. cit., p. 4.

15 L. Heron (ed.) (1985) *Truth, Dare or Promise: Girls Growing Up in the Fifties*, London, Virago.

16 D. Leavitt (1986) *The Lost Language of Cranes*, New York, Knopf. Penguin edn 1987.

17 N. Greig (1987) 'Codes of conduct', in G. Hanscombe and M. Humphries (eds) *Heterosexuality*, London, GMP Publishers.

18 M. Silverstein (1977) 'The history of a short, unsuccessful, academic career (with a postscript update)', in J. Snodgrass (ed.) *A Book of Readings: For Men Against Sexism*, New York, Times Change Press.

19 See E. Jelinek (1980) 'Women's autobiography and the male tradition', in Jelinek, op. cit. She says, 'one is struck by the number of women writing diaries, journals and notebooks, in contrast to the many more men writing autobiographies proper. From earliest times, these discontinuous forms have been important to women because they are analogous to the fragmented, interrupted, and formless nature of their lives.'

20 M. Bradley *et al.* (1971) *Unbecoming Men*, New York, Times Change Press; Snodgrass, op. cit.; J. Pleck and J. Sawyer *Men and Masculinity*, Englewood Cliffs, NJ, Prentice-Hall.

21 D. Steinberg (1977) *Father Journal: Five Years of Awakening to Fatherhood*, New York, Times Change Press.

[45]

22 J. Hearn (1983) *Birth and Afterbirth: A Materialist Account*, Achilles Heel Publications.
23 R. Fraser (1984) *In Search of a Past*, London, Verso.
24 C. Milosz (1968) *Native Realm*, New York, Doubleday; Penguin edn 1988.
25 J. Brodsky (1986) 'Less than one' in *Less Than One: Selected Essays*, New York, Viking; Penguin edn 1987. See also the other autobiographical essay in the collection, 'In a room and a half'.
26 A. Rich (1987) 'Notes towards a politics of location', in *Blood, Bread and Poetry: Selected Prose 1979–1985*, London, Virago.
27 E. Fox-Genovese (1988) 'My statue, my self: autobiographical writings of Afro-American women', in Benstock, op. cit.
28 S. Cudjoe (1985) 'Maya Angelou and the autobiographical statement', in M. Evans (ed.) *Black Women Writers*, London, Pluto. Quoted in Fox-Genovese, op. cit.
29 M. Angelou (1974) *Gather Together in My Name*, New York, Random House; Virago edn 1989.
30 R. Blackburn (1980) 'In search of the black, female self: African-American women's autobiographies and ethnicity', in Jelinek, op. cit. She comments: 'Most African-American female autobiography confess to one incident in their early years that awakened them to their colour; this recognition scene evoked an awareness of their blackness and of its significance, and it had a lasting influence on their lives.'
31 See Fox-Genovese, op. cit. She comments: 'The tension at the heart of black women's autobiography derives in large part from the chasm between the autobiographer's intuitive sense of herself and her attitude towards her probable readers. Imagined readers shape the ways in which an autobiographer constructs the narrative of her life. 'She believes this flawed relationship has improved for recent black, women writers who are . . benefiting from the slow emergence of black women readers.'
32 See Fox-Genovese, op. cit.
33 This part of the review is indebted to Chris Weedon's interpretation of 'subjectivity' as a central feature of post-structuralist thinking. See C. Weedon (1987) *Feminist Practice and Poststructuralist Theory*, Oxford, Basil Blackwell.
34 C. Steedman (1986) *Landscape for a Good Woman: A Story of Two Lives*, London, Virago.
35 From a review of *Landscape for a Good Woman* written by Mary Chamberlain in *New Socialist*, April 1986.
36 See R. Hoggart (1959) *The Uses of Literacy*, London, Penguin, and J. Seabrook (1982) *Working Class Childhood*, London, Gollancz.
37 L. Marcus (1987) 'Enough about you, let's talk about me', in *Recent Autobiographical Writing, New Formations*, no. 1 (Spring). Quoted in Wilson, op. cit.
38 D. Morgan (1987) *It Will Make a Man of You: Notes on National Service, Masculinity and Autobiography*, Manchester, Department of Sociology, University of Manchester.

[46]

CHAPTER 3

Falling apart, men's bodies, and masculine identities

I physically fell apart in February 1986. I'd been moving in that general direction for some time but I actually cracked up then. Falling apart provoked an emotional crisis about my masculine identity. In some important ways this book is a response to that continuing crisis.

This crisis took the form of a probing questioning of my gendered identity very much located in my bodily experience. It was the first time in my life that my body had let me down. I lost control of not only my grip on my body but who I thought I was. These fears and anxieties about who I was centred very much on that hidden history of denial carried around in my body for so long.

Therefore it seems right to include a brief account of the historical process of developing a sense of masculinity in my body. Then, linked but separate, an account of the physical upheavals that tore apart that deceptively settled sense of myself as 'naturally' masculine that later led to a journey of reassessment and reframing that is at the heart of the book.

I dream of a lost body. I dream of a body I desire. I envy bodies that can drift and swirl like uncoiling strands of water-weed. I dream, in slow-motion, of having a seal's body. I sense the way a seal can become a part of its liquid element, slipping drowsily through green fathoms. I can imagine the lightness of a seal's swaying rolls. I'm full of frustrated desire for the way it delights in the casual play of its own sleek movement.

All apparently very different from this gripped pressure, that was my masculine body a few years ago, and especially in a work-place context. This clenched-teeth tightening of muscles and nerves to meet the targets, goals and dead-lines that I impose and had imposed upon my life. This permanent sense of unease in my body, the ache in my lower back when the tension bites, of feeling cross-grained, of feeling at odds with my flesh, is something I live with every day.

These dreams are powerfully persuasive for they seem to offer the alluring fantasy of the unrehearsed, 'natural' body that I can escape back into, in contrast to the present, clenched pressure. But, in reality, they are empty dreams.

My body doesn't exist outside history, even though it might find pleasure in fantasizing about an uncontaminated innocence, outside time. At birth I inherited a male body (with specific biological characteristics and genetic endowments) but it quickly became a masculinized body through the social meanings and relations it encountered in learning to take part in a capitalist, patriarchal society.

Even though my body seems the most private and hidden part of me, I carry my life history in my body, almost like the way the age rings of a sawn tree trunk reveal a process through time. My personal history of social practices and relationships is physically embodied in the customary ways I hold my body, relate to it, imagine its size and shape, and in its daily movements and interactions.[1] My masculinity has been sedimented in my body over time, so one of the first things critical life-history work needs to do is to expose the interpretative frameworks, forces, practices and relationships that have gradually masculinized my body.

But before I attempt to do that, I need to look at the political forces that are working against this process of critical exposure. Historically, masculine bodies have been deliberately kept out of sight because one of the ways white, able-bodied, heterosexual men sustain their power over women and unmanly men is by the force of active looking rather than being looked at.[2] In objectifying and subordinating women's bodies through the commanding male gaze some men also shore up their sense of being on top.

Some aspects of patriarchal power are dependent upon preventing the masculine body from becoming the passive object of women's gaze. This alternative gaze can be unmanning because the masculine codes of 'Who looks at whom?' are subverted. But it isn't just the gaze that's important. It's also the social and power relations that the gazer and the gazed at exist within. In my own personal attempt at subversion I want to invite an alternative gaze to uncover the detailed genealogy of my hidden, masculine body so that the invisible practices of its making can be held up to critical scrutiny. Therefore in the following pages I want to look closely at the social constitution of my own masculine body, and point out some of the contradictions and tensions that were involved in my life history.

The first thing to say is that my relation to my own body was deeply shaped by the historical context of postwar Britain that I measured myself up against in the mid-1940s and 1950s. Therefore I'd like to start with a brief sketch of the state of gender politics in postwar Britain, and then I'd like to focus on some dominant models of masculinity that influenced me at that time.

Gender Politics in postwar Britain

In Lynne Segal's essay, 'Look back in anger: men in the 50's',[3] she sets the contemporary state of gender relations against the historical background of that time. According to her, in the late 1940s and 1950s in Britain there was a tightly controlled segregation between the sexes in terms of domestic relations and the gendered division of labour. Despite the bright and breezy tone of some of the popular and academic writing of that time in celebrating the 'new togetherness, harmony and equality between women and men in the home'[4] the reality was very different.

Men's participation in the home was very limited. Generally they kept themselves distant from housework, childcare and any activity that could be construed as 'woman's work'. Indeed a fear of unmanliness could be said to be present in some men's reluctance to dissolve the boundaries between the public and private spheres, masculinity and femininity and paid and unpaid work.

Round about this time, many women were being lured back into the home from war work. Bowlby's 'maternal deprivation' theories played a part in shaping (and were also shaped by) a political climate that created an ideology of domesticity[5] to keep women in their place, economically powerless, trapped and often isolated inside the home. It was argued that the housebound mother was urgently necessary to provide the continuity and consistency needed for a period of stabilization after the great upheavals of the war. Accompanying this move, many men were encouraged to define their manhood in fierce, and often troubled, opposition to women and homosexuals. The hunky solidity of Rock Hudson (however deceptive this appearance was!) was overemphasized in contrast to the pouting 'sex kitten', Brigitte Bardot.

Against a historical backdrop of virulent, anti-homosexual persecution in the early 1950s,[6] in both Britain and the United States, many men retreated into aggressively heterosexual identifications almost as a way of dealing with their fears of losing virility. In this politically reactionary climate of a forced repression of the slightest hint of unmanliness, a clear connection was established between an institutional homophobia and a blatant misogyny.

For example, John Osborne's sense of robust, heterosexual manliness was constructed in paranoic opposition to the threat of demanding women: 'The female must come toppling down to where she should be – on her back'.[7] Anxieties about not being manly enough were dealt with in forthright and defensive ways. Drastically simplifying, on the active side there was a strident assertion of hairy-chested, heterosexual-style practices and values, or in a quieter way a smart respectability, and on the other there was a deliberate distancing from what was seen as effeminate, 'nancy boy' culture. This often led to the production of a mutilating self-hatred in the lives of ambiguous male homosexuals, bisexuals and effeminates like me, who wouldn't or couldn't conform to the masculine ideal of 'He-Man' heterosexuality.

Some comments on the cultural politics of the 1940s/1950s

I want to focus here on some of the dominant models of masculinity that I met with in the adverts associated with muscle magazines, war films and the male film star pin-ups of that particular time.

[50]

Advertisements influenced by the muscle magazines

I grew up in a social climate of popular enthusiasm for male body-building. In the middle of the 1940s and the 1950s there was a wide circulation of muscle magazines like *Your Physique* and *Superman*.[8] I didn't read these magazines but experienced this cult of the ideal, manly body indirectly through adverts for Shredded Wheat and the Charles Atlas body-building courses published in some of the popular newspapers and comics of the time.

The Charles Atlas adverts played on my anxieties and fears and made a lasting impression. They usually centred on a contrast between a beefy hunk of a man scuffing sand in the eye of a 'seven-stone weakling', or featured a comic-strip frame showing two weedy men saying to each other: 'Gee. . .I would like to have real HE–MAN muscles!' and the other one replying, 'So would I, but it takes a long while.' The feeble maunderings of the two weeds are broken into by the powerful physique of a real photograph of Charles Atlas, all bronzed and bulging with muscles. The banner headlines of the advert are shouting, "Rot!" – says Charles Atlas. "I'll prove in the first 7 days YOU can have a Body like Mine!"'

These kinds of adverts, seen against that historical background of compulsive, heterosexual identification and linked fear of losing virility, were designed to make you feel uncomfortable in your own body. They work through this ideological contrast between the promised 'He-Man' values of toughness, muscularity and strength and the actual, personal sense of inferiority to this ideal norm. Like the 'seven-stone weakling' I felt totally humiliated and dwarfed by all these bulging muscles.

I learnt to sneer at the delicacy and neatness of my own body, increasingly feeling contempt for my cissy's body. I was generally being made susceptible to the kind of advertising that played upon my desire to be taller and bigger. It worked by first making you feel dissatisfied with what you had, then constructed a desire for an ideal, and then kept you for ever striving for perfection.

I was invited and seriously tempted to reply to a built-up shoes advert ('How to get taller over-night!'). And I hesitated over an advert that appeared underneath the stamp offers in *The Rover*, 20th August 1949: 'Be Taller! My height is 6' 3 3/4 inches. Pupils gain 1 to 6 inches. Ross system gets results. T. M. Ross. Height Specialist.'[9]

Later on in my development – perhaps around 13 or 14 – I hovered uneasily between wanting to be bigger, and a scepticism about such promises. But that didn't stop me from secretly having a go on my cousin's chest expanders. They were called Bullworkers, and I watched with envy as my cousin used them like an elastic band, pulling them right out across his back and chest. It looked easy but when I came to have a go, I couldn't even stretch them to their full extent. I never touched them again but was left with a deep sense of self-disgust.

In the end I never sent away for any of these offers or courses, but I was very much shaped by the ideology of 'He-Man' masculinity. The contrast between my actual body and the ideal fantasy of 'Getting Big!' irrationally pulled me in to adverts like the 1949 Shredded Wheat ones aimed at younger boys:

The startling thing about this advert is that it doesn't really bother to sell the product in terms of healthy eating (Shredded Wheat contained starch and roughage good for body-building) but promotes it primarily in terms of young boys' senses of their own physical inferiority and their related desire to emulate what the 'big men eat!' The advertisers knew that fantasies about

[52]

possible acceptance into the 'He-Man' club, like the ones tugging the powerless boy looking up to the confident competence of the big men heading goals, were more important than the 'crisp and tasty' appeal of the 12 'golden biscuits'.

Male heroes in the films of the 1950s

In some of the dominant models of masculinity represented by male heroes in 1950s films, I also came into contact with an ideal definition of what counted as masculine maturity and grown-upness. It had a particularly middle-class, nationalist form but it was something I was invited to aspire to.

Male film heroes in the 1950s war films, like Jack Hawkins in *Angel One Five*[10] and *The Cruel Sea*,[11] represented a supposedly appropriate model of masculine behaviour – a tight-lipped, gritty stoicism. Indeed, at one point in *Angel One Five* Hawkins growls, 'We keep going because we've got to keep going'.[12]

The kind of 'normally' mature, masculine behaviour that I was being encouraged to buy into was a behaviour that deliberately kept up a distance from any activities that could be read as 'womanly' or effeminate. Instead, it was grimly heroic, tightly bottled up and self-sacrificing. The values of determination, emotional denial and self-control were constantly held up for applause and emulation.

Personally recoiling from all this strenuously worthy effort, I felt some kind of dimly recognized, subversive empathy for more obviously uncertain, unstable stars like Montgomery Clift and James Dean. It was only much later that I recognized that their anti-heroic qualities were related to their gayness.

The other major point to make about male film stars of the 1950's is the connection between a narrow, exclusive form of national identity (sturdy, white 'Englishness' in this context) and dominant models of masculinity. A middle-class form of white, English male – Richard Todd, Donald Sinden, Kenneth More, Jack Hawkins etc. – was made singly to stand up for everything that was apparently trustworthy, decent and steadfast out of a much more contradictory variety. What is being left out and what this decent, English manliness is defining itself against is the invisible 'other' of marginalized and powerless ethnicities – of blacks, foreigners, Germans, Italians. The special claim for 'normality', represented in the tweedy calmness and self-control of these white, English, male stars,[13] is the way this interpretative framework is able to take up a centre-stage position in regulating what count as valid masculine images and identities.

My own insecurity about myself seemed to be underlined against those sturdy, English oaks, always apparently solidly stable and dependable. I could well imagine that I might have had doubts about my own credentials to fit in to this male club. With an effeminate body, and having an Italian grandfather, my doubts raised difficult questions about my eligibility to identify myself as a sturdy, English oak as well. How could I ever measure up to that stiff-upper-lip impression of solidity when I had difficulty assembling and holding myself together?

Learning to identify myself as 'He-Man' masculine at a particularly homophobic/anti-effeminate time was about trying, with difficulty, to embody force. Learning that you were 'naturally' entitled to social, legal and financial power over women was translated into learning to hold power in your body – tautening your muscles, holding yourself firm and upright, striding with a cocky strut, throwing out your chest and walking from the shoulders.

On one level, I was being invited to invest emotionally in the reassurance of a 'Hard man' identity (strong, independent, self-sufficient, 'mature', 'normal'). In insecure contexts, especially when I started going to boarding school at 12, I urgently desired safety in the stability, privilege and social recognition[14] of an identity that I could walk tall in. I wanted to be taller and bigger than I actually was and the 'hard man' identity seemed to offer a symbolic resolution to the real conditions of my life that increasingly diminished me. It seemed to offer me a virile stature that I could be proud of. And so, at moments of anxiety, I was prepared to go on half-buying into the fiction of a fixed and continuous self, and strove manfully to achieve that validated identity.

But on another level, and perhaps in supportive contexts that encouraged me to accept my potentiality for different selves in a more fluidly diverse way, I also sensed that compliance with the position offered to me in the set regime of 'hard case' masculinity was achieved at great personal cost. For me, to have slotted in to the given framework of cocky, heterosexual manliness would have also meant having to kill off other transitional selves that were also charged with meaning and value for me – selves that were able to choose warmth, understanding and intimacy, and were capable of refusing acquiescence to all this swaggering pretence.

So I was never able to fully fit in to that 'hard case' identity without many contradictory tensions surfacing. My hair registered my refusal to fit in. It was usually wild, bushy and very long, sometimes making me look 'like a girl', as some of my friends used to say. I grew up physically in-between, shaped by the complex relations between my psychological shakiness, being undersized for my age, and experiencing all of that against a cultural and historical background that strictly policed the boundaries between 'masculine'/'feminine', and that often displayed a hysterical brutality against 'deviant' and marginalized people who risked trespassing across these boundaries. As a result, I suspect my culturally constructed fear about my own bodily inadequacy was intensified by the extreme contrasts offered, and the social penalties experienced at that historical moment, by the power imbalance between the 'hard man' and the shrimp.

All of this led to a feeling of not being at home in my body, of feeling shamefully unmanly. This deficit approach to my body was exacerbated by the boarding school relations and conditions. These brought me into daily and nightly contact with the bullying fists of a 'hard case' schoolboy culture. Having to survive in those conditions meant partly buying[15] in to those dominant, masculine identities on offer within that savage regime. This context proved to be the perfect preliminary conditions for inscribing a patriarchal ideology within my body, especially through the regular, institutional practices of that regime over a period of seven years. However, it's important to recognize that this wasn't done through grafting mechanical structures onto my body from outside, but that these ideologies were 'systematically deposited and constructed on an anatomical plane, i.e. in the neuro-musculature of [my] body'.[16]

Because of my sense of physical inadequacy in that environment, I overcompensated by straining to achieve, mostly through fantasy, a Charles Atlas body and identity that would conceal, through its rigid armoury, the fearful cracks. I suppose that made me partly willing, in the contexts where I had to defend myself, to embody the ideology of 'He-Man' masculinity that existed all around me.

But that wasn't done overnight. It was constructed slowly, repetitively and daily through the institutional routines operating within certain, key frameworks of understanding. In my personal history these key frameworks were the ones of schooling, sport, heterosexuality and work.

Here, because most of these frameworks are dealt with in greater detail later in the book, I'd like to sketch in a few, brief notes about each framework:

Secondary school

At school, between 1951 and 1959, I was taught to hold my body upright, through severely controlled, disciplinary methods.[17] I can remember our gym teacher, not long out of the RAF, reading the riot act about the dangers of slouching and letting the body slump into a casual, relaxed position. He singled out one boy to make an example of. He pointed out that this boy had developed the habit of putting his weight onto one leg and leaning over to one side. What we should do, he remarked briskly, was throw our chests out, tuck our seats in and hold ourselves, proudly, upright. When local people saw us running up the high street to the gym, he said, they should know that we were grammar school boys by the way we carried our bodies.

Every day, every week, the same regulatory methods were enforced. In lining up outside classrooms, in walking in regimented 'crocodiles' to and from school from the boarding school house, in walking to and from church every Sunday, in having to take part in a 'healthy' Sunday afternoon walk, the same strict disciplining of the body was called for.

Sport

I toughened up my body through sporting activities. It prepared my body for violent clashes with other male bodies and for aggressive, competitive performance. Every cross-country run, every house practice after school, every informal game of playground football helped to develop the physical, hardship rituals necessary for the battling for honour on the sports field.

I tried to build a virile bodily presence and power in my body through sporting activities. I dreamed of possessing a triumphant goal scorer's legs, thighs and body, tuned into success and achievement. But my ambivalence towards my body and my lack of size meant that I had to settle for tricky, ball-playing skills rather than the full, *Victor Ludorum* glory. The most negative feature of playing sport for me was that it encouraged me to construct a destructive, mechanical relationship to my own body and between my body and other people. Physical, 'goal-getting' skills became detached from emotional contacts and commitments.

Heterosexuality

On one level, heterosexual relations have historically shaped me to embody superiority over women in my bodily relations. Practically, that means holding my body in a firmly decisive way that marks me off from an imaginary woman. Often that means that thrusting, driving and pushing (as an expression of phallic power) have been naturalized in my heterosexual body. That also means that there has been a pressure on me to take the initiative in sexual relations, to play up the 'activity' aspects of being a manly lover rather than being tender and relaxing. I seemed to spend time on controlling who does what to whom, where and when.

In reality, my attempts to create a virile physical presence (supposedly so that I could become more attractive to women) were always sabotaged. My vulnerability and fear, as well as my need for greater closeness, have always showed through. However my fantasies of sexual conquest and performance have always been in conflict with a need for deeper emotional understanding. That struggle has also been tied into an attempt to resist the narrowing of focus on my penis rather than finding pleasure in exploring my sexuality through the whole of my body.

Work

Historically, I've often disregarded the needs of my body to fit in to the goals, targets and deadlines of work, particularly paid work. In this way I've approached my body as a mechanical container that carries out the pressing instructions coming from my head. That's certainly increased the feeling of unconnectedness that I've already inherited in this Western culture between my body and my mind.

My emotional investment in my work identity, through compulsively straining for stardom and success, has partly fitted me into the capitalist logic of individually and competitively pursuing goals. Sometimes the goals might have been progressive ones but the methods used to achieve them were often estranging.

Compulsive activity at work seemed to offer a controlling sense of purpose and direction when other parts of my life were breaking apart. For these reasons my body was susceptible to accepting its appropriate place in a gendered organization of labour. My first wife gave me unpaid, invisible support and servicing that allowed me to keep going at such a frenzied pace in the public sphere. My ability to go on giving an obsessive, driving, physical energy to my work was dependent on being looked after in the home. And, in its turn, that obsessive energy was needed to go on fuelling a patriarchal social order.

Of course it's never as straightforward as that. As I piled more and more pressure on myself at work, my body started to give me warnings that it couldn't stand that alienating rhythm any more. These were mostly in the form of stress-related symptoms like insomnia, an incessant scratching of my scalp when I was anxious, a dry tightening of my throat, tension headaches.

Over the years I developed habits of pushing my body so hard that I lost touch with any ability to know when I had gone too far. I was unable to set physical limits to my life.

My bodily relations shifted through time. My first 20 years were a time of learning, trying and often failing to embody a 'He-Man' masculine identity, mainly through sporting, family and sexual relations and practices, and the regulatory framework of schooling. All of this left its mark on me. The social constitution of my body was massively influential in preparing me to give my 'spontaneous' consent to patriarchal power relations in the ways I've indicated above.

But after reaching the age of 20 and through the years of experiencing academic achievement at university I started to identify myself through my mind. That was also tied in to my daily working relations of being a comprehensive-school English teacher and beginning to see myself as a Hero Innovator through my intellectual achievements.

After 30, as my marriage broke up, I began to be seized by a buried grief, that probably reactivated some of the loss and grief I had experienced in my early childhood. Unable to deal with this pain, I started to seek refuge in a workaholic obsessiveness. A massive emotional investment in the work identity of a rational intellectual helped to fill up the wounding gaps in my life left by the loss of my children and the loss of another family home. So, as the years went by, I learned to avoid my pain and distress by a single-minded concentration on intellectual work. In this way, my sense of myself as a worker gave me the stability and reassurance I needed at a time of shocking disorientation. However illusory and temporary this fixed self was, it gave me an anchoring point in the shifting sands of my life at that time.

A widening split grew between my mind and my body. I felt increasingly out of sync with my body, using it to carry around my brain but being estranged from its specific needs and rhythms. It was as if I was so intent on focusing my intellectual energy that I'd become deaf to the voice of my body. Over the years this led to a general denial of my emotional life and bodily experience as I pressurized myself to meet goals and targets. That's why when I eventually collapsed physically in February 1986 it was with a sense that my body had decided to claim its revenge on an indifferent, arrogant intellect.

Falling apart

I was reconnected to the life and history of my body at the moment when I collapsed in total heart-block while teaching. It was the point at which my body dug its heels in and refused to go on obeying the imperious demands of my head.

I was late for a fourth-year class just after afternoon break. Because of my anxiety about being late, I had raced up the stairs leading to the English department. I suddenly became dizzy and light-headed. It felt as if I was being sucked into the darkening, spinning centre of a whirlpool. Before, when I had experienced dizzy spells, I had felt as if I had lurched towards the centre of the whirlpool and then veered back to the calmer fringes of the slack, outer circle. But now I couldn't stop myself from being swallowed, deeper and deeper. There was just a terrifying, revolving swirl encircling me, dragging me in. I could feel my knees buckling. I sensed that I was caving in and falling.

It was the first time in my life that my body, which I had been holding so firm and tight for so long, had completely let me down. I was scared out of my mind. I had wet myself, gashed my chin open on the floor and had been unconscious for a full eight minutes. It was the overwhelming panic of losing control of my body that possessed me. It was the shocking reversal of usual expectations; my masculine body was so used to controlling itself and others that it flipped when it felt it was being controlled by forces outside itself. It was also the fear of losing power and virility in my body, of having that defensive armoury physically embodying my masculine identity smashed to smithereens.

I was rushed by ambulance to the coronary care unit of the University hospital, Nottingham. I had never stayed overnight in hospital before, even though I was 46. That panic stayed with me over the next six days in there. Was I going to die like some of the patients who occupied neighbouring beds to me during that time? That was the central question that haunted me night and day.

All through the next three nights a woman was gabbling in her shocked, hallucinated state, two beds away from me.

'Are you there, Eric?'

'Marion?'

'Go and get me some bread and marmalade.'

A nurse tried to calm her, held her hand, and, literally, fetched her some bread and marmalade. But the woman didn't notice it and left it neglected on top of her locker for the whole of the next day.

There was an old man dying in the next bed to me. One night there was a hoarse rasping of breath, an occasional explosion of coughing and then, in the early morning, the bells rang and there was an emergency attempt to save his life. I lay listening, in mounting panic, to everything that was going on – the slamming of the heart trolley into the snoring ward, the running of nurses, the swishing of the curtains screening off his bed, the frustrated kick-start to the heart, three or four times, the concerned, muffled voices, the furtive taking of one pink carnation from the central table of flowers for the corpse to hold when later meeting his relatives.

This rang wild alarm-bells in my head. Would I get through? I was now precariously supported by a temporary pacemaker attached to a small, box battery. I obsessively watched a heart monitor register each flickering irregularity in my heart beat, and noticed how my peaks of anxiety agitated the monitoring screen.

My partner, Brenda, was there giving me close support. She slept in a visitors' room for four nights, held me, brought things for me, tried to cheer me up, asked nurses and doctors about my condition. But nobody seemed to know what was wrong with me. They ran all kinds of tests on me but nothing showed up. Then, at the end of six days, they told me that it was better for me to have a permanent pacemaker. But they didn't implant them in Nottingham. It was the specialist, regional heart hospital in Groby Road, Leicester that did. So off I went in the same clothes that I had arrived in.

Groby Road Heart Hospital

At Groby Road the doctors weren't interested in giving me a pacemaker before they'd investigated me thoroughly. So over the next six weeks the doctors ran a battery of tests on my body that again didn't come up with any solid proof of what was wrong with me. They suspected that I had endocarditis, a bacterial infection in the heart that might have developed in conjunction with my leaking heart-valve, a family legacy from my mother. But the classic, unmistakable symptoms of that condition – black flecks on my finger-nails – weren't there.

I became intensely aware of my body's moods, its daily movements, its sudden swings, my distinctive heartbeat like a personal thumbprint, its aches and pains in a way that previously living through my rational intellect had distanced me from. Lying in bed all day I sensed every little event through the finger tips of my nervous system. I hated having my blood taken for tests, sometimes twice or three times a day. I felt the needle sharply puncturing my vein and then the slow coaxing and pumping of my blood into the tube.

Then they ran a long series of ultra-sound tests on my heart. I remember being asked to lie on my side and an instrument like a microphone being stabbed right into the area of my heart. It was wincingly cold on my warm flesh. The machine imaged an internal picture of my faulty, leaking valve and the magnified slurping and sloshing sound of my blood echoed in my ears and filled me with terror. I felt a deep fear of being invaded in a peculiarly intimate space where I had lived for so long, hidden away.

I also remember panicky attacks of sudden light-headedness during that time. Because my heartbeats were being screened on a monitor I was painfully self-conscious about my heart rhythm. Any slight flutter of my heart, stumbling pauses and hesitations in the beat, would send me into jerky tremors of anxiety. And then, looking up, there the tremors would be, wobbling their crooked way across the monitor. So there was a constant inseparable link between my nervous anxiety and my heart rhythm, each influencing each other, back and forth, forth and back.

However there were consolations. One of the advantages of sharing a two-bed cubicle in the modernized fever hospital at Groby Road was the possibility of close contact with the other person in the cubicle. Even though I was very ill I tried to keep up my interest and curiosity (which were very real) in other patients' lives.

One of my companions was a lorry driver called Mal. The pressure of piecework, flogging himself to achieve bonus rates, had contributed to putting him inside Groby Road. He told me that he used to get up at 2 or 3 o'clock in the morning in order to get through London and down to the south coast before the morning rush hour.

Driving an Artic,[18] he usually took 20-ton loads of coke and coal from the Nottinghamshire/Derbyshire coalfield down to the Kent coalfield and then, often in the same day, went across to Port Talbot and Llanwern. The pressure of constantly racing the clock, and coming home totally exhausted, had finally damaged his heart.

He was fed up of always having to push the speed along, getting to the Kent coalfield in four and a half hours instead of the eight hours he was allocated. He had got used to the bonus in his pay packet and found that he was caught in a trap. To get more out of the piecework system he frequently had to work a 90-hour week, fiddling the logs, claiming an overnight allowance and getting back to Leicester before midnight.

Also my surrounding context had a great influence on my relation to my body. At Groby Road all the doctors and consultants were men. All the nurses and cleaners (except for two male nurses) were women.

Within that very rigid, patriarchal institution, my male consultant and the other male doctors who did the daily donkey work gave me the sense that I didn't own my body. They spent a lot of time talking amongst themselves about me rather than to me. They talked about my physical condition as if I, personally, wasn't there. I became invisible to myself when they were around.

[62]

One day on a visiting round, just before the consultant came into the cubicle, I overheard them discussing the state of my heart: 'Yes, there's a horrendous calcification of the septem wall'. I knew they were talking about me because I had seen the white calcification shown up in the ultra-sound image of my heart. The specialized, technical language intensified the sense I had that I was being viewed as a clinical object, somehow detached from my felt sense of myself as a living, breathing person who could exercise choices.

My feeling of bodily objectification was also deepened by the nurses' meetings. At the end of each nurse shift (three times every 24 hours) there was a ritual handing over of information. There were whispering voices outside in the corridor. They were summarizing and commenting on my condition for the next shift to take over – talking about my body and my moods, repeating fleeting points that I'd made during the course of the day, repeating the times when I needed medication, and so on.

Even though I was still extremely wobbly, I think this context of being talked about as a detached body provoked my resistance. It strengthened my determination not to allow myself to be passively contained within the all-controlling, expert power of the male consultant. All through that time I kept on asking him questions about my condition. I tried not to take anything on trust but, as far as I was able, to participate actively in the treatment and decisions that were being made.

My partner believes that I came through that time because I kept on making myself 'awkward' in the eyes of the professional experts, writing down questions when I was too ill, joking, being irreverent, challenging established authority. In my own groggy way, it was my attempt to take charge of my body, rather than just passing it over, like a carcass, into the hands of the experts.

Body scanning, catheterization and heart surgery

The exact causes of my illness were still a mystery to my doctors. As a result, my consultant suggested, as the tests hadn't shown up anything, that I needed a much closer, internal investigation of my heart and body.

[63]

After so many years of bodily invisibility, this period felt like a time of alien invasion, of having my body colonized and prodded by machines that penetrated far inside my body. My fear of losing masculine control and being de-armoured was acute. I had learnt to be the penetrator and the fucker. Now they were fucking me, penetrating into my secret places. My purchase on a safe, heterosexual masculine identity was being eroded.

The first experience of invasion was being body-scanned at Leicester Infirmary. I had to lie flat in a white gown on a mechanical trackway, like the Frankenstein monster. Then slowly the trackway fed me into the dark, inner mouth of the scanner. There was a moment of real, claustrophobic panic as I moved, gradually, into the blind centre of the machine. My body felt as if it had been dismembered into separate sections and areas as X-ray photographs were taken from as many different angles and perspectives as possible. It was a moment of total, physical disorientation as my body was whirred around, tilted back, raised upwards, turned on its side. In my mind, my body broke up into little bits.

The catheterization was even more invasive. A fibre-optic catheter, like a long worm with a searchlight, was fed into the chambers of my heart. The doctor gave me a local anaesthetic and made an incision in my groin so that the catheter could wriggle its way up one of the main arteries into my heart.

I think I can remember the despair I felt when the doctor realized he was going up a tributary vein not a main one and had to slowly remove the catheter, step by step, and start all over again. When he eventually reached the inside of my heart they ran several tests on me to find out its actual condition. I can remember flinching away at the injected dye that was flushed through my arteries to check whether they were furred up or not.

Still none the wiser, and perhaps noticing my deepening depression and anxiety at the long wait, my consultant recommended that they should operate on my damaged heart valve and have a proper chance to find out whether I actually had endocarditis. I reluctantly agreed.

The preparation for the operation forced my body into a starkly naked exposure, almost literally and metaphorically. First I had to shave off all my body hair from my chest, armpits and lower stomach and then all my pubic hair as well. I protested to the nurses at this who agreed, privately, that they thought it was a waste of time. But they told me that this particular surgeon was a stickler for this kind of detail and they would get it in the neck if they didn't comply. And so I had to go on with it, cursing over the hospital razors as I kept nicking my skin, and then had to have several antiseptic baths.

Of course my time during the operation and then my later recovery in the intensive care unit are blurred, a confused time of severe physical disorientation and tearing, ripping pain. But what was significant was the way, not only that my external covering of hair was shaved off, but also that the protective shield of my historically constructed, masculinized body (the tensely held pattern that shaped my neuro-musculature) was smashed into and broken open. In the process of the heart surgery my chest was physically unzipped, my sternum broken and my heart repaired and reconstructed. I awoke with a new plastic valve busily and strangely clicking away inside me.

After the operation

I really fell apart, emotionally, after the operation. I was told three days after it that the surgeon had confirmed that I had a bacterial infection in my heart. So I was immediately put on this massive dose of antibiotics injected straight into my veins through a venflon (a needle connected to a plastic tap for intravenous injection). To make matters worse I was told by my consultant that I would have to stay in hospital for at least another six weeks.

This was the bottom point of that long time in hospital for me. I felt total despair. I was now in Ward 11, the convalescent ward. All around me there were already signs that the people who had been operated on at roughly the same time as myself were beginning to move around and were visibly getting stronger; whereas I not only had to fight for survival after the operation but I also had to take on this fresh assault on my life. After all the tests, investigations, traumas, shocks of the previous seven weeks I felt absolutely drained of energy and the will to go on. I felt every necessary bodily movement was just too much for me. My bodily cage felt devastated and there was this terrible burning pain, like a spiky thistle with sharp edges, flaming away inside my ripped chest.

One of the nurses fixed up a bandage hoist with one end attached to the end of my bed and the other left close to my hands. They kept on trying to encourage me to lift myself into a sitting position from an exhausted, pillowed slump. I felt unreasonably irritated by their false cheeriness. I just wanted to be left to fester in my misery.

I gave up asking questions about my body. My life seemed to be cramped inside a closed box, with the predictable routine of four injections every day and the fuss of meals. Every late afternoon my burning fever would return and my temperature would soar. And there was an increasingly difficult search for a vein that wasn't clapped out. The constant pain of inserting venflons began to haunt my dreams. All my veins were over-used, after all those tests, and beginning to close up. Doctors would literally spend hours searching my arms, wrists and the backs of my hands, trying to pat and then smack a vein into prominence. After several futile goes at inserting the venflon, with the agonizing pain of getting the needle out of my mottled arm, at last the venflon would be effectively put in only to close up after a day and a half.

I asked to be put back into Ward 12 where I knew the nurses and the cleaners. But instead of bringing me back to a cubicle they put me into a small, side ward for seven men. My depression deepened. I was surrounded by men waiting for operations who were trying to control their mounting panic by putting on bright, brave faces. There was a television positioned at the head of the ward, and every morning for about three hours we all watched, dozed and half-watched 'Good Morning Britain'. The TV presenters' determined cheerfulness, prattling on about daily facts, personalities, weather and trivia, drove me further and further into an endless tunnel of despair. I felt a murderous rage swelling in my body, but I was too ill and depressed to express it. I just sank back and allowed myself to disappear into a drowsy slur.

At the lowest point of my depression I cracked up, emotionally. Just after the ward sister had realized her mistake and moved me back into a small cubicle, I started to cry. At first in apologetic, strangulated sobs but then wildly, uncontrollably. I still don't know exactly what I was crying for, but the slightest thing would set me off.

I seemed to be open and vulnerable, in a way that I had never experienced before, to other people's grief, sadness, fear. They never acknowledged these feelings in their talk. I could just sniff them out, like some disciplined tracker dog, beneath all their protective foliage. One minute the other person in the cubicle would be telling me his story about how he got to Groby Road, and the next minute I would feel a stinging and smarting behind my nose and then my cheeks would be streaming with tears. It was like a great dam cracking open in me after all those years of holding myself tight.

All those influential models of ideal, masculine maturity – that stiff-upper-lip stoicism and self control – started to fissure. I didn't need to keep reaching upwards towards the false solidity of these sturdy English Oaks! I could begin to learn how to change that clenched, tensed control in my body. Of course it didn't occur as neatly as that. It's a part of a long complex process of change and reconstruction, both personally and socially. But it was this crying that seemed to point the way towards another way of being and relating in the world. I've only begun to understand the importance of that emotional cracking up four years later.

Getting better

My body began, very grudgingly, to get better. After about two and a half weeks on the antibiotic treatment my afternoon fever still didn't come down. So my consultant upped my dose. He confessed to my partner that he was throwing everything he could at me. It was almost more than my body could take. Later he admitted that he wouldn't have known what to do if my body hadn't responded.

But respond it did, day by day, ever so gradually. My afternoon temperature started to come down over the next three and a half weeks and my health began to stabilize. However, at the same time, the venflon agony increased. Nearly all my veins had shut down under the intense battering they had been getting over the last 14 weeks. I had had enough pain. My nervous system felt as if it had been shot away.

I would have to go through a long-drawn-out ritual of agony before the doctors managed to find a working vein. They even asked me to sink both my arms in a bucket of hot water so that the veins would begin to stand up more conspicuously. Then they would carry out the close inspection of every part of my wrists and arms for a suitable spot. I can feel again now the sharp puncturing of my flesh over and over again, the aching of the needle in the vein and the more sustained pain as the vein gave up and closed down.

I was in such agony and anxiety about it that the consultant agreed to my refusal to take any more injections. I think he saw my fatigue. He transferred me onto a tablet dose that ended up as 16 pills taken four times a day with two injections of gentamicin in my backside as well. That went on for another two and a half weeks as I continued to recover.

After 16 weeks in hospital, an appallingly long time, I was let out to go back home. I still had to take the pills for another three weeks, and the injections were given to me every evening by the district nurse. The consultant recognized, as I did by this time, that I could only heal properly and gather my lost health at home. But for the next three months I had to keep going backwards and forwards between hospital and home.

These return visits to hospital weren't only detailed post-operation check-ups but were also connected to a careful investigation of my blood to see if it was still contaminated by the bacterial infection. After a few minor hiccoughs I was given the all-clear. So in mid–August 1986, about 25 weeks after I had collapsed in total heart-block, I was eventually recalled to Groby Road Hospital for another three days to have a permanent pacemaker implanted.

My bodily crack-up provoked me to take on a critical reassessment of my traditional bodily relations and masculine identity. My body reasserted its claims for a fuller representation in my existence by disrupting the illusion of my coherent, unified, rational intellect and shredding it into small fragments.

This shocking invasion blew up the fantasy dream of 'He-Man', masculine power in my body. It forced the actual state of my damaged body into critical visibility. And without creating another fantasy of total, harmonious reintegration between my mind and my body, it showed me why it was necessary, while living within the fragments, to bring my bodily experience and my emotions into a closer creative contact with my intellect. That process is still continuing, bumpily and unevenly.

Physical breakdown is a terrifying experience for many men because it connects the masculine body with weakness, dependency and passivity – all the supposedly 'feminine' qualities they have spent a lifetime defining and defending themselves against. Often for the first time in some men's lives it opens up fearful cracks in the 'hard case' front of heterosexual masculinity. Breakdown, illness and injury can also be a strategy for renegotiating dominant, heterosexual, masculine identities that have become imprisoning for some men, like me, who have never felt completely at home within those kinds of conventional investments. In another way, falling apart helped me to negotiate the conflict between wanting to give up traditional power without losing face. It offered my partner and myself a safe place within which both of us could revert to temporary, secure identities, without giving up the combined struggle to change gendered inequalities. Very occasionally we could resort, as a temporary breather, to much more rigidly dichotomized identities. For example, I could enjoy my official permission to take to my bed and admit my dependency on my partner, at the same time as my partner might take fleeting pleasure in looking after me and getting closer, if it didn't go on for too long.

Falling apart turned out to be a way of refusing more thrusting, driving and pushing. And it also helped me to choose to make more confident investments in my other, transitional selves. With official legitimacy, I could turn my back on more patriarchal pressure, and start to put energy, in a different collaborative way, into 'changing men' issues at both a personal and social level. I have begun to set myself new physical limits, and have started to restructure and repace my life: with difficulty, it has to be admitted, but I am moving in that general direction.

Before the 25 weeks of my breakdown were up, I didn't need to be reminded that I could afford to give up my ambiguous attempts to achieve a 'He-Man' strut and identity before it finally did for me.

Notes

1 Here the argument is indebted to R. W. Connell (1983) 'Men's bodies' in *Which Way is Up?* Sydney, Allen & Unwin (Sydney, Australia), and his section on 'The body and social practice', in R. W. Connell (1987) *Gender and Power*, Cambridge, Polity, where he says, 'My male body

does not confer masculinity on me; it receives masculinity (or some fragment thereof) as its social definition.'

2 See R. McGrath (1988) 'Looking hard: the male body under patriarchy', in A. Foster (ed.) *Behold the Man: The Male Nude in Photography*, Edinburgh, Stills Gallery.

3 The whole of this section is indebted to L. Segal (1988) 'Look back in anger: men in the 50's', in R. Chapman and J. Rutherford (eds) *Male Order: Unwrapping Masculinity*, London, Lawrence & Wishart.

4 ibid., p. 70.

5 See D. Riley (1983) *War in the Nursery*, London, Virago, for a critical perspective on 'Bowlbyism' in the 1950s.

6 See the section, 'Homophobia and the fear of unmanliness' in Chapman and Rutherford, op. cit., pp. 84–5; G. Rubin (1984) 'Thinking sex: notes for a radical theory of the politics of sexuality', in C. Vance (ed.) *Pleasure and Danger*, London, Routledge & Kegan Paul, pp. 270–1.

7 J. Osborne (1960) 'Sex and failure', in G. Feldman and M. Gartenberg (eds) *Protest*, London, Panther. Quoted in Segal, op. cit.

8 See section, 'Heroes for sale', in Foster, op. cit., pp. 27–8.

9 Published in a weekly comic called *The Rover*, 30th July 1949.

10 Directed by George More O'Ferrall (1952), Great Britain.

11 Directed by Leslie Norman (1953), Great Britain.

12 See A. Medhurst (1984) '1950s war films', in G. Hurd (ed.) *National Fictions*, London, British Film Institute.

13 See A. Medhurst (1985) 'Can chaps be pin-ups? The British male film star of the 1950s', in *Men in Camera*, Ten-8 photographic magazine. No. 17.

14 All of this discussion is indebted to the 'Identities/Subjectivities' group in the Cultural Studies Department, University of Birmingham, 1989–90.

15 'Identity, continuity or coherence is often *bought* by cutting or stretching ourselves to fit in with some powerful source of recognition, some heavily installed or institutionalised model.' From M. Clare and R. Johnson (1986) 'Nationalism, narrative and identity'. Unpublished paper presented to the Conference of the Association for Cultural Studies, 22 March.

16 See E. Dempster (1988) 'Women writing the body: Let's watch a little how she dances', in S. Sheridan (ed.) *Grafts*, London, Verso.

17 See M. Foucault (1984) 'Docile bodies', in P. Rabinow (ed.) *The Foucault Reader*, Harmondsworth, Penguin.

18 An articulated lorry.

CHAPTER 4
Family background

My father and mother met while they were both working in the 'Silver Wings' café in Cardiff some time around 1936. They were both born in the South Wales valleys; my mother in 1912 and my father in 1910. My maternal grandparents were both from Manchester, and my grandfather from that side had worked as a manager of a cinema, as well as on the Great Western Railway.

On my father's side, my grandfather (Gaudio Amarilli) had emigrated from a small town in northern Italy to Cardiff near the end of the last century. He had worked his way up in the icecream/coffee-bar business to owning several cafés in Abertillery from 1900 to the middle of the 1920s, and then later in Nottinghamshire.

To gain acceptance in the local community he used a business name (Jackson) which he later officially took on when he changed his name at the time of intense Italian unpopularity in Britain following the Italian invasion of Abyssinia in 1934.

My father helped in the Abertillery cafés when he was a boy, and then branched out on his own when he began to work in Cardiff. My mother was soon pregnant with Shirley and that pressurized both of them into what was then called a shotgun marriage. In 1937 they left the really severe economic depression of South Wales for the anonymity and greater possibilities of London. My father found a job driving for a 'ladies' clothing firm and they lived in a flat in a tenement block just behind Euston station.

Those two years between 1937 and 1939 were very lonely ones for my mother. She was very isolated looking after her baby in difficult conditions, uprooted from her family and with Dad frequently absent during the week. That's why, when war broke out in September 1939, she was positive about the chance of getting out of London and rejoining her family in a rented house in Paignton, South Devon.

When war was declared my father joined the Auxiliary Fire Service in London (deciding that that was a wiser choice than joining the armed forces and possibly having to fight against his father's people). My parents gave up the flat because Dad could live in the fire station; and Mum, who was now pregnant with me, was evacuated to Paignton.

So there I was born in February 1940 in an extremely feminized household. Along with my mother and my two sisters (Anne was born in 1942), there were my two aunts, Joan and Minna, and my mother's parents who spent some of their time looking after the two boys of Joan's failed first marriage.

We lived in one room of this overcrowded rented property from 1940 to 1944, with Dad coming down for rare flying visits. In 1944 we managed to rent a series of rooms, with a back kitchen, over a shop on the main Paignton to Torquay road. That's where I remember hearing tanks rumbling through all night in 1944, just before the D-Day landings in Normandy.

I went to Oldway Primary School, Paignton, from 1945 to 1951. I passed the 11-plus and started to attend King Edward VI Grammar School, Totnes, as a day boy, taking a bus every day from Paignton to Totnes (about five miles, but about seven miles in all from my home). In 1950 my mother gave birth to a fourth child, Susan, and as a result her physical condition noticeably deteriorated.

In 1952, when I was 12, my mother died from heart disease and suspected endocarditis. So from 1952 to 1959 I went to the grammar-school residential institution, Kennicott House, paid for by the county council where about 45–50 boys boarded, mainly from isolated farms in north Devon or bronchial asthmatics from other parts of the country.

From about 1953 my father lived with Violet Holdaway, who also offered her house to us during the long holidays between terms. Shirley, Anne and myself were all now boarding at Teignmouth and Totnes and we only saw our Dad intermittently during parts of the long holidays. The rest of the time, until we all went off to higher education, we were handed around various real and imitation 'aunts and uncles', who took turns in deciding on whether they were going to adopt us. And then in the end they didn't.

Staying with Violet Holdaway didn't work out, either for her or us, so in 1956 Shirley and I left to stay with Aunt Minna during the holidays. From about that time I became a weekly boarder, staying at Kennicott House during the week and at my aunt's during the weekends and some of the holidays.

In 1959 I continued the educational route out of the working class by going to Leicester University.

A feeling of panic is very much with me now, of not knowing where to start in all these unconnected scraps of family history. An autobiography is as much about what I choose to forget, to avoid or to conceal as it is about what I choose to make public. Indeed, what I leave out is as meaningful as what I put in, and, in some ways, the shadows of the absences are always lurking behind what is named. For many men, the calculated avoidance of pain in their public face memoirs is as resonantly implicit in their silences as the selected scraps they choose to share as representative.

I suppose I could have started in the randomness of intensely felt, family moments; of straining on the pot to gain the approval of my mother, of pressing my nose against the shop window and feeling the waves of want, want, want sweeping over me for the lead soldier, of waking up in the middle of the night with the hollow, sinking feeling that I'd done it again and sensing my pyjamas and bedclothes sopping wet.

Or I could have started with the history of our family pets; of a pet rabbit that dug a hole under the telegraph pole in the back garden, of a pet budgie that could prise off tin lids with its beak, or a hedgehog (found in the local woods and brought home) that we later discovered with all its innards squashed out flat on the main road outside our front door.

But this appearance of spontaneous authenticity is very deceptive. At first sight, it seems that these casual, unguarded details give us more of the immediate sense of what it felt like to be there then, and of what I valued then. But as I have already indicated in the introductory section on the dialogue between past and present, there is no pristine, pre-social nugget of memory that is just waiting to be uncovered and appreciated, that hasn't been worked over, again and again. What we are left with is a fictional reconstruction of life events that we lend significance to, in accordance with the way our present emotional investments in certain identities shift and change.

From this alternative perspective I can decide to choose a critical framework (my anti-patriarchal, anti-capitalist viewpoint) to inform my selection of representative moments from my life history.

I suppose what matters most is making explicit my present-day values and priorities, and to show how those interests have shaped this process of selective reconstruction. So that the reader isn't sold a fake authenticity ('This is how it was. .'), but allowed to see into the inner workings of a process of transformation and recasting that is much more open to choice and historical change.

It's time to start. I'm going to make a beginning in my reconstruction of a childhood nightmare that seems to summarise something of an important, emotional structure in my life – a structure of loss, grief and the connected, obsessive search for greater closeness.

The nightmare that haunted the boy's dreams coincided with his father's homecoming. It came at the moment in his life when he had to learn to sleep alone in a small, cramped box room, far away from the merging comfort of the double bed.

The nightmare was always the same. He felt that he was physically shrinking against the massiveness of the surrounding cupboards, wardrobes, chest of drawers. He became smaller and smaller in his bed, while the room's ceiling and walls started to close in on him. His eyes started to ache with the burden of taking in the swelling bundle of his thrown off clothes (blackly silhouetted in the shadowy gloom) draped across the back of a chair. The walls pressed in on his senses and suffocated him. He was nothing against the leaden bulk leaning down on him. He wouldn't cry out again, but he had to get out of there, to breathe freely again.

The boy braced himself for half a second, staring up at the car headlights criss-crossing his bedroom ceiling, and then cautiously lowered himself out of his bed. He crept out of the door and across the dark landing, the same wonky floorboard giving him away again. His feet were like blocks of ice on the cold lino as he slowly inched the door open to his parents' bedroom. He stopped still for a moment listening anxiously to his mother's breathing. It was as if there were cords that attached him to the soft rise and fall of her breathing.

On the other side of the bed from the doorway his father stopped snoring, groaned and harumphed noisily, turning restlessly in the bed. With held breath the boy edged himself

*under the sheet and eiderdown, on his mother's side of the
bed closest to the door. He snuggled into her safe, warm
thigh. She had half-wakened, knew who it was without
checking, murmured, sighed and went back to sleep. He
couldn't believe his luck, this time.*

*The boy slid his left arm under the pillow and nuzzled
his nose down deeply into the warm, pillow scent of his
mother's hair. He was the right size again. He could go to
sleep here, and forget his fear. The snoring bulk of his father
moaned again, loudly, and shifted over in the bed away from
his wife and son to face the wall again.*

Presenting this text as a seamless flow, as an apparently spontaneous outpouring of recollections, unmediated by viewpoint,
would be deceiving the reader. What I want to try and do is to
invite the reader to understand the process of producing this book
from the inside, to share some of the difficult choices over how a
critical autobiography is put together.

I've already mentioned the blurring of the boundaries between
truth and fiction in critical autobiography. Here in this piece on
getting into my parents' bed at night the fictional reconstruction is
clear. Using my adult, retrospective priorities as a 50 year old man
looking back over his childhood, I'm working from an extremely
shadowy and heavily reworked viewpoint. I'm using my present,
adult understandings of how I felt I was emotionally rejected and
abandoned as a child at my father's homecoming to fictionally
reinvent the anxious isolation of the small boy I might have been
at five years old.

The danger with this way of working is that adult, retrospective
categories can weigh too heavily in the process of selecting the
life stories that fit into those categories. In this chapter I'm very
aware of this creaking weight. My attention is so fixed on the
feminist-influenced arguments about the family being a breeding
ground for gendered and class-related inequalities that they seem
to take precedence over the life stories, so that the social/political
comments and the stories seem very detached and unconnected.

In this chapter, the awkward transitions between chronological
documentary, carefully wrought, fictional scenes, and sociological
analysis are probably a result of still being confused about the
possible significance of that time, and being uncertain how to

combine the needs of the whole book (the documentary piece on my family background), the anti-sexist focus on looking back on my family, and the emotional pain of some of my family stories.

These might be some of the reasons why I decided to write this scene in the third person. On one level it gave me a protective distance from an area of my childhood experience that hurt too much. Holding it at arm's length allowed me to approach it in a way that didn't make me too rawly exposed.

On another level it allowed me to announce that this wasn't just a personally eccentric story. This use of 'the boy' suggests that there were other boys, at this particular time, who found their fathers' homecomings displacing. There were common features about the story that placed my personal feeling of isolation, fear and obsessive search for warmth into a wider historical frame. Perhaps the use of the words 'the boy' also alerts the reader to the gendered status of my relationship to my parents and this nightmarish moment.

Choosing the more anonymous use of the third person, against the first person, also might broaden out the range of its potential reference. It meant that I wasn't just locked into the narrow perspective of the first person, but had access to wider critical options and perspectives.

It's very difficult to think clearly about your own family. There are so many intense emotions just lying under the surface of everyday life. Also critical issues are often fogged by a traditional mythologizing of an ideal, nuclear version of the family[1] achieved at the expense of a multiplicity of other forms.

My family was very much one of those marginalized other forms, with an eccentric yet specific class, regional and historical identity. I grew up in a respectable working-class family, driven by war conditions into a semi-evacuee, housesharing arrangement between 1940 and 1945.

It was an arrangement that defied easy categories; it must have been an extremely feminized household, with the radical potential of war work for women temporarily opening up new possibilities in the job market. Certainly it was my two aunts, Joan and Minna, who must have ruled the roost during that period, as my grandparents were both in their 70s when war was declared.

It was through Joan's initiative that the rented property, a large, rambling house in Great Headland Crescent, Preston, Paignton, had been acquired. She was one of the first women to break the male monopoly of working on the local buses. I can still vaguely remember the photograph of Joan as a bus conductor, with one foot jauntily astride the first step of the Devon General singledecker bus.

With Minna it was roughly the same. She had a bold, laughing, extrovert energy that, weekly, took her to Swindon during the war, where she worked on making parts for Lancaster and Stirling bombers. Both sisters had been influenced, in varying degrees, by growing up around an industrial, labour history within the South Wales valleys. Joan was the more sophisticated thinker, having won a scholarship to Cardiff High School for Girls, but Minna was full of a passionate, at times wild, resentment at social inequality.

Minna and my mother shopped at the local Co-op for most of their lives. (Minna once told me, later on, that she wouldn't have got through the war if it hadn't been for the tick she was allowed to get at the Co-op.) And later, on weekends from the age of 16 to 19, I think I can remember something of the thwarted frustration of Minna's Labour-voting household, getting the *Daily Herald* during the week and the Co-operative movement's newspaper, *The Reynold's News*, on Sunday, while situated within the Tory stronghold of Torbay.

Mum was the quiet one of the three sisters. She didn't put herself forward as much as the other two. On the surface, she seemed to be more content in conventionally identifying herself through marriage, the family and homemaking. But she also had suppressed longings for fashionable glamour (I remember one pageboy hat she bought with a bobble stuck on top), and a love of going to the pictures every week.

At one of the peak moments for cinema-going in Britain (between 1946 and 1951) she used to collect us straight from primary school, and arrange to meet Shirley outside the Regent cinema in Paignton (Shirley by then had started at secondary school). I remember my belly always grumbling out for food at embarrassing moments, munching the jam sandwiches while my eyes were glued on the screen, or craftily nibbling away at the Lancashire hotpot or rock buns that Shirley had made during her cookery class that afternoon.

My mother's passion-starved yearnings seemed to be satisfied by the horror films of the day, like the Sherlock Holmes adventure,

[77]

The Scarlet Claw. I remember being absolutely terrified by the scenes of misty, lurking menace when the claw struck out on the surrounding marshes. I was also paralysed with fear at the scene from *Green for Danger* when a nurse re-enters a hospital at dead of night. She starts to creep down this corridor when she sees a masked surgeon, with a raised scalpel in his right hand, coming towards her. My mother didn't seem to be worried at all about the possible effect of the films on us, or the fact that I had nightmares about *The Scarlet Claw* for several months afterwards. She had a need to get away from the daily grind, even with the bind of having her kids around her all the time, to treat herself at least once a week, and that she did.

And a regular grind it certainly was. It must have been incredibly hard sleeping in a single room with two and then three children under the age of five, and taking sole responsibility for her own family's care and (with her mother) domestic labour. Joan was out all day and Minna only came back for occasional weekends some of the time. So most of the daily work must have fallen on my mother's shoulders.

Within the unequal divisions of home and work, private and public spheres, I think my mother must have struggled, in her own quiet way, against the conventional assumption that her body was just there for producing babies, and her time of pregnancy, childbirth and childrearing automatically called for the support and protection of a male breadwinner. Certainly my elder sister felt that one of the most urgent forces in my mother's life was her fear of getting pregnant again. That must have been a fear of having no life of her own apart from the repetitive routines of childrearing and housework; and possibly mixed up with a fear of dying in childbirth, because of the strain put on her damaged heart. From this angle, perhaps the prospect of my father's permanent homecoming in 1945 might have filled her with alarm as well as positive anticipation. The sense of widening differences between them might have centred on the conventional habits of a partly hidden but happy-go-lucky Catholic boy (who certainly wasn't used to worrying about contraception) colliding with my mother's suppressed desires to have a space and a life of her own. I can't be sure about this but it does make sense of the edgy relationship they had, and my sister's and my own shadowy recollections of that time.

[78]

The other major feature about my family life between 1940 and 1959 was its interrupted, discontinuous character. My father was absent from 1940 to 1945, and after my mother gave birth to her fourth child (Susan in 1950) her heart condition, and suspected endocarditis, rapidly deteriorated. For the last 18 months of her life before she died in 1952 she was either disabled but dragging on, in hospital, or convalescing (for six months?) in a fireman friend's cottage in the country between Paignton and Totnes. As a result, I only experienced a more traditional, nuclear family unit, with its narrow, self-enclosed way of organizing itself, for five or six years, from 1945 to about 1950/51. From 1952 to 1959 I went to the Devon County Council, residential part of the grammar school that I had gone to in 1951. That discontinuity and deep sense of homelessness had a lasting effect on me in the years to come.

Perhaps the first thing to say about the family as a social organization is that, in its claustrophobically intimate conditions, it promotes intense and powerful emotional attachments to parental figures. These initial interactions[2] with my parents, and the deeply ingrained patterns of emotional attachment that go with them (or lack of them), are constantly influencing the way I relate to other people in close friendships, and the way I behave today. Some of these central patterns of attachment in my own life can be seen in the nightmare scene about the ceiling closing in on me, described ·earlier.

Because of the lopsided history of my first five years, which overemphasized the intersexed relations between my mother and myself (see Chapter 6 and 7 for a fuller treatment of these themes), I developed a clinging, over-close attachment to my mother. It felt so desperately needy that if my independent growth as a boy had demanded that I dump my attachment to my mother then I would have preferred not to grow up at all. My overpowering sense of oneness with her did feel as if there were cords that connected me to the 'soft rise and fall of her breathing' for ever. Some of the implications of that for the construction of my masculinity are spelt out later on in the book.

Separate from that, but interlinked, were my interactions with my father. In a way he never had the chance of being allowed in on the inner sanctuaries of his family at his permanent homecoming at the end of the war. Both the matriarchal household, and the special relationship I had with my mother, shut him out. I experienced him early on as a 'harumphing' presence, turning contemptuously away to face the wall, away from the soft pampered intimacies (as he must have perceived them) between his wife and coddled son. He was significant to me, in the early years, as a conspicuous absence (his positional and symbolic status[3] was sometimes referred to, as in 'If I told your father what you're getting up to now, he would be really angry'). It was the estranging distance of his dealings with me that comes through to me now. It was only much later in my life that I was able to develop some sympathy for him as a mutual outsider.

In my own life the family that I grew up in was an important breeding ground for both social-class and gendered relations. Through particular incidents from my own personal history I'd like to try and investigate both areas, linking together as much as I can comments about social power and the psychoanalytical.

Looking back now, and trying to understand a particular 'structure of feeling'[4] associated with social class (its atmosphere, its power differentials, its bitter flavour in my mouth, its implied social relations), I can rework one specific incident like this:

My mother had promised my elder sister a 'big treat' on the special occasion of her birthday. My sister was very excited by the possibility of what this treat might turn out to be. My mother hinted that it might be something to eat and, immediately, we imagined vast Knickerbocker Glories, great slabs of cake and endless bottles of foaming ginger beer (a favourite drink of my sister's).

But the real 'treat' turned out differently. Mum took us to a posh café/restaurant on the top floor of the largest and most prestigious department store in Torquay at that time. (Rockhey's it was called). I think I can remember the solemn-faced, black-uniformed attendant in the wood-panelled lift calling out the names of each floor as we went up to the top floor.

It was a hushed, soft carpeted place of potted palms and waitress service. Women in fancy hats and fox furs were taking a long time over sipping their tea, and a head waiter

*hastily directed us to a side table out of sight of the people
entering through the glass doors.*

*I can only guess what my mother must have gone through
when she saw the menu. There were vol-au-vents, and all
kinds of tiddly bits dressed up to look expensive. They must
have cost the earth! She must have realized that she'd made
a mistake, but one look at my sister's face told her that
she had to see it through. When the waitress arrived she
was ready. Avoiding the waitress's eyes, she ordered some
tomato sandwiches and a pot of tea for three.*

*We kept quiet but all our wild imaginings went crashing
to the floor. All our extravagant visions of Peach Melbas
and Knickerbocker Glories took a nose dive when we saw
the woman return with one, small silver salver. Inside there
were six, dainty tomato sandwich triangles with their crusts
cut off. A doily covered the inside of the salver and a handful
of cress was sprinkled over the triangles. The waitress asked
if there was anything else we wanted. She gave us a funny
look, hesitated, then went away.*

*We ate the sandwiches in silence, drank the tea, and left
quickly. Nobody commented on anything, or mentioned the
birthday. To my knowledge, it has never been referred to
since that time, by any of the family. But I can still remember
the hurt of that funny look, and the shame flaming my
cheeks.*

This scene has a significance for me – in terms of class insecurity
and put-down – that it could never had had then. Now my
more consciously worked-out, interpretative system (seeing the
family as an important institutional site for generating class and
gendered inequalities) selects this scene as one of crucial social
recognition. This is the moment when I recognized my own
social powerlessness in relation to another social world that had
its 'crusts cut off'.

My present critical perspective has lent this scene a dramatic,
revelatory importance. The story is loosely based on a moment
from my life that I actually lived through. But it's a scene that's very
dimly lit and blurred for me, associated in some complex way with
a vague unease. But here in my retelling, the fictional elaboration
has dressed the scene out in the light of my current social values.

All the invented details about the interior of Rockhey's – the potted palms, the fox furs, the vol-au-vents – have been filtered through layers and layers of other cultural events and systems of interpretation. They weren't just discovered there, completely intact, as I rummaged around my mental loft. Instead, they have been reworked through other codes, stories, memories, like glimpsed scenes from Noel Coward and Terence Rattigan, *Upstairs, Downstairs*, the memory of my granny's fox fur, vague recollections of *Grand Hotel*, Max Jaffa's Palm Court trio, suggestions about the 'vol-au-vents' from my partner, and other caricatured scenes from Bournemouth and Torquay.

But what holds these random details together and arranges them in a particular way in my retelling is my present viewpoint. The organized pattern of feeling in the piece comes through my relating this moment to many other times and moments in my lifetime – starting at grammar school, at university, tipping a taxi-cab driver, sipping sherry with the professor – where I've also experienced that sinking feeling of being out of my social depth. And it's that interpretative viewpoint that controls the pressure behind the choice of the word 'hastily' and encourages us to linger over the 'funny look' of the waitress.

The danger is in misrepresenting personal histories as a series of special dramatic moments of illumination and recognition. What is probably more shaping, but more difficult to show, is the slow drip, drip, drip of everyday social practice, custom and relationship, rather than these special moments. In family terms I mean the daily practices of who goes shopping, who does the cleaning, ironing, cooking, washing up. So perhaps I ought to be a little more wary of selectively reconstructing a life history in terms of its grand, story moments?

This was one of the first times that I became consciously aware of being a part of the bottom of the league, of a working-class family group that was always short of money and status, in relation to more affluent social groupings. But I don't want to give you the wrong impression that my family life was characterized by spectacular hardship and poverty.[5] In fact it was a very contradictory place, partly providing relative comfort and safety and occasional scarcity, panic and limited horizons.

We managed because of my mother's usual thrift and careful planning, and the fact that my father was prepared to turn his hand to odd jobs, outside the regular fire-service time, like painting and decorating, sweeping chimneys and playing in a small band that worked around the Torbay area, in small hotels and pubs.

Seen against this background of my mother's customary cautiousness, it was a strange decision for her to take us to Rockhey's. But perhaps again it fits in with her occasional desire to break out of the daily grind, and claim a brief space for herself in a different world of fashionable elegance? I'm not sure. But its effect upon me was to provoke me into measuring myself socially against the 'funny look' of the Rockhey's waitress, the lift attendant, the women in 'fancy hats and fox furs', and a completely unknown social world with its 'crusts cut off'. Family (with its economic and social placing – my sister remembers my father's wage as being about £4.50 a week in the late 1940s) and social class came together there in the sense of shame and inadequacy that I felt in relation to those other figures.[6]

That socially learnt undervaluing of myself has remained with me through all the stages of my upward social mobility through grammar school, sixth form, redbrick university, school teaching and teacher training. The class-based fear and anxiety about my adequacy and credentials to do what I was doing, that lurked just below the surface, prodded away at me through one, persistent, central question: 'When will they find me out as an impostor and fling me out?'[7]

But the social undervaluing of myself, learned in and through the family, was made more complex by the presence of two other factors: the egalitarian, educational aspirations of growing up in that woman-dominated household at a time of positive reconstruction and the 1945 Labour government (and particularly the way my mother's hopes for me were influenced by that contact and context); and the difficulties I met with in building a masculine gender identity in myself.

In terms of my mother's educational aspirations for me (backed up, in some ways, by the Butler Education Act of 1944), she never just prepared me to slot into my appropriate class position in the world of work and the existing social order. There was a new sense of possibilities in the air. Rigidly held social divisions seemed about to crack apart. Accordingly, my mother encouraged Shirley, Anne and myself to become enthusiastic, weekly users of the public library,[8] and that proved to be an incredibly valuable source of other perspectives and experiences, and (along with comic reading) also helped me to become a fluent reader.

In learning to look upon myself, in certain contexts, as a potential high-flier, I must also have taken advantage of the male-supremacist assumptions in that culture that privileged any sign of unusual endeavour in a rising 'Boy Wonder' who might go far (see Chapter 7). That expectation also hooked up with my mother's pushing of me forward as a possible extension of herself, and a possible living through me of some of her most frustrated ambitions and fantasies.

However there were many contradictions in the ways I looked at myself. The systematic undermining of myself as an autonomous person, to which class relations contributed, was also reinforced by my increasing self-doubt and ambivalence about viewing myself as an adequate boy/man. I couldn't, wholeheartedly, prise myself apart from the seductive closeness of my mother's bed, to positively identify myself with a father who was not only physically absent, but who also could be snortingly contemptuous about all the qualities I valued in myself. (See Chapter 6 for a much more detailed exploration of these issues.) So we see that class and gender relations were intertwined in their powerful and lasting effect upon me.

The family represents one of the most important social institutions in daily producing and often perpetuating gender inequality. It does this through the gendered division of labour, through playing a major part in constructing a system of unequal divisions between home and work, private and public, paid and unpaid work, 'feminine' and 'masculine'. And these gendered dualities are also integral in creating the possibility for power and profit central to a capitalist, economic system.

In the case of my own family, these socially produced splits between my mother and father were exacerbated by wartime conditions. My father, separated from us by 200 miles, was economically privileged through my mother's unpaid labour, and by being a male breadwinner. However he lived without the immediate support of his wife and family, and managed to survive through terrifying Blitz conditions. My mother's dependent and inferior position, in comparison to my father, was clearly associated with her narrow, isolated role of having sole responsibility for childbirth, childcare and domestic labour. But she was also partly supported by being part of an extended, feminized family household. And her increasing irritation with the suffocating narrowness of this position has been hinted at in her weekly cinema-going, and the 'big treat' at Rockhey's.

The system of male power over women is buttressed by the 'naturalized' segregation of distinct yet unequal spheres of activity and passivity.[9] As a result most men benefit from these exclusive domains which are organized in favour of men's interests. Michele Barrett and Mary McIntosh make this point clearer: 'The principle of the wage-earner and his dependents, of the husband who contributes cash while the wife contributes household labour, is not a division of labour between equals, but an unequal exchange in which the man's interests predominate.'[10]

The snag with this general critique is that, although my father did benefit from and take for granted all my mother's household labour, he didn't fit easily into this overall, critical approach to the family. He is caught between the contradictions of fulfilling the symbolic and ideological role which a sexist society in general and my mother had created for him, and not coming up to scratch as a fully paid up patriarch (through his hovering on the margins of the family, and his lack of social power in the labour market). In my imagination the head of the table position where he ought to be sitting is always empty.

Some of these contradictory tensions are captured in the memory of having, on occasions, to collect my father's wages on Thursday mornings. My father didn't carry himself around the family as a strutting patriarch and economic provider. It was always an inadequate wage he earned, and it wasn't ever enough to qualify as a 'family' wage that would provide comfortably for the whole, growing family. As a result he didn't earn the right to wear the authority of adequate breadwinner. Also the legacies of his sustained absence, the influence of the matriarchal household, and the special relationship between my mother and myself wiped out the pretence of him ever wielding any real domestic authority[11] in the home as well.

This is born out by my mother's constantly worried attempt to manage our domestic affairs. She would start to scribble after tea on Tuesday or Wednesday evenings, sometimes on the back of blue sugar bags, in her weekly attempt to 'reckon up'. To see if she could make ends meet. Then later that night there might be raised adult voices booming through the floorboards. They only ever seemed to argue over money. On the following morning I was often asked, as a last resort, to go into Torquay by bus to collect my Dad's wage packet.

I hated going. I always protested like mad. Most of my reactions were about having to face the pay clerks in the office at Torquay Fire Station. They'd always try to make me feel small, picking on my embarrassed mumbling and holding it up for public inspection before the other people in the queue.

'Speak up, son!' they would say, 'We haven't got all day, you know', or 'Stop mumbling into your beard!'[12] But it's only now, on reflecting on the past, that I can detect other forces at work there as well.

I think that part of my squirming discomfort also came from an indirect awareness of a general state of economic insecurity that was always there in the air, of always having to be at the mercy of how much my father brought into the house each week, and of often-repeated family catchphrases that almost ritually prepared you for the worst: 'Money doesn't grow on trees, you know' or 'I don't know where it's going to come from, I just don't.'

I think that background of economic insecurity seeped through to me as an atmosphere of distrust in the future and cautious watchfulness, of not being able to release my longings fully because they might turn out to be too pricey.

Although my father wasn't a full-blown, strutting patriarch he wasn't a nurturing father to me, either. Some of the contradictions of his position, caught between conflicting forces, and his relationship with me, are taken further and looked at more closely in the next chapter.

Notes

1   The origins of this ideal come from the mid-nineteenth century bourgeois form of the family that gave rise to the nuclear variety in contemporary ideology. See M. Barrett and M. McIntosh (1982) *The Anti-Social Family*, London, Verso.
2   'The Scarlet Claw' (1944). Produced by Royal William Neill, USA. 'Green for Danger' (1946). Produced by Sidney Gilliat. Great Britain.

3 The argument here is indebted to Tom Ryan (1985) 'Roots of masculinity', in A. Metcalf and M. Humphries (eds) *The sexuality of men*, London, Pluto.

4 See A. Brittan (1989) *Masculinity and Power*, Oxford, Basil Blackwell, p. 30: 'instead of a real father-figure, sons identified with the symbolic representation of the father, a representation interpreted and defined by the mother'.

5 A term that rescues emotion from being trivialized as free-floating feeling, arising from spontaneous origins. Here the term recognizes that feeling is partly shaped by social forces, and partly 'relatively autonomous'. From Raymond Williams, (1961) *The Long Revolution*, Harmondsworth, Penguin.

6 The working-class family that I came from was another of Carolyn Steedman's marginal, 'borderland' families that wasn't a part of the 'classic' working-class autobiographical tradition of spectacular hardship and poverty. Talking of her own family she says: 'Not only was it not very bad, or only bad in a way that working-class autobiography doesn't deal in, but also a particular set of emotional and psychological circumstances ensured that at the time, and for many years after it was over and I had escaped, I thought of it as ordinary, a period of relative material ease, just like everybody else's childhood.' See Carolyn Steedman (1986) *Landscape for a Good Woman: A Story of Two Lives*, London, Virago.

7 Influenced by a working-class, Leeds woman's recollections that on her first day of teaching she thought that the authorities would fling open her classroom door and denounce her as inadequate.

8 'My life was formed only by means of the public library which provided me with my only uncensored access to books.' Denise Riley (1985) 'Waiting', in L. Heron (ed.) *Truth, Dare or Promise*, London, Virago.

9 This part of the argument is indebted to Michael Kaufman (1987) 'The construction of masculinity and the triad of men's violence', in M. Kaufman (ed.) *Beyond Patriarchy*, Toronto Canada, Oxford University Press.

10 Barrett and McIntosh, op. cit.

11 On page 124 of Bob Connell's *Gender and Power* he cites Anne Parson's study of a non-Oedipal 'nuclear complex' in Naples. He says: 'Cultural and psychological evidence here shows a family pattern where the mother is central, the father has little domestic authority and the mother–son and father–daughter relationships are emphasised more than same-sex identifications.' The study referred to is Anne Parsons (1964) 'Is the Oedipus Complex universal? The Jones-Malinowski debate revisited and a South Italian "Nuclear Complex"', *The Psychoanalytic Study of Society* 3, pp. 278–326.

12 I'm not sure how far this incident is unconsciously influenced by a similar scene of collecting his father's wages in D. H. Lawrence's (1913) *Sons and Lovers*, Harmondsworth, Penguin.

CHAPTER 5

Relations with my father

What has the Man not been able to talk about?
What is the Man hiding?

(Friedrich Nietzsche)[1]

Generally, men have not been able to talk about the emotional histories of their relationships with their fathers (or lack of them), or the parts of themselves that they have disowned. In a great deal of autobiographical work written by men there's usually a masking overemphasis on their relationships with their mothers at the expense of their fathers. Often the mother is idealized, put on a pedestal, or reduced in human size as she is squeezed through the narrow lens of the pressing, emotional needs of men. Again and again, she is seen as a self-sacrificing, passive victim,[2] giving up everything so that she can service her adored son.

In contrast, there is a frequent gap where the father ought to be. Usually he's there in the family group only in name; distant, removed or seen externally, only in terms of his working relations. Nothing is said about fathers' buried emotional lives; all those locked up affections, sensitivities, intimate longings, suppressed tenderness. All of that starved and disturbing life is kept well hidden.

I want to try and change that traditional approach by breaking open some of these silences. I want to take a longer look at my father, in order to understand the shocking isolation of his death, pursuing the reasons why he acted like he did, and generally trying to rewrite my relationship to him. In doing this I want to redefine some of the over-rehearsed autobiographical episodes dealing with the contact between him and me that I've carried around with me inside my head.

[88]

In taking this approach I've made sure that I haven't neglected my mother. She's solidly there in the opening chapter on the family, in the chapters on sexuality and language, and scattered through the rest of the book in small details, asides and references.

When I first started to write about my father I half-sensed that something wasn't quite right. It was difficult to get at him. He seemed to be constantly evasive, as if there was nothing really there to get hold of – only a bold face as a defensive shell to laugh at the world with and avoid intimacy, or a front defined by his public labour that seemed to close down the possibility of other kinds of questions.

I had to start somewhere so I grabbed what was to hand. I tried to fit him into an Oedipal frame of interpretation, and I started one early piece of writing off like this:

> I'll get even with that bugger, whatever I do. He comes back after so long away and takes my place in her bed. In the black uniform of the AFS he comes back, unexpectedly, and takes up my space.

Although there was some anger inside me it still didn't feel right. There was just something too worked up about this way of talking about him. There was a recoil inside me from the pressure of feeling that I ought to feel anger against him.

Slowly, over the months of trying to rework through therapy my relationship with him, there emerged the sense of feeling something much more muddled about him, that included some strands of anger but that didn't represent the full range of my feelings for him. He just wouldn't stay still within a straight Oedipal reading. He kept on bursting out of that crippling straitjacket.

Gradually I've begun to recognize that there are much more contradictory and ambivalent features about my father's position in my early family life and his relation to me. Through this I've gained a more critical approach to the limitations of a conventional, Oedipal interpretation. And that's allowed me to own up to the fact that the primary emotion I now feel towards my father is one of deep sadness, flecked by traces of anger.

Some of the sadness comes through in an incident over a toy fort. Looking back from my present vantage point, it seems significant that many of my reworked memories about my father are about him bearing me gifts, presents, suggestions that are then turned down by me. It gives me a way of understanding his need to win a place in the affection of his kids after a long absence. It's as if he wanted to persuade me (a mother- and woman-defined boy), through his offerings, to allow him into my suspiciously guarded, inner reaches after his awkward homecoming. Perhaps he also felt that his rightful position had been usurped by my upbringing in a woman-centred household, and he was trying to fight back.

The toy fort was one of my Dad's Christmas presents for me (perhaps for my seventh or eighth Christmas). I remember discovering it on the floor at the bottom of my bed on Christmas morning. It was a blue-grey fort with sawdust particles mixed up with the paint. The sawdust gave it a slightly scarred, rough texture to the touch. Apparently Dad had made it during his evening shifts at the fire station, putting it together laboriously from old packing cases.

It was bristling with gap-toothed turrets, a drawbridge that you could pull up with a string, and defensive parapets surrounding a tight square with narrow firing slits cut into the walls. It was the product of a great deal of work and energy, and I felt flattered by my Dad's positive caring. I said how much I liked it, over and over, as if to convince him that all his labour had been worthwhile. (Perhaps my Mum had put me up to that?)

At first I played with it, dutifully, positioning all my lead soldiers around the fort at strategic points, but it was all frozen and dead and I soon lost interest. The only aspect that really caught my imagination was seeing the fort as a part of a *Beau Geste*[3] narrative. For a while, I imitated Gary Cooper in propping up dead Foreign Legion soldiers (my lead ones) by the parapet slits to fool the marauding bedouin outside the fort. But even that waned fairly soon.

What the toy-fort episode really reveals are the implicit hopes about the kind of son my Dad really wanted. The fort is really a present for the kind of action boy my Dad would, in some ways, have liked to have made presents for – a robust, practical, no-nonsense son who would have revelled in the conventional boy's activities of fighting and competing.

But perhaps my father himself, in his choice of present, was also trying to fit into the traditional expectations of a masculine culture? (Every day of his working life he was surrounded by the all-male fire-service's insistent culture of manliness.) On coming back from London and finding his son being turned into a milksop, and finding his own privileged position undermined by my mother's sisters, perhaps that combined erosion of his authority had provoked my father into playing up the more manly aspects of his own character in relation to me? Indeed I would go so far as to suggest that the sight of my blond curls and sissyish, effeminate ways made him feel uncomfortable within his own ambivalent grip on his own masculinity. He retaliated by overcompensating for his fear of his own emotions by playing up a 'normal' heterosexual face.[4]

Viewed from this perspective I suppose some of my sadness comes from the lost opportunities of closeness and contact between my father and me. An awareness grows in me that we might have had a chance of meeting within our unguarded, more vulnerable sides if the continuous striving to achieve an acceptable, manly face hadn't wedged us both apart.

This personal disowning of parts of ourselves (in my father and myself) also connects up with a history of disowning on my father's family side. In fact the emotional disowning within the historical circuit of grandfather, father and son also leads to a social disowning between fathers and sons.

The defensive lies that close off the private from the public spheres, kept hidden between grandfather, father and son, form a major part of the institutionalizing of patriarchal relations, and plays a part in keeping that system intact. But before I can concentrate on the relations between my father and myself it's important to bring into visibility something of this family history of concealment:[5]

Jackson or Amarilli?

I've never felt at home within my name. And within the oppressive weight of the lying that goes with that name. Jackson. The conventional son of a Jack. An effective maker and doer in the world of work. A sturdy son of traditional masculinity. What's he got to do with me?

Jackson is the name of a boxer. Len Jackson[6] of the early decades of the twentieth century, at least that's how the passed down, family story goes. He sounds like a real man – a robust man of steel, a man of action. I suppose that's why he must have been chosen. Anyhow, with his brawn and his fists, the boxer stole my real name away. (That's how I perceive it and feel it now, looking back in 1989). I feel that my real name is the name of my Italian grandfather – Amarilli. A flower. The name of an Italian country girl. But Gaudio (that was my grandfather's first name) had to shut out all of that Amarilli part of his nature in order to fit into a society that would have labelled him an alien,[6] either for his girlishness or for his foreignness; indeed a vicious society that would have projected its own fear of effeminacy[7] onto unmanly foreigners who were only good at making icecream, rather than hewing coal.

But what could he do – my grandfather – arriving with the rest of the cheap, migrant labour from Colorno in northern Italy, some time at the turn of the century, at Tiger Bay, Cardiff? What he did was what most other first-generation immigrants did, at that particular time, to save their skins. He split himself into two, keeping his true identity a secret in insecure, public contexts, and publicly turning his back on any traces of his distinguishing culture, religion, language, history and his own feelings in order to appear normal.[8]

Gaudio became a closet Italian hiding his feelings and identity and taking on a British name in the place where he worked so that he wasn't marked out as an alien. He dumped Amarilli for Jackson during his working week, kept silent about his longings and buried himself in his work, a work that all immigrants recognize if they can get it – a desperate willingness to work all hours of the day (like Asian cornershop owners today) to gain an economic security, and respectability, a toehold in an imperialistic and masculinized culture. All that remained of Amarilli was kept firmly sealed behind the Sunday family door and the Catholic church.

In doing all this, Gaudio allowed himself to be defined, used, named by a racist Britishness, and a brutal, men-on-top society. He got used to living the daily lies of a double life: that he was handy with his fists, that he could sort out the drunks from the Newport and Cardiff trains who staggered into his *brachi* (café/ice-cream parlour) in Abertillery late at night, that he was like Len Jackson.

[92]

In the end, in most public situations, he allowed the dominant culture to swallow him up. Gaudio changed his name through deed poll so that his sons could make their ways in that commercial world without insult or suspicion. Amarilli got gulped down by a xenophobic culture that was used to incorporating foreign intrusions. Before the going got too hot for 'dirty little Eyeties!', round about the time of the Abyssinian[10] war with its daily fear of being officially classified as an 'alien' and being sent to an internment camp, Amarilli was obliterated by Jackson.

My increasing sadness about my lack of closeness with my father, and my emerging sense of the missed opportunities between us, was brought to a head at the time of visiting him in hospital just before he died in 1972.

I had been rung up by one of my sisters and told that my father was dying of cancer of the liver. The following morning I travelled down to Paignton hospital to see him. I hadn't seen him for maybe five or six years.

I arrived in his ward at about five o'clock the next evening. There was a long table set out at the bottom of the ward where some of the patients were sitting eating. I got half-way down the room when one man half-rose from the table and turned towards me. I didn't recognize him at first. He was so changed.

I was shocked to see my father's face worn down to skeletal sharpness. He had lost all his flesh, and he was so very thin, frail and bony. His hair, which had been intensely black and brylcreemed in the piano-playing photograph (see p. 105), was now totally grey. His eyes were staring at me, searching me out.

I think he knew he was going to die. And he met that savage fact with customary bravery and stoicism. I felt embarrassed in front of him. I made a feeble effort to reach out to him, to get beneath the mask. But how could I think I was entitled to do that? I had spent the last 30 years keeping him at a distance. How could I change things now when probably the effort to preserve the mask was the only thing that was keeping him going?

I think I tried to talk about his childhood but he deflected me with a weak joke. Even in his dying he wanted to show a brave face to the world. It was the brave face that shut me out this time, like I had closed the door on him when he came back from London in 1945. The tables were turned now but no one benefited from it in our separate loneliness.

It was the shocking isolation of his dying that got through to me, even though I've repressed the exact details for a good number of years. We were never able to say one truthful word to each other. We were both more intent on holding the sham of bravery together than wanting to meet in an admission of our uncertainties and fears. That's why, today, I feel a strange, sad sense of mutuality with him, mixed in with occasional spurts of anger. The mutuality comes, I think, from the way we both denied the emotional principle in our lives.

Now I want to hug him to me in our shared contradictoriness but it's all a bit too late for that.

I only have a very hazy notion of what my father's upbringing was like, but he was certainly one of my grandmother's favourites. I think he learned to get his own way with women through being charming and pleasing to his mother. In some contexts, he showed more emotional expressiveness than the usual dour containment of many British men. Indeed he always seemed to be more comfortable around women. He could relax and drop his guard with women – laughing, teasing, flirting and joking. And he really came into his own as the charming ladies' man, full of dash and vivacity, seen through his piano playing, his old-time dancing, his wit as life and soul of the party and constant teasing.

I think he must have sensed his own emotional ambivalence (that choked-down range of sensibilities, sensual pleasures and emotional openness – perhaps the Amarilli part of his inheritance from his father) in a deeply repressive, misogynistic culture that defined manhood in terms of its denial of the feminized Other.[11] Afraid, like his father before him, that he might be denied entry to the male club, or fearful that he might be interrogated too closely about his masculine identity, my father overcompensated by building a masculine front that shut me out. Along with the front went a fierce patrolling of the boundaries between his 'masculinity' and 'femininity'. He was trapped, like I was, within the false and distorting dichotomies between 'masculinity'/'femininity'. Therefore he was segregated from the world of feeling and sensibility. He partly disowned his own emotional side, or Amarilli part of himself, that might give him away in the homophobic, fire-brigade world of men. He was also positioned as a male breadwinner in the public domain of business names and external exchanges, split off from his private, home world of love, affection and tenderness.

The implications of all this, in his relationship with me, were that his denial of his emotional side led to a denial of me. He just couldn't afford to meet me within the risky vulnerability of his own unguarded feelings. Just as his father, Gaudio, had disowned the Amarilli aspects of his own make-up, so my father, Don, denied and kept buried his own emotional complexities. So instead of respecting my difference as a sensitive, emotional boy, uneasy within the pressures of conventional masculinity, he imposed the traditional hopes and wishes of having an action boy for a son on me.

In a way he wanted to re-masculinize me through his gifts of toy forts, garages and Hornby-Dublo train sets. Through this he seemed to want to get back at the sissyish influences, between 1940 and 1945, that had been blurring the boundaries between rigidly separated 'masculine' and 'feminine' features in me, and that were undermining his own belief in his image of himself 'as manly provider. These influences were the women-dominated household that he must have seen as usurping his given place, and the special relationship between my mother and myself.

Another important aspect of this denial in my father was the cultural dimension of being a second-generation 'Eyetie' trying to find acceptance in a heavily repressed, patriarchal British culture, especially in the world of the 1930–50s. Growing up in a coalmining community in Abertillery, South Wales, where tough physical labour gave a man a dignity and clearly defined identity, it must have been especially difficult to live with his own sense of emotional contradictions within the dominant cultural values of that community.

What I'm really talking about here is the tendency of certain 'masculine' cultures in Britain and elsewhere to project their denied emotional side onto 'foreigners' (like Gaudio Amarilli),

[95]

especially Mediterranean 'foreigners'.[12] This process of projection is precisely caught by Arthur Miller in his play *A View from the Bridge*[13] where a tough New York docker, Eddie Carbone, projects his fear of his own denied emotions, and his suppressed sexual desires for his 'baby' niece, Catherine, onto two Italian immigrants, Marco and Rodolpho. The dam in Eddie finally bursts out when Rodolpho starts to take Catherine out. He complains about the effeminacy of Rodolpho to the lawyer/observer/narrator figure, Alfieri:

EDDIE: The guy ain't right, Mr. Alfieri.
ALFIERI: What do you mean?
EDDIE: I mean he ain't right.
ALFIERI: I don't get you.
EDDIE: Dja ever get a look at him?
ALFIERI: Not that I know of, no.
EDDIE: He's a blond guy. Like. . . .platinum. You know what I mean?
ALFIERI: No.
EDDIE: I mean if you close the paper fast – you could blow him over.
ALFIERI: Well that doesn't mean —
EDDIE: Wait a minute, I'm telling you sump'm. He sings, see. Which is – I mean it's all right, but sometimes he hits a note, see. I turn around. I mean – high. You know what I mean?
ALFIERI: Well, that's a tenor.
EDDIE: I know a tenor, Mr. Alfieri. This ain't no tenor. I mean if you came in the house and you didn't know who was singin', you wouldn't be lookin' for him you be lookin' for her.
ALFIERI: Yes, but that's not —
EDDIE: I'm tellin' you sump'm, wait a minute. Please, Mr. Alfieri. I'm tryin' to bring out my thoughts here. Couple of nights ago my niece brings out a dress which it's too small for her, because she shot up like a light this last year. He takes the dress, lays it on the table, he cuts it up; one-two-three, he makes a new dress. I mean he looked so sweet there, like an angel – you could kiss[14] him he was so sweet. .'

Singing, dancing, having long, wavy hair, enjoying doing traditional, women's work, blurring the rigid divisions between 'masculine' and 'feminine' – all of these things are seen as dangerously threatening to a precariously achieved masculine identity. In my father's case his grip on his own masculine sense of himself was so wobbly that my blond curls that made me look like a girl, my embarrassed shyness, and my closeness to many women, especially my mother, must have challenged him in a roughly similar way to Eddie Carbone. As a result, he responded by playing up his manliness and virility when he was around me, so that I always sensed the weight of his disappointment in me as not measuring up to the kind of boy he partly wanted me to be.

I can remember the bitter edge of his scorn when I tried to express myself as an emotional boy. Between the ages of 13 and 14 I seemed to be continuously grieving inside for the loss of my mother and my home. Also the pain was deepened by having to go to a bleak, alienating boarding institution, and having to adjust to a totally different household than I was used to when I stayed at Violet Holdaway's house during the long school holidays. We used to have row after row in an extremely tense atmosphere, and after a while I just couldn't stand it any more. I was drenched with grief, and my eyes used to fill up with tears at the slightest dig. Especially with my father. I couldn't have an argument with him without dissolving into tears that were half grief and half anger at myself for letting myself down so badly.

One day, after one such argument and tears, my father became totally exasperated. Suddenly he turned on me and yelled, 'Why can't I ever talk to you without you snivelling and crying?' The aggressive edge of his contempt scraped me raw inside. I can still feel the cutting sense of hurt to this day.

Crying was a difficult thing for me to do, as an adolescent boy. I was caught between partly valuing my sensitivity while, simultaneously, striving for a greater manliness. But when I let myself go and sobbed for the loss of everything I loved in the world at the time, it felt like the most emotionally honest thing I could have done. But to my father it represented yet another disappointment. I could never pull myself together to present a brave face to others, like he did in his own dying, when the brutal weight of his disappointment in me came through to me again.

My father benefited from some of the conventional power and privilege of the male breadwinner role, but in other ways his social and symbolic authority within the family was eroded in the historically specific conditions he found himself within (see Chapter 4). His lack of social power in the labour market (as an inadequate wage-earner) and his marginal position in the family circle meant that he had to look elsewhere for a compensatory status and self-respect.

He was all at sea within the traditional position of the strutting patriarch, but in an alternative sphere of confidence he appeared to be at home as an entertainer/joker[15] figure, playing in the band, organizing 'do's', children's parties, special occasions, and enjoying being the wag on coach trips, and in old-time-dancing circles. Within the working world of men my father was very wary of allowing his feelings and desires to become visible in any way. He kept all that trapped part of his make-up severely cut off from the men's world. It was only through the socially approved entertainer role that he could let himself go and release his ladies' man charm, charismatic energy and emotional flamboyance.

But the entertainer/joker role was more contradictory than I'm making out. I think it must have bolstered my father on two levels. It gave him permission to open out a fuller range of sensibilities than he was able to do in everyday life through dancing, artistic skill, performance, piano-playing etc. It also offered him a chance to develop a set of confirming power relations between the sexual authority of the jokey, flirtatious 'master of ceremonies' and the mainly female audience.

In terms of a compensatory sexual and social authority, because of the relative absence of more traditional, patriarchal roles, I think my father must have felt strengthened and confirmed by the sense of being in charge that he was able to generate in his quipping, teasing relationship with his audiences. I have spoken to women who knew my father in his entertaining heyday and they all remark how attractive, charming and animated he was as a piano player, and possibly seductive '*master* of ceremonies'.

I think he must have felt bolstered by the sense that, if he had really wanted to, he could have had any of the number of women who were interested in him. The trick was to improve his self-esteem without having to endanger his security by doing something about it. He trembled on the margins of sexual desire and had the visible evidence that he could have scored if he had wanted to, while remaining firmly in control of what went on. It was a position where he could flaunt his authority and power, in total contrast to the diminished role he played within his family and at work.

Christmas party at Torquay Fire Station

The time that really demonstrates my father's inventive flair as an entertainer was when he organized 'do's', special events, Christmas parties at the fire station. (The old Torquay fire station was situated in an old limestone quarry up Market Street. You entered from the street, through an archway, into an asphalted courtyard overhung by scarred limestone cliffs.)

It might have been 1946–7 when Dad was master of ceremonies and chief organizer (or so it seemed) for one particular Christmas party for the firemen's kids, accompanied by their mothers in many cases. Dad was in his element as the person who was holding everything together. He revelled in the role of wisecracker, full of extravert energy and repetitive banter, asides and set jokes. Soon he had the whole audience eating out of his hand, and many of the firemen's kids swarmed around him, giving him the attention usually associated with a favourite, funny uncle. But not me. I cringed back, out of sight, wincing away from his forced charm and joviality. I was embarrassed by his creaking jokes, his streak of showperson's vulgarity (once he'd poked corny and sexist fun at my sister being in a girl guide patrol called the 'Blue Tits').

Dad handed us all paper hats to wear with witty slogans on, and then we all played oranges and lemons, hide and seek and musical chairs. I really didn't want to leave my mother's side but Dad blustered and cajoled so I eventually joined in, but with yearning glances towards the direction of my mother.

Halfway through the party, after the jelly and trifle, Dad told us all that Father Christmas was coming with a sack of toys but that we'd have to go outside into the courtyard if we wanted to see him arrive. It was bitingly cold but we didn't seem to notice it. When we all got outside one of the firemen pointed up to the top of the surrounding cliffs and shouted, with his hand pointing upwards, 'There's Father Christmas!' At the same time a searchlight from one of the fire engines leapt out into the dark and focused on a hooded figure waving at us all from the top of the cliff.

Suddenly a fire-engine escape ladder started to whir skywards, extending its many sections of ladder towards Father Christmas. He clambered on and started to come down towards us. When he began to come near we were ushered back into the station to see him 'come down the chimney' (I think my father had rigged up a cardboard chute down which Father Christmas dropped). Then with a flurry of red and white, Santa plopped out from the chute, wriggling and out of breath.

It was unmistakably one of my Dad's imaginative brainwaves, done with exuberance and great panache. But again I couldn't let myself enter into the spirit of the event. Instead I squirmed with embarrassment. I think I didn't want to be publicly known as Don Jackson's son. But I also knew in my bones that my Dad couldn't resist bringing us in to the public spotlight.

A few moments later I was proved right. He was a fire-engine driver and wanted to show me off as his son, perhaps because he'd been away a long time and wanted to make up for lost time. He came over to me and said, 'David! Come out and ring the bell on my fire engine!' There was a photographer around from the local evening newspaper and perhaps my Dad had wanted to create a striking photo opportunity?

He wanted to parade me, out in the glare of public attention and in front of all the other firemen, as *his* son: in a way, to declare that he'd played a part in producing me. After having been shut out of the womanized intimacy of the Great Headland Crescent household, and with a difficult homecoming, here was his chance of showing that I was a part of him, that I wasn't just a whining 'mummy's boy'.

I sensed that Dad wanted me to be proud of his work, his zest, his engine driving, like any 'proper', self-respecting boy would have done. He wanted to see me ringing his bell, clanging it wildly and eagerly, like any robust son that he could have been proud of, would have done.

But I cringed back again from all this public spotlighting and displaying of me into the folds of my mother's skirt. I didn't want to be put on show, like a caged animal, as the privileged son of that charming and dashing Don Jackson, who could have first go at ringing the engine bell any time I wanted! So Dad shrugged his shoulders, gave my mother a stern look for producing a milksop, and went over to ask another fireman's son, who was all agog with excitement and anticipation.

My occasional anger with my father came from the way he under-valued my different qualities and inner resources. His grip on his own masculine identity was so insecure, and his authority and status so weak, in a socio-economic sense, that he found it difficult to tolerate any deviation from a compensatorily, traditional image of the robustly masculine.

As a result, he had high hopes for me as a certain kind of son – practical, down-to-earth, energetically active in making and doing in the public world, thrusting, outward-going. Any other resources and qualities – especially other qualities of emotional awareness, sensitivity, reading and writing skills, intelligence, responsiveness to natural beauty – were all bundled up in his mind as signs of effeminacy and to be avoided. He couldn't bear anything in me that tied me even more closely into being a 'mummy's boy'.

Consequently, he didn't respect my difference from him. Instead of wanting to understand who I was in my own terms, he unconsciously set about invalidating my own sense of myself, and my different ways of making sense of the world; not deliberately, but because he couldn't see beyond the familiar territory of his own customs, expectations and fears.

Now in 1989 I vacillate between accepting and distrusting my emotional side. The distrust comes partly from a sense of class inferiority, and a lack of confidence in my feelings that I learned indirectly through my father's disappointment in me.

This distrust of the full spread of potentiality in me is reactivated in certain contexts. This moment, now, while I sit here thumping the typing keys, builders are below my window, banging and sawing outside. It is as if they represent the dominant version of what it is to be a real man. Against the sawing, drilling and banging, my intellectual labour seems to be puny and effeminate. Although I value what I'm doing in my head, emotionally, I feel apologetic that I can't meet them halfway within a manually active life. They induce in me something of the same kind of undervaluing of the different resources I possess that my father used to produce in me. And that undervaluing often leads to a deeply compulsive need to prove to the bangers and sawers that I'm really OK, that I can, if I want to, qualify for entrance into their club. But the form that need to prove myself usually takes is a competitive sparring through language (see Chapter 7).

There are two particular incidents from my personal history that illustrate my father's undermining of my emotional qualities. One is about the time when I heard that I'd passed the 11-plus, and the other is about another gift from my father – this time a secondhand Hornby-Dublo train set.

Passing the 11-plus

That barbaric system of dividing children into a three-tiered education service (grammar, technical and secondary modern) at 11-plus was ruthlessly exposed by the way our primary school headteacher organized the announcement of the 11-plus results.

One morning in the assembly hall of Oldway Primary School in 1951, immediately after prayers, the headteacher separated the passes from the failures by reading out a long list of children's names (the failures – unknown to them) and telling them to go back to their classrooms where their teachers would be waiting for them. I didn't know what was going on. I thought I might have got into trouble but, any rate, I knew it must be extremely important. There was a strange hush in the hall.

When all the failures had gone, Miss Fleet, the headteacher, turned on her most beaming smile and told us we had all passed to go to the grammar school next year. Again we didn't know what it meant, but at morning playtime that day I joined the other 11-plus passes cruising around the playground, arm in arm, jubilant and excited. Already the passes felt at least three feet taller than the failures. And there was a boy called Lester (who later became a famous referee) sulking and crying in a deserted corner of the playground and saying, 'I didn't want to go to that *snobs*-dump, anyway!'

My father met the news of my 11-plus success with his usual ambivalence. He didn't respond with the present of a watch or a bike that would have (and did) come from conventional, proud, middle-class fathers. And, of course, I didn't expect that. He didn't even slap me on the back and congratulate me. (Perhaps I always wanted some warm, physical contact with him?) Instead he expressed a puzzled doubt about the very possibility of me passing, or doing well in anything. Perhaps the authorities had made a mistake? Perhaps they'd got my name muddled up with somebody else's? Jackson was quite a common name, wasn't it?

What he did next totally knocked the stuffing out of me, and took away any developing belief in my own abilities. He rang the grammar-school secretary to confirm that they hadn't made an administrative mistake – and was told that I was in the first 20 of a first-year intake of 60-odd boys.

I think he was jealous of any educational achievements on my part that deepened the bond of intimacy with my mother and the world of women. He couldn't bear my unmanly interest in reading, writing, my emotional commitment to things – things that he, wrongly, associated exclusively with the 'feminine' sphere. I think he must have felt excluded from this world of intimacy and fought back through a contemptuous undervaluing of who I was or who I might become.

The Hornby-Dublo train set

My Dad used to haunt auction rooms hoping to pick up a bargain. One day he came back triumphantly brandishing a prize. He'd managed to pick up a secondhand Hornby-Dublo train set at a very reasonable price. It was a massive layout involving a complicated network of signals, bridges, points and tracks. At first he helped me to join together the tracks in the attic, but after a few evenings he left me alone and I soon got bored with this aimless and perpetually smug engine, circling the layout, over and over again.

The only way I could get any further pleasure from that train set was to create disruptive gaps in the smooth running symmetry of the circuit. I wasn't at all taken by all that boys' talk about gadgets and technical knowhow, like, 'Oh that's a 6-4-2 wheel arrangement on that Great Western Railway tank engine. Did you know that?' I'm not sure why I wanted to disrupt the neatness. Perhaps it was one way of crying out my need for a personal response and closer contact with my father. Not being able to do that in a straightforward way, I might have resorted to an antagonistic way of grabbing his attention.

Therefore what I did was to lend that blank, repetitive circuit the invented drama of a disaster story. From then on I spent hours stage-managing giant crashes; changing track directions or points at the last minute, or raising the level of the track, so that the engines used to smack into each other, tilt over crazily and lurch off the table top. Perhaps I was really shouting out to my father, 'Why can't you give me your attention?' Or perhaps stirring up his anger would have been a sign that he was capable of responding, emotionally, to me?

For a brief time, I seemed to come alive through the perverted ingenuity of dreaming up new plans for a spectacular wreck. But even that palled and I abandoned it to gather dust for a few months. My father protested to my mother about the way I was using it, or not using it. And then one day I came back from primary school and found it gone. My father had packaged it up again and taken it back to the auction room.

The spectacular crashes were my own creative bids to struggle free of the cramping pressures on boys who ought to be caught up in the fascination of technical details, facts and figures, unrelated to social relationships, as a preparation for a future role as a handyman or Mr Fixit in the house, the garage, the shed or under the car.

There's a picture of my father in the family photograph album that makes me want to skip on to the next page. He's playing a piano in a trio made up of accordion, drums and piano. His black hair is parted down the middle and sleekly brylcreemed. He looks the part of an entertainer. His eyes are lit up and he's half letting go of a grin. It's the practised smile of somebody who's used to sparkling in company, perhaps who only came fully awake through the sparkling.

Whereas the accordionist is turning away from the camera, my father has the cheeky directness to look straight at it. He looks as if he welcomes its gaze, because he has a youthful face, aware of its own charms. Proud of his exuberant energy, it's the face of a potential womanizer. Perhaps that's why I want to turn away from it? I have disowned that face for so long it's difficult to see it again in a new way. I have almost got used to its distance and absence. So much so that I have been slow to recognize how it resembles my own.

I'm now in the process of seeing that face afresh because I think I now understand the costs of concealment that went into presenting

Family album: father playing the piano.

that face to the world. Like my own face, and that of so many other men, it's a front that's built around an emotional withdrawal from an alternative world of intimacy, more vulnerable relationships, and disclosure through acknowledging fear and uncertainty.

The brave, brylcreemed front helped my father to get by every week. It's a face that allowed him to be emotionally disengaged at home when the going got rough. He could retreat behind it when challenged, and it helped him to gain acceptance in the wolf pack world of men.

Through recognizing the similarities and correspondences, as well as the differences, with my father, I've begun to change the way I feel towards him. Sadness has now generally replaced anger as I've started to own the common features that exist between us. This newly discovered mutuality is organized around the buried parts of ourselves that we both detached ourselves from in our daily living. I begin to know him in a different way than the sceptical son distrusting the sparkling, brylcreemed smiles of the entertainer. He's now more real to me, and closer, in our mutual denial of our emotional sides. And I also recognize him and myself in the process of overcompensation that goes with that fear of being found out in our unmanliness and ambivalence.

My own relationship as a father with my own son has been directly shaped by this family history of concealment and defensive lying on the men's side. The disowning within the father of his buried emotional life (partly inherited from an estranging relationship with his own father) often leads to the father or son rejecting one another. That's how the circuit of estrangement and disowning was kept going through my grandfather Gaudio (denying his Amarilli part), through my father (denying his emotional flamboyance) and through me (burying my feelings and contradictory desires in workaholism).

In the context of my first marriage (from 1962 to 1973), which was also a shotgun marriage like my parents', my denial of my emotional side took the form of not being able to develop an image of myself as a nurturing[16] father taking pleasure in sharing the children and the housework. This inability seems to have many possible roots.

First, the legacies of my own lack of a relationship with my father, and the total lack of positive images of fathering I received from those legacies, made a central contribution. My absence from the daily experience of household labour (because of the institutional life at boarding-school where all boys were regularly serviced by women cleaners, kitchen workers and a matron) and my interrupted family life also played a part. But perhaps most significantly of all, my own shaky grip on my masculine identity pressurized me into overcompensating for that sense of emotional ambivalence by building my absorption in a reaffirming achievement, success and performance through my work as an innovatory English teacher.

I was defined and led by work rather than focusing on the alternative priorities of building an equal partnership and deepening my relationship with my wife and kids. There was a sharply drawn segregation between the male breadwinner and the female childcarer and homemaker. Within that split there was no chance of blurring the boundaries between my 'masculinity' and my 'femininity' by building an alternative image of a nurturing father. I certainly benefited within the lopsided power relations of the breadwinner/housewife binary system, but I was also trapped within its mutilating constraints.

The only father image that I could visualize, as a result of my faulty relations with my own father, was the grotesquely inadequate part I tried to play during the period between about 1964 and 1968. I think I can remember wearing a navy-blue, middle-aged man's cardigan bought from Marks & Spencers, with chunky, mock-leather buttons running down the front, and trying to look the part of the manly provider. All I lacked was a pipe and slippers and the artificial concoction would have been complete. But it was like wearing borrowed clothes. My much more contradictory and ambivalent identity wouldn't fit inside them. There was nobody there inside the navy-blue cardigan and the buttons gave me away. Just as when I tried to imagine my father sitting around the family table at meal-times, his chair was always empty.

My son Peter, born in January 1963, is the only male member of the historical family circuit to have allowed his emotional side to become publicly visible through his appearance and style. Supported, in some ways, by the gender-bending street style of the 1980s, and directly influenced by the androgynous presentation of self of rock stars like David Bowie, Peter's appearance has often formed an implied critique of dominant representations of

[107]

masculinity. In his personal relations he has also seemed to be more gently drifting than the usual thrusting and controlling man. When I think of him now, I see him at the time when he was wearing bangles and decorative rings, dangling earrings, chiffon scarves, make-up and perfume.

My first marriage broke up in 1973 so I only knew Peter closely for the first eleven years of his life. From then on I only saw him for occasional weekends and half of the long holidays. At first, perhaps for the four or five years after our separation and divorce, my children always came down together in a threesome. Then they arranged to come more individually, often with friends from home, or in Peter's case I used to take him walking for weekends in the Lake District, staying at Kendal Youth Hostel.

Peter dropped out of a university course in microbiology at Aberystwyth after the first year and soon became part of a hippy drug culture moving on every six months or so, between Aberystwyth, Todmorden (where we lived during the last five years of our marriage) and then Nottingham.

At this moment he seems more happy and settled, living in a long-term partnership in Todmorden. But writing this I feel full of grief in losing contact with him. I have tried many times to talk about what's going on between us but he sees this as my usual 'ear-grinding' and doesn't seem to want to notice that I'm in the process of changing. The last time I saw him he said he didn't see any point in talking. I haven't seen him for nearly a year now and he never rings.

Perhaps my past disowning of my buried emotional life, and primary identification of myself through work, has played a significant part in my son rejecting me.

My obsessive commitment to work probably came from it offering a compensatory controlling power and self-affirmation that I couldn't realize in my personal and social relationships outside work. Whatever else failed in my life I seemed to have this last certainty around to give me a spurious direction and purpose, and a way of hiding away from emotional blockages that were too disturbing and painful to look at.

My marginal position in my own home, and my complete lack of domestic credibility, meant that like my Dad I had to look elsewhere for a compensatory status and self-respect. Work offered me a way of regaining a proud face. So I ploughed most of my energies (some of which could have gone into childcare and housework) into keeping up the public face of a dynamic, innovatory head of English.

Everything else could be crumbling around me; my relationship with my children, my contact with my partner but I still had the bolstering image of my workplace identity to fall back upon. The powerful image of the dynamic whiz kid, way ahead of the others, top of the first division in the innovation league, was still there holding me up.

Perhaps it was this controlling, driving energy to achieve things through work, and to construct an image of myself that was adequate for my fantasy aspirations, that cut me off from my son; or at least played a major part in that process of rejection. Despite my protestations to the contrary, he probably sensed the crushing weight of my unspoken disappointment in having a son who didn't want to identify himself through work, who didn't have the driving pressure of a social mission[17] pushing him on. But I'm not sure whether he would agree with this.

Although to me it seemed that Pete lacked a social purpose or a significant commitment to anything, he was happy to define himself in the way he wanted to be. So he might have resisted, like I had done before him, my attempt to define him in my own terms. He didn't seem to want my version of a meaningful life imposed on him. As a result he turned away from me and deliberately avoided that sense of being put down and reduced in size when he was around me.

That undervaluing of my son, going on when I was most obsessively hooked on working priorities, has now changed. I don't want to control or define him. That's the last thing I want to do. I now urgently want to understand who he is in his own terms but, perhaps because of that past history of rejection and undermining, he has decided to close his ears to me.

If some men are ever going to break the established pattern of concealment and defensive lying (between fathers and sons, sons and fathers) over generations, they have to start interrogating those absences, gaps, empty chairs where the father has slipped out of view. Then they have to learn how to start meeting their loved ones within the risky and often dangerous area of the feelings and relations that they can't talk about. Instead of heroically soldiering on, withering inside but keeping the brave face going, even in their dying, men need to understand that more satisfying and equal relationships come before success. Then they need to go on to appreciate that they can only build relationships through knowing how to let other people in on their buried lives, alongside changing the traditional, gendered divisions of power and subordination.

The process of writing this chapter represents in itself a revaluing of my own suppressed emotional side. It does this through its movement towards disclosure, towards dethroning the stoical father in his grip on my own and many men's imaginations. He continues to hide away within this split between the public and the private, where he can continue to detach uncomfortable, personal knowledge from public actions and statements. The maiming practices of male power are often made possible and sustained through this split. How else can we explain some men's abilities to carry through exploitative and violent actions?' It's only through the numbing repetitiveness of living the daily lies of a double life (like Jackson/Amarilli in his split, business/personal existence) that they can bear to go on living with the competitive woundings and mutilations.

A much more integrated approach that started to connect up the public and the private in men's lives, and that insisted on no separation between what we publicly professed to believe in and our everyday behaviour, would surely lead in the direction of social and personal change? Reconnecting men to the emotional histories that they aren't able to talk about has to be one of the most important starting points for activating that kind of felt, critical stocktaking that often leads to changed ways of relating and acting, and helps to develop a commitment to changing men in the social world. This chapter is a tentative starting place for that kind of personal reconnection.

Notes

1 Quoted in Alice Jardine (1987) 'Men in feminism: odor di uomo or compagnons de route?' in Alice Jardine and Paul Smith (eds) *Men in Feminism*, London, Methuen.
2 See Carolyn Steedman (1986) *Landscape for a Good Woman*, London, Virago, where she develops a critique of Richard Hoggart's and Jeremy Seabrook's interpretative approach to working-class lives, especially women. She says they both delineate 'a background of

uniformity and passivity, in which pain, loss, love, anxiety and desire are washed over with a patina of stolid emotional sameness'.

3   The film was produced in 1939 by William A. Wellman. USA. *Beau Geste* is about the life of a supposed coward, played by Gary Cooper, who joins the Foreign Legion to regain his lost masculine honour. He does so in a climactic scene where he is the only one left alive in a desert fort besieged by bedouin. Singlehandedly, he fools them and wins the day by propping dead bodies up in the firing slits.

4   To reinforce this point see L. Segal (1990) *Slow Motion: Changing Masculinities*, London, Virago, pp. 159 and 314, where she refers to the 'homophobic ideologies of such institutions', and, 'that bastion of male preserve, firefighting. . .'

5   'A whole history of disownment, of children rejecting parents and parents rejecting children.' From David Leavitt (1986) *The Lost Language of Cranes*, New York, Knopf; Penguin edn 1987.

6   I still don't know whether this family story about the boxer name has any basis in fact.

7   The fear of an 'alien invasion' was high around about this time, when between 1881 and 1900, 2500–3000 Russian and Polish Jews settled in England *each* year. See L. Sponza (1988) *Italian Immigrants in Nineteenth-Century Britain*, Leicester, Leicester University Press.

8   The connection between imperialism and an ideal of manliness is pointed out by Mrinalini Sinha (1987) 'Gender and imperialism: colonial policy and the ideology of moral imperialism in late nineteenth-century Bengal', in M. Kimmel (ed.) *Changing Men*, London, Sage. For further evidence see *Truth*, vol. 34, no. 879 (2 November 1893): 'Foreigners are in fact, deceitful, effeminate, irreligious, immoral, unclean and unwholesome. Any one Englishman is a match for any seven of them.'

9   This pressure to assimilate is brilliantly explored in Adrienne Rich (1987) 'Resisting amnesia: history and personal life', in *Blood, Bread, and Poetry*, London, Virago. She says: 'The pressure to assimilate says different things to different people: change your name, your accent, your nose; straighten or dye your hair; stay in the closet', and: 'To assimilate means to give up not only your history but your body, to try to adopt an alien appearance because your own is not good enough, to fear naming yourself lest name be twisted into label.'

10 'The period of prosperity for Italians at the beginning of this century was shattered by World War Two, when the Italian speaking minority were classified as "aliens", and many were interned in detention camps on the Isle of Man, or were deported to Australia or Canada'. From Linguistic Minorities Project (1985) *The Other Languages of England*, London, Routledge & Kegan Paul.

11 See Jonathan Dollimore (1986) 'Homophobia and sexual difference', *Oxford Literary Review*, vol. 8, nos 1–2.

12 Compare British anti-French sentiment between 1688 and 1714, when French culture was seen as feminized and foppishly over-refined.

[111]

See Michael Kimmel (1987) 'The contemporary "crisis" of masculinity in historical perspective', in Harry Brod (ed.) *The Making of Masculinities*, London Allen & Unwin, pp. 136–7.

13. From Arthur Miller (1958) *Collected Plays*, Cresset Press, London.

14. A passionately contradictory action, it's both a sign of a hard, masculine culture's extreme contempt for any suggestion of softness (like Middlesbrough-born Brian Clough later kissing the two supporters he'd thumped after they had run across his pitch), and a use of the bantering form to express suppressed homo-erotic desires, while appearing to deny them. See the *Sun* newspaper reporting of this incident, February 1989.

15. Perhaps, on one level, my father was tapping in to a continuing historical tradition of Italian immigrants working in Britain as street performers and entertainers (organ grinders and street musicians etc.) See Sponza, op. cit. On another level, perhaps he was using the joker/entertainer persona to express a range of illicit desires that couldn't be negotiated in his normal, public-world relations? Thanks to Antonio Melechi for this point and many others in this chapter.

16. The nurturing, caring father represents for me an image of masculinity which has positively reintegrated its isolated 'masculine' and 'feminine' elements. I use it here as a deliberate critique of the stoical father.

17. The evangelical fervour of that approach to English teaching during the 1960s and 1970s (a legacy of an Arnoldian/Leavis version of English studies) is well documented in Chris Baldick (1983) *The Social Mission of English Criticism 1848–1932*, Oxford, Oxford University Press.

CHAPTER 6
Sexuality

This chapter is the most difficult for me to write. Sexuality is still an area of so many present contradictions and confusions in me that it's not easy to know where to start. But the very continuity of these unresolved conflicts perhaps offers a kind of starting point. More specifically I refer to those infantile, unconscious desires and unrecognized, emotional attachments that have lasted into my adult life. Without some critical attempt to understand my sexuality as having traceable origins in my childhood relations, and as something that is deeply enmeshed within a web of social forces, then the 'hydraulic model'[1] of male sexuality (that male sexuality is a naturally gushing force and has an uncontrollable and addictive power in men's lives) will go unchallenged in me.

As well as arguing that my sexuality was socially constructed, I also want to focus my attention on the pattern of emotionally charged attachments and relations within my lifetime. So here I attempt to combine together social and psychoanalytical approaches to investigate some of the major themes of my sexual development.

Bearing in mind the complexities of telling this story, a chronological history of my sexual growth might be the easiest way of organizing that continuity.

The first five years: early relations with my mother

Viewed from a past/present dialectic, my present search for a sense of lost completeness can be understood in terms of exploring the psychoanalytical origins of my early relationship with my mother and how that emotionally charged pattern was later strengthened, particularly between the years of 12 and 16 in the boarding school.

[113]

In my present situation in 1990 my partner and I physically embrace in a close, cuddling position sometimes after making love together. My right arm is deeply burrowed under the pillow supporting her head, with my left arm cradled around her. Our legs entwine round each other as well. So physically interwoven are we that I feel as if our separate arms and legs are indistinguishable.

That deeply nourishing sense of fusion is strangely entangled with that overpowering sense of oneness I felt with my mother, in that early period. However, in 1990 the difference is that once compulsive search is now in the process of being reworked as an explicit need that we have shared with each other, and as a result have more control over, rather than an unconsciously addictive drive that we can do nothing about.

Of course it's extremely difficult to reconstruct a time about which I have little conscious memory. All I can do here is to trace back the fleeting shreds of atmosphere, incident and emotion in terms of my present vantage point and world-view. From such a standpoint it feels right to suggest that these relationships might then have existed. There is also the testimony of other members of my family to consider whilst applying to them the same kind of interpretative reconstruction.

I don't want to repeat the points made in Chapters 4 and 5, but it is important to sketch in here the social as well as the more personal background. For some of the first five years of my life my family was virtually a single-parent unit. In late 1939 my mother left the flat in London to share a house with her parents and sisters (in Paignton, south Devon) far away from the threatened German bombing of London. My mother was pregnant with me, and nursing her first child. My father had just joined the Auxiliary Fire Service in London so he stayed on there and only came down for the very rare flying visit over the next four years.

In a male-dominated society, partly exacerbated by wartime conditions,[2] my father lived the life of a single man again, but in a terrifying environment, while my mother bore the brunt of childcare/domestic-labour responsibilities. In these pressing circumstances it's perhaps not too surprising that my mother, in claustrophobically close proximity to me, and excluded from regular physical, emotional and social contact with my father, should turn the full intensity of her loving affection on me, her only son, born in February 1940.

My mother was afraid of the dark, and frightened about the wartime blackout. Perhaps she kept on worrying about what was happening to her husband in London, worrying about the flames, the bombing and devastation, but also worrying about his charming ways around other women. How did he spend his nights? Did he sleep with anybody else? Also, since their shotgun marriage in 1937, my mother wasn't sure that she trusted him, alone and on the loose, around other women. In this context it's possible that she compensated for all those nightmarish fears and anxieties by using me as a substitute lover, as a physical comfort to have her son in bed with her during the long nights when she didn't get much sleep. Perhaps she also saw me as a possible extension of herself, in that through me she might be able to realize some of her most frustrated ambitions and desires. In all of this it makes more sense for me now to reconstruct her, not just as a passive victim of these social constraints (isolated and cooped up in the house with two very young children not knowing whether she would ever see her husband again), but as a more resilient person, grappling in her own way to get back at the injustices of those social arrangements, and perhaps even getting back at my father through me.

Here I'm not wanting to blame my mother but to point out how, in a sexist society intensified by war conditions, her survival energies were concentrated into a form that made a lasting impression on me. By this I mean she 'confused her relationship to [me] as an infant with a sexual relationship to [me] as a male'.[3] What that felt like was being so powerfully connected to her that I feared losing that snuggling sense of oneness when she wasn't around. Later, I became emotionally needy around women but, at the same time, resented being dependent on or being tied down by them.

Of course some of this can be put down to the common, intersexed features of many mother/son relationships within the lopsided assumptions of a gendered hierarchy. In this culture, 'objects of desire are generally defined by the dichotomy and opposition of feminine and masculine'.[4] As a result, in being cared for by a person of a different gender my maleness and oppositeness as a sexual other became of critical significance, particularly when my mother was deprived of all everyday emotional and sexual contact with my father at a time of extreme emotional distress.

But my overwhelming, clinging attachment to my mother, and that later pattern of being emotionally needy around women and expecting them to fill gaps in myself, can probably be explained through an early relationship of physical closeness and sensual oneness that must have trembled on the edge of substitute adult male/female sexual love. From my present perspective it feels right in reconstructing that time – a time of extreme emotional hunger and distress in my mother – as one which exerted an influence over her to find a compensatory emotional attachment that would give her some comfort.

I was so wrapped around in the folds of my mother's body that the boundaries of self and not-self didn't exist for me. The sense of complete fusion and oneness meant that I didn't have a sense of self apart from her. But, simultaneously, I was also threatened by the fear of a possible withdrawal of that warm, protective nest. I was clingy around her because I was anxious, if she vanished, like in the peek-a-boo game, I would be annihilated. I didn't have a sense of who I was outside my contact with my mother, so if she disappeared I became totally wiped out as well.

This partly explains my continuing ambivalence in trying to build a male gender identity and sexuality. Through all the reasons stated above (particularly my closeness to my mother and the sustained absence of my father) I found it extraordinarily threatening and painful to prise myself apart from the seductive warmth of my relationship with my mother in order to build a separate, masculine sense of self through identifying with a distant father. The really painful thing was having to repress my closeness with and dependence on my mother in order to become 'masculine'. This led to a later over-straining to assert my 'masculine' identification at the expense of a feared softness or anything that could be interpreted as dangerously 'feminine'.

Therefore I wasn't able to experience myself as a male without a deep ambivalence, conflict and self-doubt.

My father's return (five–six years old)

When my father came home from London to live permanently with us (some time in 1945) I was evicted from my parents' bed where I slept with my mother. In that wrenching away from the merging with my mother's body I awoke through language (see Chapter 7) to a world organized around a binary opposition between the sexes.

In the first years of my life, I was fluidly polysexual,[5] curious about the workings of bodies (arses, earholes, orifices were there to explore!) but not very much concerned with sexual differences. But from four or five onwards (with the related shock of seeing my Dad's penis for the first time) I became much more genitally focused, entering into a cultural/symbolic world where male and female sex differences and sex organs became linked to a set of hierarchical social and power relations.

Perhaps I experienced my father's return as a flexing of social and physical power that gave him the apparently 'natural' right to expel me from my mother's bed and get in there himself. It seemed to me at that time stupidly unfair that my mother should prefer and privilege him over me. After all, I was there first in the bed and in my mother's affections. From about that time bodily relations and sex organs started to have a wider social significance for me. My father's breadwinner status, symbolic supremacy and his penis represented power, strength and activity (in a male-dominated society) in the competitive rivalry for my mother's love. My sense of possible personal disintegration tied in to the withdrawal of my mother's body (felt as an intense sense of loss and fear that resulted in a long period of bedwetting) began to be understood in comparative social and phallic terms: I had a measly, little 'winkie' and could never challenge his thick, murderous-looking shaft.

This culturally learned, comparative fear of phallic/social inadequacy formed the basis of a lifetime's 'castration anxiety' in me. The fear that I was a weakling, a sissy, a 'half pint' was experienced in my self-critical view of my own body. It was this anxiety and fear of not measuring up to the virile, heterosexual norms as represented by my father that produced an ambivalent striving in me towards a genitally-focused masculinity, in an attempt to distance myself from my 'sissy' traits associated with my mother.

That left me in a deeply contradictory position. It makes sense to me now to interpret that time as being one where I was being tugged in two ways at once between a desperate striving towards a full-blooded heterosexual masculinity, mostly working at a symbolic, fantasy level (through disowning my feminized aspects), and a continuing closeness with my mother that didn't allow me a fully achieved separation from her so that I could form a differentiated identity as a boy and man. This resulted in all kinds of tensions and conflicts undermining my grip on an independent, masculine identity. Ironically, the more I sensed my inner shakiness and vulnerability, the more I strained to be accepted as a 'proper', thrusting boy. And that insecurity was exploited by the surrounding influence of patriarchal institutions, like the family and schooling.

Indeed the social construction of a split in me between activity/passivity[6] meshed in with the divide between phallic power and castration anxiety at the point of my father's entrance into my life. But also, at roughly the same time, my movement into the world of primary school in 1945 deepened those splits even further with an institutional and even architectural reinforcement between masculinity and femininity. In particular, it was also through the separate girls' and boys' entrances of the primary school that I became aware of myself as a divided thing called a boy, and learnt the ritual banter and insults that went with these different constructions.

The social meaning of our biological differences was being learned through having separate boys' and girls' desks, toilets, places to hang our coats, boys' and girls' playgrounds (with the boys' playground physically elevated above the other one), separate changing rooms, being lined up separately in the playground after morning and afternoon playtimes, having our names listed separately in the school register, and the different ways we were talked to and related to by the teachers: 'Have we got any Big Boys willing to lift some tables for me after the bell goes?' or 'Girls! Miss Brocklehurst would like a few volunteers today to wash up the staff room cups!'

But as I learnt to play up my more assertive aspects in order to gain confirmation of my masculinity, that repressed softness and tenderness linked to the relationship with my mother always had a way of seeping through. For example, I found the transition from the comforting home nest to the world of school very difficult to get used to. Sometimes in this disturbingly unfamiliar world of strange voices, rules, smells like sweat, pee and cabbage, I used to panic at the disappearance of my mother. To fill up this gaping hole I used to take a handkerchief with the smell of my mother on. Often at moments when I felt myself being seized by a sinking hollowness in the pit of my stomach, I used to bury my nose in my handkerchief and reassure myself with long, deep sniffs of home and my mother's body. The scent was warmly mellow, unlike the cabbagey smell, and reminded me of my mother's hair on the pillow when I was cuddling up to her in the nights before my father came back from London.

Sensual pleasure: play and experimentation (seven–ten years old)

The hold sex has over men arises from the fact that sex is linked with motives and forces other than the need for sexual satisfaction.

(Andy Metcalf)[7]

Male sexual relations often act as a roomy holdall in the lives of men, into which all kinds of other needs than just sexual satisfaction are crammed – needs like touching, sensual playfulness, intimacy, tenderness.

I don't want to give the impression in all this that my developing sexuality was totally focused on masculine confirmation. In fact it was much more multi-stranded than that, and especially so at certain times of my life. The years between seven and ten were just one of those times.

In terms of the direction of this chapter, I can selectively reconstruct that time as seeming to include more moments of innocent touching, playfulness and curiosity than after 11 – like the Saturday-morning scenes in my parent's bed with my two sisters.

After the Saturday-morning torture of the weekly dose of California syrup of figs to keep our bowels regularly open, I can remember the sensual delight we used to have in burrowing down into the comparative vastness of our parents' bed. We used to enjoy wriggling down into the hollowed out shapes of our recently arisen parents' bodies. We spent the precious time sharing secrets, telling stories, laughing and giggling under the bedclothes, but, most lascivious of all, tickling the soles of each other's feet.

Shirley and I used to take opposite ends of the bed, and Anne used to lie sideways across the bed, so that with an effort and some squirming, we could all tickle and be tickled. Sometimes the soft finger caressing used to pierce right through me, to the point where I had to cry out for the almost painful pleasure to stop. But at other times I could just manage to hang on to my self-control as the inner crevices of my toes were stealthily explored.

Occasionally I used to let rip a loud fart and yell out, 'HMS Vanguard firing a broadside!'[8] Then there were groans, thumps and protestations from my sisters, and we all used to flap the bedclothes to get rid of the creeping whiff. Sometimes I used to shake up the old, lingering smell so that we could all get in another last sniff and moan before it vanished.

The playful intimacy between my sisters and myself was most in evidence in the 'coalmining' game we invented for those Saturday morning forays into the usually forbidden zone of our parents' bed. In the protected secrecy of the game I could give up most of my fear of effeminacy. I remember wriggling right down under the sheets and blankets, often interlocking our arms and legs as we burrowed, until we were right down at the bottom of the bed with the blankets firmly tucked in, half suffocated.

Down there we had to hack out the coal and pass it back in buckets along a human chain to the surface. We always took it in turns to perform these different tasks. The game usually ended with a pit accident when we imitated a rock fall, yanked out the tucked in bedclothes, and draped ourselves over the end of the bed, half in and half out, gasping for air until we dropped on the floor.

All the time that I was writhing down into the tunnels of the bed I used to draw in deep breaths of my mother's smell; the softness of her hair intermingled with the homely heat of her body on the sheets.

The sexual experimentation during this time was also more of a puzzling-it-out, innocent variety as well. One playtime at primary school (I must have been about seven or eight) a boy called Derek and I locked ourselves in the classroom with a girl called Gail agreeing that we'd show her ours if she would show hers.

It was all very much a non-event as far as Derek and myself were concerned; gawkily we unbuttoned ourselves and took out our winkies as if we were peeing. Gail seemed to glance at them and then looked away in what looked like boredom. I didn't know whether she was really embarrassed, shy or secretly excited. Whatever she felt she managed to disguise it very well.

Then it was Gail's turn to show us hers. She quickly pulled her knickers down and we moved in a bit closer to get a grandstand view. But there was nothing to see. There just seemed to be a sunken folding of her skin at the bottom of her stomach. We gazed at it for a little while then we looked away. We couldn't see what all the fuss was about down there.

Not one word was spoken through all this exchange of glances and we never referred to it again.

Masturbation, homo-erotic activities and homophobia (11–15 years old)

The pattern of desire and emotional attachment produced in me in my first five years became intricately interwoven with the tightly repressed, homophobic atmosphere of the boarding school I went to, especially between the years of 12 and 16.

At the age of 12 my mother died and my whole world broke apart. My hope for continuity and stability vanished overnight. It was as if she had permanently withdrawn the possibility for me of ever feeling warm and close to another person again. Her death threatened the very foundations of a separate identity, apart from her. It was in this shocked state, dragging an enormous, bottled-up grief behind me, that I was sent to boarding school.

My whole being was crying out for love and affection but all I found was the steely, disciplined order of the school's rules and regulations and, with the other boys, the vicious banter and teasing of a bully-boy, heterosexual culture (see Chapter 8). I remember lying in bed at night and staring up at the plaster-frieze ceiling. I couldn't sob or cry out. All I could do was keep my body rigidly still, and stare, stare at the ceiling, trying to make sense of it. After a few nights of lacerating misery I found that the only way to get by in that kind of climate was to pretend to forget my grief and to join in and try and become one of the lads.

For that to happen I had to repress even further that fluid, wideranging play of sensuality and loving tenderness, in order to emphasize the robustly active parts of myself so as to gain approval from the male club. That meant throwing myself into sporting activities, and learning the codes of verbal sparring.

In terms of my sexual development that meant learning to focus a great deal of attention on my penis, in my humour, boasting, teasing as well as my anxieties. Practically it meant learning to masturbate in the dormitory, almost every night. Without any possibility of affectionate relationships, my desire turned inwards on myself. At first that expressed itself through a curling up in bed after lights out and hugging myself with my hands tucked in under my scrotum, and with my knees bent. But soon, with soft porn magazines like *Spick* and *Span* around, and masturbation going on all around me, I started to fondle myself.

There was such a terrifying vacancy inside me (after my mother's death) that I comforted myself, and borrowed a masculine identity from the ruling norms of tough-guy, heterosexual life, through gradually learning to arouse myself into a stiff erectness. In that context the frenzied yanking and the final hot spurt of semen into a balled up handkerchief gave me a spurious sense of ego-bolstering activity and strength and I suppose briefly confirmed me in my wobbly masculine identification. But it was only a temporary satisfaction. With the quick surge of prick-joy over, a hollow emptiness took its place, and the semen stickying my fingers smelt of wallpaper paste.

That was probably the start of my gradual estrangement from my body. My penis began to become detached from my heart and lovingly reciprocal relations, and instead became an illusory means of a comforting sensation of positive activity. This shoring up and comforting through sexual stimulation (partly satisfying my longing for contact, touch, warmth) couldn't last because the semen wasn't the shared seed of loving tenderness, but rather the guilty seed of concealment and secrecy that gave rise to a long, buried history of screwed up handkerchiefs in the backs of cupboards and drawers throughout my life.

Accompanying this masturbatory focus on my penis went a sexualizing of women's bodies from about 13 onwards. The original desire for my mother (like sucking at her breast) became displaced onto women as sexual objects, like the fashion models displaying women's underwear I later masturbated over in the Marshall Ward's mail catalogue. Through this eroticizing of parts of women's bodies I fantasized a more manly, dominating control over compliant women that seemed to keep my castration anxiety at bay. That's how, on one level, I became so susceptible to reproducing the traditional relations of heterosexual male power over women, except that it was more contradictory than that.

[122]

My ambivalence about my conventionally masculine identity (and my longing for close physical contact with loved ones) made me more wideranging in my sexual experimentation at the time. In some ways I was able to sustain something of the sensual playfulness that I've mentioned above through a homo-erotic playing around in the dormitory and school. In my early years at the boarding school there was sexual experimenting with other boys that developed a strange kind of intimacy and physical closeness which we kept quiet about but weren't too ashamed about either. Indeed, in an oblique way, these intimacies seemed to question the dominating form of boy/boy relationship in the dormitory.

With two boys in particular I can remember a hesitant approach to some kind of ambivalent affection through hands slipping in under bedclothes, to fondle, stroke and then to quietly masturbate each other. On one occasion there was a continuation into the broad daylight of the school day. One boy, who had a bed next to mine, continued the masturbation game in the chemistry lab.

One of my trouser pockets (short trousers they must have been!) had a convenient hole in it, and this friend used to inconspicuously sneak his hand into my pocket and caress my penis through the hole, while the teacher was demonstrating the latest chemistry experiment on the dais underneath the blackboard.

Homophobia is thus an integral component of heterosexual masculinity, to the extent that it serves the psychological function of expressing who one is not (i.e. homosexual) and thereby affirming who one is (heterosexual).

(Gregory Herek)[9]

My early, relatively fluid sexual potential became trapped within the false dualisms of masculinity/femininity and heterosexuality/homosexuality between the ages of 12 and 16. Increasingly guilty about the homo-erotic play, I relieved the anxiety about my ambivalent masculine identity through consolidating my grip on the seeming 'normality' of heterosexual masculinity at the expense of a threatening homosexuality. That's why Gregory Herek rightly suggests that homophobia isn't a marginal matter, but an integral part of the way heterosexual masculinity is constructed. 'Hard case' masculinity not only defines itself positively through assertiveness, virility, toughness, independence etc. but also negatively by defining itself in opposition to what it is not – feminine or homosexual.

Gradually over this period I succumbed to this pressure to identify myself in the homophobic terms of what I was not. As a result, I not only tried to bury deep within myself any giveaway traces of softness, weakness, gentleness, effeminacy but I also tacitly acquiesced in the rampant, institutional homophobia of my school life.

To confirm my manliness in public I needed to join in on the constant jokes about 'queers', 'browners' and 'nancy boys', and show disapproval about boys and teachers who showed traits of weakness like our physics teacher (who was also a Church of England clergyman). He became the butt of the most barbed homophobic abuse and constant jibes. He was a totally ineffectual teacher, who was always trying desperately to keep order. Panicking, he used to veer from screaming threats to trying to get in with some of the boys. Knowing he couldn't get through to the 'cocks' of the class, he used to sidle up to the loners, odd ones, vulnerable ones like me, and try and butter them up.

What I had noticed about him (and what made me turn away from him and have nothing to do with what was going on) was his sly, insinuating intimacy of manner, creeping up behind us, placing his ample bum on the lab bench next to our stools and bending down to us to whisper confidentially to us in a soft, lisping voice. It was a practised preacher's voice saturated with 'concern', asking us about home problems and offering well rehearsed advice.

'Browner' was the name we gave him for that. Meaning, I suppose that you had to watch your arse-hole, a sly finger up your bum, when he was sucking up to you. Totally unfair, of course. I can't remember any specific action of his that warranted such an attack, but it was more the combination in him of weaknesses defined against a culture of virulent homophobia.[10] It was his lack of manly discipline and assertive teacher authority, his possession of feminized, ecclesiastical connections, and his immediately suspect, 'intimate' manner that labelled him in our eyes, 'queer' or 'browner' or, at least, out of place within the expected norms of conventional masculinity that we were all trained up in. In retrospect, I feel deeply ashamed of how I just went along with the others in their attack on him, and hid inconspicuously, in the male club.

The pressure to confirm my heterosexual virility against the undermining activities of 'queers' (the 'queer' in myself as well as outside) came to a head in my life around about that time. That meant a stricter policing of the boundaries between heterosexuality and homosexuality, and that produced a great deal of tension in me about being associated, in any way, as 'one of them'.

This fear of negative labelling (which gnawed away at the heart of my masculine identification) became focused on moments when I was sexually approached by other boys or men. Two particular incidents stay with me.

The first came on one of my weekend visits to my aunt's in Plymouth. Every Monday morning during term time from about 1954 to 1956 I used to catch the 6.40 from Whitleigh Estate back into town, to link up with the bus back to Totnes.

I used to sit upstairs and I became friendly with a man in his fifties, passing the time of day, him wanting to know where I went to school, what I thought of Plymouth Argyle etc. Every Monday he used to come and sit by me, but over the weeks I started to become wary of him and wonder what he was up to.

His talk became spicier and he kept looking at me in a strange way. It was when he told me a story about his boss possessing a drawerful of 'French letters', with a knowing leer on his face, and started to pat me on my left knee that I couldn't stand it anymore. From then on my flesh crept when I thought about him. So I went out of my way to avoid him; catching the 6.20 bus, always going downstairs, deliberately sitting with somebody else.

From that time on I tried to shut out of my life those sexually 'other' and frightening elements that threatened to unsettle my precariously achieved sexual identity.

The second incident affected me more deeply, during my period at university when I was about 19 or 20. Initially I was very disappointed in university life. It didn't live up to my fantasies of intense, intellectual conversations late into the night. But one person stood out from this general banality – a person called Brian in his second year reading biology. I suppose I was attracted by his total lack of conventionally masculine behaviour; he was always questioning his sexual identity, risking emotional disclosure, and exploring work, life and relationships.

We used to listen to Bartok and Stravinsky, endlessly talking, drinking coffee till late into the night. But one particular night we

[125]

went on longer than usual and Brian suggested that I shared his bed with him. I was too sleepy to be alarmed at that suggestion. It seemed to flow out of our emerging closeness. And any rate I was dog-tired so I just went along with it.

When in bed I turned my back towards him and tried to get some sleep. But soon I felt his arms coming around me in a close embrace. I think he was just being tender and wanted a cuddle but I was seized by total panic. I held my breath for a few more minutes with Brian caressing my back and with me tensing up all over my body and gripping on to the outer edge of the bed, until I couldn't stand it any longer. By now I was completely possessed by fright. Suddenly I tore the bedclothes back, flung my clothes back on as fast as I could and fled.

I think Brian was as surprised as I was. Afterwards, he wrote to me several times. We talked about it but something had snapped within me. My inner voices kept on warning me, 'Get out of this as fast as you can!' As a result we were never able to get the relationship back on the old, unself-conscious footing as before. From then on I was always slightly embarrassed and ashamed around him.

The thought that some men were attracted to my softness, my blond hair or my vulnerability frightened the life out of me. The only way I could deal with that anxiety was to try and slam the door on it for ever, together with playing up the 'tough guy' features in myself. But as we have seen before, what is denied and repressed has a habit of coming back in other forms in later life.

Heterosexual conquest and performance (16–19 years old)

My sexual feelings were messily entangled between the ages of 16 and 19. There was still a longing in me for contact, softness, intimacy and a hunger in me for a relationship that involved emotional understanding with a girl. But the other pull in me towards masculine confirmation was so strong that I couldn't bear to make myself vulnerable enough to stand a chance of forming such a relationship. The result within me was a deeply divided sexuality, at once yearning for closeness but employing a predatory sexual approach that was linked to an ego-bolstering emphasis on performance and conquest, and keeping control of the situation at all costs.

My fear of girls (and the 'girl' in myself) was disguised by the compulsive sexual routines of 'trying to get my end away' that I learned from around about the time of being 16–19. It was as if I had built a male ego and status from colonizing and invading the female body that kept me firm and upright[11] from the terrors of dissolving away completely, and the fear of losing my grip on the strict boundary policing that kept me masculine. As Cynthia Cockburn comments: 'The dread of women emerges as a terror men feel regarding the precise location and integrity of their self-boundaries, and their identification of woman with what lies outside those boundaries and threatens to overwhelm them.'[12]

From about 17 onwards, on Saturday nights, I used to go to a dance hall on Paignton seafront called 'The Casino'. (From 16 I had become a regular weekly boarder and so spent weekends in Paignton with an aunt.) What obsessed me at that time was which girl I could take home after the last waltz and how far I could get. The later bragging, sexual-conquest story was an important part of gaining status within the competitive rivalry of the male club.

The whole person of the girl used to be fractured into objectified parts, as I used to go through an automated ritual of sexual advances. First holding hands, then kissing, French kissing with the tongue. If the girl was responsive I launched into an assault on her breasts, now not the nurturing breasts of my mother but the eroticized playthings of sexual conquest. I tried to feel her up through her clothes, wriggling my hand into her bra cups, eventually after some complicated manoeuvres unhooking her bra and kneading her bare breasts. Then, later, the final assault on slipping my hand down over her stomach, into her knickers and fingering her.

Of course it never happened exactly like that; there were always sharp protests from the girls, with a restraining hand or an emphatic, 'No!' Some of the girls I took out strongly resented being treated like dummies but that didn't seem to modify my technique. I went on obliviously, imposing this mechanical 'sequence of invasion'[13] on most of the girls that I walked home with, pausing to sit on park benches or snog in shop doorways. As a result any chance of really relating to the girl as a total person vanished out of the window.

[127]

The reputation of being sexually fast kept my fears at bay, but it also cut me off from any possibility of developing tenderness and intimacy with a girl. Looking back now from my present perspective it becomes more and more clear that in forcing my version of sexual desire upon girls I was controlling and using their bodies to hold my manhood together.

However some girls I knew at the time took the initiative and stubbornly refused to play my sexual games the way I wanted them played. Especially one called Wenda.

I met her at a Saturday-night barbecue party on a beach between Paignton and Brixham. I was 18 and went out with her for just under a year. She refused to go along with my controlling, willed intentions but, instead, she chose me. She was standing in a small group of girls and as my friends and I joined the party Wenda moved towards me and presented me with a bluebell. I might have misinterpreted the gesture because we'd had a few pints to help us face the party but it felt like I had been chosen out of the group and Wenda was in charge.

What really attracted me to her was that she was witty, lively and wouldn't jump through my hoops. She was also sexually uninhibited when she was relaxed, and made me feel that she liked my body as much as I liked hers. Once my controlling tendencies had been seen through, and my invasive approaches had been blocked, my tenderness could flow alongside an often humorous sex-play (that Wenda sometimes initiated).

One incident from that time seems to sum up what often went on between us. One Sunday Wenda invited me to go back with her and her family to the small town in Somerset where she had been born. When we arrived there in her father's black Wolseley Wenda suddenly decided that she wanted to show me where she had played as a child growing up.

The day was stiflingly hot as we walked down sunken country lanes with earth banks closing us in, across some fields to a cluster of gorse bushes that Wenda remembered playing around. A small, secret clearing of grass opened up just inside the outer circle of bushes.

When we got inside and lay down on the grass Wenda immediately dared me to take my clothes off. But I wouldn't if she wouldn't. So we went on enjoying the verbal foreplay, the teasing and the challenging.

Wenda was so determinedly unprepared to lie back and think of England that all my fantasies of sexual domination evaporated in that itchy heat. The more solidly she insisted on her round-edness as a person who enjoyed teasing me, the less I became obsessed with the driving push towards 'getting my end away' at all costs, even though as a virgin I was still desperately seeking my first fuck to give me credibility with the rest of the gang.

In the end, I remember both of us stripping off to our underpants and knickers, and relaxing into the stickiness of the sex-play as we quietly stroked and probed each other's bodies. What stays with me from that time is the elated sense of physical wellbeing; my shudder of physical excitement as Wenda ran her fingers down my back, the soft down at the nape of her neck, the buzz of the insects all around us and the warmth of the sun on our bare skin. And then we dozed off with my head on her thigh until it was time to get back.

In all of that period of time we went out with each other we never once had sexual intercourse with each other, although we came very close to it several times. Perhaps because of my sexual insecurity and lack of experience I was happy to let Wenda control how far we went, and she clearly wasn't ready for doing it with me. Perhaps she didn't want to become a 'notch on my cock'[14] and be talked about as the object of my first conquest? I just don't know. But she probably sensed my emotional ambivalence and didn't want to risk such a significant act with somebody who might forget the process of loving her in my desperation to become initiated.

In fact my first complete, sexual conquest was a terrible disaster. I wanted to be thought of as sexually sophisticated to cover up the fact that I was really a virgin. That made me fixated on the hunt for my first fuck.

Consequently I was on the lookout, just after Wenda and I broke up, for a girl who was an easy lay. Stephanie was the girl who filled the part in my fantasy scenario. She had a notorious reputation in the world of the 'Casino' (probably mostly fictitious) but I knew we fancied each other by the way we both eyed each other up on Saturday nights. We both had a reputation for being 'fast' and I suppose we were drawn together because of these stories. I think we both wanted to find out whether they were true or not.

[129]

I tried to prepare the Grand Event very carefully. I even managed to calm my fears enough to run the gauntlet of a chemist's shop (particularly all those women assistants!) and stutter a request for some Durex. With all that arranged, I asked Stephanie out one evening in the early autumn and took her for a walk around Oldway Mansion, a large hall and grounds near Paignton.

I knew, step by step, how that fantasy Grand Event ought to have gone. I'd read about the scene often enough in Mickey Spillane, Hank Jansen, Moravia's *Woman of Rome*. I thought I knew all about the predictable rhythm of that scene, from the 'less serious' to the 'really serious' necking. That was probably the trouble. I had such intense anticipations that the real event was bound to be a letdown.

We ended up on a park bench behind the tennis courts. I was frightened and cold inside, as I moved through the mechanized routine of sexual advances. Stephanie didn't offer any resistance. On the contrary, she seemed to be very well practised in all these things. She even helped me to pull her leopard skin pants down. And then she quickly and expertly unzipped me and pulled my penis out. Perhaps it was her confidence that made me even more trembly in that I felt that she was undermining my controlling grip.

My legs were shaking now, involuntarily, and I was in a state of intense panic. I fumbled with the condom, not knowing which side the teat should go on before Stephanie showed me how.

Then we both seemed to realize how impossible it was to remain on the park bench. We slipped off the hard laths of the bench, with our pants around our ankles, and spread ourselves out in the damp leaves and chestnut husks.

I was semi-paralysed. I didn't know what to do next but wanted to cling on to the impression that I'd done this before. Stephanie, I think, understood what was going on and simply guided my penis into her.

But I was so emotionally uptight, hovering on the lip of the grand climax, that I suddenly ejaculated into the condom as I began to move inside her. All I can afford to remember from that time was the bitter shame afterwards, of not being able to meet Stephanie's eyes, and throwing the condom off me into the damp leaves.

That was the first time in my life (but certainly not the last) that the pressure to perform sexually at the right time produced such a build-up of anxiety in me that I crumbled. (The reader might notice, even now, that in order to deal with the shame and embarrassed loss of face in this episode, I've had to borrow some of the conventions of literary autobiography. There are probably other ways of telling but here I needed the security and disguise of established forms.)

Sexual crisis

This logic of competitive virility had its own self-destructive elements concealed within it. For many years I kept my relationships with women sealed off in separate compartments of my life. I either used them as mother-substitutes (like my first wife) or projected fantasies of wildly abandoned sex scenes onto objectified women (always brought down to earth in the few casual affairs I became involved in). But the force of internal contradictions – feeling shitty about using women to mother me, yearning for long-term intimacy yet feeling a mixture of a temporary sexual high in the affairs, and then an intense distress afterwards – cracked open the separate cells of my sexual concealment. I couldn't go on feeling so secretive, exploitative, fragmented. Every day the widening gap between my conscious understanding of what I was doing and my actions depressed me. So I was forced into reassessing the compulsive nature of my sexual behaviour, and trying to bring the divided parts of myself back into relation with each other again. Critical pressure from a feminist partner also accelerated the movement within me towards reassessment.

After a long period of wavering and mounting distress this state of inner fissuring grew into an overt crisis. From May 1984 to September 1985 I lived apart from my long-term partner, and we began, very painfully, to uncover my secret sexual history that I'd kept hidden from her for so long. But I was still very confused: vacillating between wanting to open up honestly and, at the same time, wanting to cling on to confirming masculine fantasies about performance, power and control.

This is extremely painful to write – for both my partner and myself. What we include, what we decide to edit and leave out has been negotiated with her. Some things are just too hurtful to include here. And, anyway, we're not talking about literal truthfulness, but a carefully edited version of significant moments that seems to sum up the central social and personal relationships of that specific moment, in terms of the main values and priorities of this chapter and the book as a whole. That's why there is some telescoping of life-history events here.

Again we're not talking about transparent recall, but selective reconstruction over the time and space of a whole lifetime, and the principles that inform that selection are guided by what is personally bearable for both of us. The notion that the individual male writer has the privilege to confess all, in a freefloating, uncommitted way, at the expense of the loved ones around him, is at the heart of a male supremacist world-view.

Here the attempt to make more explicit and visible the buried sexual history of one man may be useful to others in so far as, through its carefully selected, particular details it also helps to provoke critical reflection on the common features (social forces and relations, and personal patterns of emotional attachment and desire) that go into the making of masculinities within different locations, historical moments, contexts and relationships.

I was still ashamed and found it extremely difficult to own up to what I had done and take responsibility for my actions and my partner's pain. Looking back now, it seems that my need to go on viewing myself as a 'High Plains drifter' (because of my sexual insecurity), capable of scoring and pulling birds when I wanted to, kept me insulated from what my partner was going through.

The crisis came to a head at the moment that my body and my feelings revolted from the life that I was leading. One particular incident seems to sum up some of the general tensions of that period for me.

It occurred one evening when I was still living alone when I arranged to meet a woman, who had come to several of my WEA classes, for a drink. Halfway through the evening she turned towards me and said, 'What I could really do with now is a really good fuck!'

In retrospect, what I should have replied was, 'Well if you're looking for a *really good fuck* you'd better go elsewhere', but because of my insecurity about my sexual adequacy, I felt flattered and easily complied.

To be honest my body was in a really bad state at that moment.

For two months I had been nagged by the dull ache of a nervous stomach, and whatever I did for it it wouldn't go away. Indeed, my whole physical being was centred on the ache and my state of emotional distress rather than sexual pleasure. But instead of sharing these worries with her, I tried to ignore what my body was saying, and concentrate on this flattering invitation. *Real* men were always ready for it at any time, weren't they, irrespective of how they were feeling?

I suppose it was this widening split between my present state of feeling (anxiety and grief mixed together) and a mechanized routine of sexual approaches that gave rise to that disastrous evening. We went back to my house and quickly got undressed. But my body wouldn't follow the sexual instructions of my head. It just wasn't engaged in what was going on. My penis remained limp and only half-listened to the shouts of sexual arousal. And meanwhile I was slowly brimming over with a sense of self-disgust, isolation and humiliation.

No longer could I go through the sexual motions without feeling something for the person that I was with. In shrinking retreat from the present demand to perform on cue, my body was at last crying out for reintegration into the loving web of affection and shared feelings. No matter how loud I cursed it inside my head, my estranged penis defiantly refused to join in any more games of conquest. That bodily refusal, I realize now, was more like a scream of protest from my whole being which was learning to put loving closeness before performance.

The long struggle: re-making sexual and loving relations

The conflict between my need for masculine confirmation through sexual conquest and a desire for a grown-up relationship has begun to be resolved over the years. Now I'm involved in the long struggle of knitting back together the different parts of myself through the questioning, challenging and loving of my relationship with my partner.

At the centre of this process of reworking for me is the redefinition of what counts as male sexuality and a questioning of what seems most 'natural' in heterosexual relations. Dimly, I have become

[133]

aware that the 'natural drive' of my sexual behaviour – and especially thrusting, goal-oriented behaviour inevitably centred on penetration and orgasm – is a defensive carapace built to protect my fears of revealing my shaky grip on my masculine heterosexual identity.

Earlier in this chapter, I tried to trace the origins (mainly through the relationship with my mother) of why I now cannot experience myself as a man without deep ambivalence, conflict and self-doubt. That sense of my own emotional neediness has been difficult to admit and recognize in my own life because it eats away so voraciously at the foundations of my masculine identification and my power. As a result, I have compensated for these eroding fears of emotional dependence, long-term involvement and vulnerability by clinging on to those ego-bolstering habits of activity and strength found in the 'natural drive' of masculine, heterosexual behaviour.

As Wendy Hollway rightly suggests, 'men's strategies of resistance to the vulnerability they feel through "needing" a woman are precisely ways of exercising power: a power conferred on them by the positions available to men through the system of gender difference'.[15]

I have now become aware that because of my need for self-affirmation and 'exercising power' in a world that I suspect might be crumbling away at any minute, I have over-concentrated on my genital sexuality which has tended to stand in for my whole, masculine identity ('A man is what his sex is')[16] and confused sex with loving. But how to change all of this? I can't just force my fantasies and desires to obey my conscious will to change. Attempting to move away from this crippling focus, so that I can move in the world in a different way, has meant therapy and counselling (the results of which you see on these pages), opening up with friends in a different way, consciousness raising, rediscovering my original potential for a more fluid, wideranging play of sensual possibilities and relationships. Some of these new ways of relating are summarized here in a series of 'snapshot' impressions.

In a quarter-filled bath I take turns with my partner in massaging the other person's back. I like smoothing baby oil into the valley running down my partner's back. It's the slow stroking and caressing I enjoy, and learning to touch gently with the tips of my fingers down the curve of her back. Then again she tells me where she wants to be touched, and I change the rhythm to a stronger, kneading movement at the top of her back and taut neck. Acknowledging the separate reality of her needs, rather than imposing my pushy, sexual needs on her all the time, helps me get into closer touch with her.

I can give and receive at once, and gradually I'm learning to open up to go with the movement between us rather than controlling what we do through predetermining a sexual agenda. Now I seem to be more confident in switching from active to passive behaviour without too much anxiety.

In the past I've always been scared out of my wits about touching other men, in case I get labelled as 'one of them'. But over the last five years I've learnt to be more physically affectionate with other men. Some of this behaviour is still stilted and embarrassing for me but, slowly, touching and relating to other men is helping to take the burden off my relationship with women. Now I don't immediately look towards women for conventional nurturing, contact and support when I'm in a disturbing situation. That mutual support and contact is always there between my partner and myself but I try not to exploit it as I used to do. Close male friends are there as well for regular sharing and support.

Through a greater physical closeness with men I seem to be able to share more of what's going on in my emotional life with close male friends. By doing this I prevent the emotional build-up in myself that often pushes me towards manipulative behaviour, and I have begun to develop lasting, affectionate relationships with men.

One particular example will clarify what I'm saying. Last year after a difficult workshop on life-history work within a 'Changing Men' conference at Nottingham, I felt quite depressed and hurt about what had happened. But knowing one member of the group I was able to find comfort in a prolonged hug that seemed to release some of my inner tension and distress. It ended up with both of us sobbing on each other's shoulders. It felt warm and supportive, and gave me permission to show the bottled-up distress that I was feeling. In the past I would have looked solely towards women to supply me with some of that emotional nourishing.

[135]

In trying to unlock the damaging split in me between a traditional, fixed notion of masculinity/femininity, I've found the attempt to relate to women in a warm, understanding but non-sexual way important. It's also been important in the way it's backed up the reworking of the relationship between my long-term partner and myself.

With difficulty, I've managed to build this kind of new relationship with a woman friend over the last five years. What it's helped me to do is to learn how to relate to women as total personalities rather than sexual objects. Taking the sex out of the relationship has enabled us to build an emotional and intellectual understanding, without being forced into the old predatory or needy patterns.

The central change in this new form of relationship (for me) has been that the focus has shifted from my pressing neediness dictating the terms of the relationship to one of mutual respect for each other's independent resources. I don't want to push this woman friend into doing things for me, or liking her for what she can give me. It feels much more like feeling affection for the other person's difference from you. I know that sounds unlikely but, in fact, that's quite a precise account of how we've related to each other over the five years.

For her the benefits of this kind of relationship are that the other person doesn't become a substitute parent-figure. She doesn't get hooked in so easily, as in sexual relationships, to that unconscious pattern of infantile desire and emotional attachment. That makes it easier for her to build a friendship that enjoys recognizing the separateness of the other person while still feeling on the same wavelength.

Forming such a relationship with another woman can also have spin-off advantages for the mainstream heterosexual relationship, as long as there's trust there as well. From my perspective it can help the mainstream relationship prevent that claustrophobic narrowing of interests and relations that often comes with the movement into an exclusive couple.

As a result I don't expect all of my needs to be satisfied, or even acknowledged, within the confines of the mainstream relationship. Non-sexual, yet intimate, relations with another woman has broadened out the possibilities of developing friendships with women as strong, independent friends without either the dependence on women for nurturing or sexual gratification.

In all of this the slow struggle continues. In the past I allowed myself to be compulsively driven in my sexual behaviour, but now, through this process of making my contradictory feelings and actions more critically explicit and visible, I'm moving towards taking charge of my emotional needs, desires and feelings where 'choice, change and diversity'[17] are starting to replace gushing urges and irresistible drives.

Notes

1 Referred to in J. Weeks (1985) *Sexuality and Its Discontents*, London, Routledge & Kegan Paul.
2 The experience of the Second World War was a contradictory one for some women; for some (like my Aunt Minna) war work made them feel more independent and strong, even within a male-dominated society, while for others, like my mother, it seemed to increase their domestic/childcare burden.
3 All of this section is influenced by N. Chodorow (1978) *The Reproduction of Mothering*, Berkeley, Calif., University of California Press, especially 'Pre-Oedipal mother–son relations', pp. 104–8.
4 See R. W. Connell (1987) *Gender and Power*, Cambridge, Polity.
5 See M. Kaufman and G. Horowitz (1987) 'Male sexuality: towards a theory of liberation', in M. Kaufman (ed.) *Beyond Patriarchy*, OUP (Toronto Canada). Coining the word 'polysexuality' rather than 'bisexuality', they describe it as: 'a fluid capacity for sexual excitation and discharge through any part of our body including the brain, with its ability to fantasize, and through the various senses, touch, taste, hearing, sight and smell'.
6 See ibid.
7 From the introduction to A. Metcalf and M. Humphries (eds) (1985) *The Sexuality of Men*, London, Pluto.
8 A Royal Navy warship that we had all seen visiting Torbay in south Devon.
9 G. Herek (1987) 'On heterosexual masculinity: some psychical consequences of the social construction of gender and sexuality', in M. Kimmel (ed.) *Changing Men*, London, Sage.
10 This was the background against which a closeted, gay music teacher committed suicide rather than face up to allegations about his sexual relations with boys from the school.
11 See K. Theweleit (1987) *Male Fantasies*, Cambridge, Polity.
12 C. Cockburn (1988) 'Men, masculinity and socialism', in J. Rutherford and R. Chapman (eds) *Male Order: Unwrapping Masculinity*, London, Lawrence & Wishart.

[137]

13 This phrase comes from J. Wood (1984) 'Groping towards sexism: boys' sex talk', in A. McRobbie and M. Nava (eds) *Gender and Generation*, London, Macmillan.

14 A. Metcalf and P. Morrison (1980) 'Sex in long-term relationships', *Achilles Heel*, nos 6/7 on sexuality.

15 See W. Hollway (1983) 'Heterosexual sex: power and desire for the other', in S. Cartledge and J. Ryan (eds) *Sex and Love: New Thoughts on Old Contradictions*, London, Women's Press.

16 Havelock Ellis, quoted in Weeks, op. cit.

17 Ibid.

CHAPTER 7

A critical language autobiography: patriarchal power, social class and language

Here are some fragments from my broken, discontinuous language history. These language shards have been carefully selected to represent some of the key themes of my shifting language uses, especially over the last five years.

(a)   The scene is a conference on education. I'm feeling particularly unsure of myself. I've recently split from a long-term relationship. I'm unsettled and very depressed.

A male speaker finishes his presentation and there is an invitation for any questions from the floor. After four or five questions I stand up and ask a pseudo-question, which is really a concealed statement. It's an aggressive intervention that cuts abruptly across what's been said before, that doesn't attempt to join in a continuing conversation but is really an attention-seeking ploy to claim superiority for my perspective and to undermine and upstage the speaker's contribution. I'm so intent on making my point that it's as if I've shut my ears to everything around me.

The conference is silenced and the organizer makes the suggestion that we break for lunch. I still feel high on winding myself up to make a public contribution, but another feeling of hollowness and shittiness is also gathering inside me, in the pit of my stomach.

[139]

(b)   The gap between my language and feeling is sometimes glimpsed through the way I stumble through sentences. Sometimes there are long pauses, waverings, rephrasings in mid-sentence, incoherences. I let the ends of my sentences trail away into an unfinished limbo.

(c)   When I feel relaxed in using language – mostly in one-to-one conversations with other men who are struggling to change as well – I can speak in a vulnerable, intimate way that helps me to share with the other person. When my attention isn't focused on talking for victory, I can hold my silences, listen creatively, and sometimes reach out to the separate reality and differences of the other person.

With close friends I can risk emotional disclosure. I admit that I feel frightened of speaking in public these days to a group larger than ten. It's in situations like that, when the anxiety builds up in me because of that public pressure to perform, that I go to pieces.

(d)   With some men, usually those that I've known for a long time and who aren't particularly interested in changing themselves, I might still occasionally greet them with a friendly punch on the shoulder while mock-bantering with them: 'You old bastard. Long time no see. What have you been up to then?'

Perhaps I really want to touch them in a softer way but a mock punch conceals my embarrassment, and keeps my defensive armoury intact. And it certainly keeps me within the old frameworks.

(e)   In 1982 I wrote an educational book that in its use of language vacillated over the question of sexist bias in pronouns. Mostly I used 'she' if a person was being referred to, but at times a few 'he's' crept in.

In 1983 I brought out another one that used 'she' consistently throughout the text, but trembled, uncertainly, on the verge of using 's/he'.

In the end I didn't use 's/he' because of the awkwardness of it on the page, but meanwhile my critical awareness about male-as-norm assumptions about language use was growing. Leafing through a feminist dictionary[1] I found this:

[140]

For a boy, internalising the generic interpretation of masculine pronouns is part of a continuum. He becomes aware that a symbol which applies to him is reflected throughout the animate world; a link is strengthened between his own sense of being and all other living things. For a girl, no such continuum exists.

(f) At times, when my wife and I meet another couple in a pub for a drink, I catch myself coming in too fast at the end of what somebody else is saying. To me it looks like an occasional misreading of the cues of turn-taking, of not knowing whether the person has finished completely.

But to my wife, a person I have often interrupted in the past, it feels as if her right to finish what she is saying, at her own pace, is violently grabbed away from her. It seems as if I'm so eager to come in and make my statement that I switch my attention from the interpersonal skills of turn-taking to the internal marshalling and monitoring of what I've got to say. My immediate demands ('Now all listen to what I've got to say!') take precedence over the more relaxed, reciprocal build-up of conversation.

(g) In therapy I'm learning, very painfully and slowly, to unblock frozen feelings, like the deeply repressed feelings around my distant, continuously absent father. Here's a journal entry that I made on 6 September 1988 after a session when I had tried to pursue an image I had of him:

An image of my fireman father blocking the doorway in his black uniform. A looming presence, choked up and untouchable. Staring down at me.

Wearing this fireman's great-coat made out of worsted cloth, silver buttoned and belted, he looked impregnable. Buttoned right up to his neck. Not letting anything out but very well protected.

One evening his uniform was spattered with dissolving flakes of snow that quickly vanished before the heat of the coal fire.

And then the photograph of me sitting on his lap. I must have been two and a half or three and this must have been on one of his infrequent flying visits from London to see us. I don't seem a part of his lap. I'm squirming, flopping sideways as if the coarse cloth of his uniform is scratching my skin.

(h) At moments of unexpected excitement I let drop an occasional 'Fucking hell!' This swearing in a Standard English speaker sounds like an affectation. But I think there are quite a few other things going on there.

On one level it's a legacy from a culture of male supremacy, where the association of the active force of 'fucking' privileges me as a male, but there's a class dimension as well. As I've moved further and further away from being a part of the language norms of vernacular culture, through my upward movement to the grammar school, sixth form, university, school teaching and teacher training, I've clung on to certain non-standard forms to mark my class unease and hostility at the socially mobile process of having been uprooted from one class and moved up to the middle class. Partly, it seems like a gesture of regret for the loss of the close-knit solidarity and support of adolescent, peer-group norms.

Or perhaps, as Jennifer Coates[2] suggests, I might be one of Labov's[3] 'linguistic lames', their speech reflecting neither the vernacular norms of their peer group nor the standard norms of the legitimized culture. It hovers between the extremes of the (working-class, male) vernacular and prestigious (middle-class) Standard English.[4]

(i) During 1986–88 I was working as a school tutor/teacher trainer within a secondary-education school-based curriculum development in Sheffield.

As a part of equal opportunities' work in secondary schools the organizing group put on a Gender and Education day in July 1987. As a practical way of investigating and challenging some of the taken-for-granted language behaviour of men and boys in mixed-group activities I introduced a check-list[5] of common, negative features. And I asked women and men to apply them to their own experience of working in mixed groups.
Some of the key features were:

(i)   Hogging the show – talking too much, too long and too loud.
(ii)   Speaking in capital letters – giving one's own solutions or opinions as the final word on the subject, often aggravated by tone of voice and body posture.
(iii) Restating – especially what a woman has just said perfectly clearly.
(iv)   Focus transfer – transferring the focus of the discussion to one's own pet issues in order to give one's own pet raps.
(v)   Condescension and paternalism – 'Now do the women have anything to add?'

And positive, alternative possibilities were also suggested:

(i)   Limiting our talking time to our fair share.
(ii)   Not interrupting people who are speaking.
(iii) Not speaking on every subject.
(iv)   Not putting others down.
(v)   Nurturing the democratic group process.
(vi)   Interrupting others' oppressive behaviour.

Many teachers responded to these check-lists with a shock of recognition. And I certainly include myself in those shock waves. I could relate the examples of my language behaviour, above, to quite a few checklist features myself!

The fragmentariness of my language history is a consciously diverse arrangement; it represents a kaleidoscopic variety of constantly changing language styles, uses and interactive contexts to match a subjectivity which is similarly 'precarious, contradictory, and in process, constantly being reconstituted in discourse each time we think or speak'.[6]

Also in this arrangement there is an implied critical attack on the myth of the unified, stable individual who expresses her/his fixed identity in an authentic, internally coherent, *single* language. Alternatively, I can view myself as having at my disposal a wide range of language uses and varieties, shifting as material circumstances and institutional frameworks collide against each other and change. These language uses offer me conflicting ways of making sense of my personal and social worlds, from the men-on-top assumptions of my language behaviour in the education conference (a) example above, through to a language of uncertainty (examples (b) and (c) above). But, before we go any further, what are we talking about when we refer to language?

This chapter will deal with language as primarily social behaviour and will largely ignore a narrowly mechanistic definition (the formal features of grammar, syntax, phonology and lexicon). What I want to focus on is not only the way language shapes and organizes our sense of ourselves in the world, but also the social and 'cultural norms of spoken interactions'.[7] More precisely I want to explore the 'gender-differentiated communicative competences',[8] as in example (f) above, where my habit of interrupting conversations effectively silences the women in the group.

What I mean by 'communicative competence' here is the tacit social understandings between speakers and listeners which help us as language users to get by in the outside world:

Imagine someone who speaks at the same time as others, who doesn't respond to questions, who looks away when addressed, who stands embarrassingly close to another speaker, who doesn't laugh when someone tells a joke. . . such a person might use well-formed sentences, but we could all recognise that they were incompetent in an important sense. It is this knowledge of how language is used in a given society which constitutes communicative competence.[9]

It's the lack of these social understandings between speakers and listeners in group interactions that results in some of these negative checklist features that we've already met with in example (i) where men go all out to 'hog the show' or maintain their power and control by constantly using 'focus transfer' rather than dwelling and building on what's gone before.

I also want to argue for a dialectical model of the relations between language and material reality. I want to try and walk a tricky tightrope between the unproblematic position of (a) language as a transparent, expressive medium *reflecting* social reality, and (b) language *constituting* social reality for us, in terms of language acting as a classificatory system or grid through which we give meaning to our inner and outer worlds.

Although I have more sympathy for the (b) approach it probably gives too much importance to language. I agree with Deborah

Cameron[10] when she rejects the idea that 'language alone determines perception and reality'. Instead what we might have is a dialectical relationship between being partly shaped and a more active, personal shaping. On one hand I was partly determined by the already existing linguistic, classificatory systems and related 'communicative competence'[11] and interactive systems that I found myself within, *and* on the other there was the active individual negotiating of modified language practices and interpretative systems as my material conditions shifted and changed. The systems changed as conditions altered, and vice-versa, within a continuously interrelated cycle, without any necessary pre-givens.

For a particular example of this, consider the changing authority[12] of fathers in society today. The language and imagery of paternal authority (e.g. a frowning, bearded patriarch seated at the head of the Sunday table, carving the roast beef) is gradually changing in relation to families, styles of leadership and management etc., as the male-breadwinner ethos is increasingly dismantled. Male supremacist assumptions in the language of hierarchical, male authority are being increasingly questioned in the presence of single-parent families, with more and more men becoming unemployed, and with deskilling[13] practices and bureaucratization undermining men's automatic sense of power and authority at work. But change here doesn't happen in a simple fashion. Some of us still cling on to and are shaped by the powerful legacies and frameworks of this paternal history (like deference towards 'strong leaders' in group interactions) but, at the same time, we reach out towards more open/non-hierarchical models, as our social conditions alter.

What this dialectical approach does is to turn its back on a disempowering, linguistic determinism, opens up language as a site of political struggle, and emphasizes the active participation of the individual and collective groups as potential agents of change.

I now want to look, in greater detail, at some of the most important struggles and conflicts between competing discourses[14] or frameworks through my personal history, and how my language uses were shaped and remade in varying contexts and social relations. Here I would have liked the organizing emphasis to have been on the different themes within my language history, but I have had to compromise to include more of the chronological, linear movement of my development than I had hoped.

Patriarchal power framework

'I knew you must be a boy. You wriggled and kicked so hard
when you were in your Mum's stomach.'

'They called you "Bull" Jackson when you were in Paignton
hospital. You hollered and bawled so loud they could hear you
right down the corridor.' (Told in an approving voice.)

(Family stories passed down to me by my Aunt Minna)

Patriarchal power relies on the social understandings that we
bring to bear on references to sexual difference. And those social
understandings are primarily constructed through language.

It was through language that my sexual difference was organized
and differentiated into the 'common-sense' assumptions of masculinity, to know that hollering, gripping on tight with my fists
and lively wriggling were understood, within a male-dominated
society, as only to be expected and welcomed from a boy. I
learned to view myself as somebody who had a 'natural' right
to special treatment and servicing very different from the ordinary
and commonplace expectations of other people's lives (especially
girls and women).

And all through that childrearing period which privileged the
robust activity of a boy, I gradually began to be shaped within
the 'binary prison' of the 'male and minus male'[15] relations of the
language system that I'd inherited.

Framework of gender identification

My gendered sense of self was partly shaped through language.
Before, I was merged with my mother's body in a furry cocoon,
with no sense of the boundaries of self and not-self. It was like being
immersed in a warm bath for ever. I was totally at home, with no
sense of my own difference to estrange me from this loving nest.
It was just suck, sucking all day.

I awoke to myself (or partly so) through my father's re-entry into
the family. I was thrust out from the soothing fusion of my mother's
bed and split into parts. I started to become self-reflective and gendered (or nearly so) at that moment through a variety of different
social forces, including language. But not unproblematically.

[146]

It's important at this point to acknowledge my debt to Lacanian thinking, and my differences from it. I was partly placed within a symbolic framework and a related language and social system (at the point of having to withdraw from my mother's body) which put men at the centre of the universe and compensated for my sense of loss by offering the future promise of strength and vitality. The source of this power, according to Lacan, is to be found in the privileged possession of a phallus (a cultural and symbolic construction of immense authority and mastery).[16]

I unconsciously assumed that I had a 'natural' right to be privileged and serviced by women (that was the established order of things wasn't it?) but I'd rather emphasize the power of social forces in my assessment of where these assumptions come from. Instead of the phallocentric assumptions of Lacan, that give too much importance to language and the male genitals in constituting a gendered sense of self through an awakened awareness of the phallus, my sense of myself as a boy came, I think, from the social and patriarchal relations of power and subordination interacting with a symbolic framework of phallic power within which I grew up.

Instead of being statically positioned as a gendered subject within a dominant, patriarchal symbolic framework (which prevents any political change), I would prefer to make sense of my developing awareness of gendered identity through a more dialectical model of the relations between language, symbolic framework, power relations and social forces. From this perspective, all through my life, there has been a dynamic interaction between the way I have been shaped and placed within the patriarchal framework, and my active attempts to subvert and reconstruct these given relations as my material circumstances and relations changed.

An example of this interaction between language and social forces can be seen in my confused and contradictory relation to the changing patterns and power relations within my family life.

My attachment to my mother was still so overpowering, my father so hated and so weak and distant as a future model to identify with, that I didn't wholeheartedly embrace the patriarchal order represented by him. I envied his social power but also couldn't bring myself to identify with my arch rival for my mother's love.

There were thus unresolved confusions and tensions within my general acquiescence in patriarchal authority. I began to become differentiated as masculine (within that symbolic, cultural and political order which taught me to expect privileged treatment over women and to enjoy the benefits of that system) but also at the same time I felt deeply uncomfortable within that semi-identification.

Indeed, erotically, I was still so stuck on my mother that I've gone on half-accepting and half-resisting that identification with my father. Words became my tool to fight back with, to keep on sparring with him for that lost sense of merged completeness that he seemed to have taken from me. Admittedly she seemed to prefer him to me in her bed but surely she could see the power of my language? Could she afford to ignore my prowess in reading and writing? It's these questions that keep me striving to outshine other male speakers, like the one at the education conference in incident (a) above. A context of deep insecurity where I feel the shakiness of my masculine identification linked to a social network of dominant, heterosexual male power is the particular chemistry that reactivates some of these compulsive habits.

The fear and anxiety in me about being wrenched away from the merging with my mother's body created a missing centre, a fearful gulf in me that threatened to destroy my whole world. As Cathy Urwin[17] says: 'Both the absence of satisfaction itself and fear of the loss of the source of satisfaction creates anxiety in the child. Like Freud, Lacan sees the attempt to master [sic] this anxiety, and ultimately to control desire, as the impetus behind the acquisition and use of language.'

In looking closely at my present uses of language I certainly can detect some points of connection with these comments about the origins of language. Although my language developed out of social interaction (the loving gestures, waves and shouts of interpersonal responsiveness), the emotional charge and investment of my language use seemed to grow out of the avoidance of an all-engulfing pain of separation from my mother. Language partly allowed me to keep the pain at arm's length by displacing the pain and anxiety into the use of language itself.

'Mastering anxiety' (notice the gendered nature of the process) through language has had destructive repercussions in later years. In learning to anaesthetize pain through language as a distancing device a wide gap has opened up between my mouth and my heart. And in some cases words have been used by me to buttress, defend and pro-tect a wounded self. Connected to this, the language of masculine control (bossing, asserting, lecturing, advising, interrogating and debating) has made me feel better mainly at the expense of women and, to a much lesser degree, other more vulnerable masculinities. At moments when my inner world has threatened to crack apart, the language of masculine control has managed to keep me intact, although I recognize that confronting and challenging the source of those terrors would have helped me (and others) much more.

The possession of language also changed my customary relations with my parents. Language gave me a weapon to take on my father in the competition for my mother's love. I didn't have his relative authority or his physical strength but I began to see that I could outshine him through my word-power. And not just outshine but put down and humiliate him in public. Out of these emotional origins came my language of competitive performance that has kept me on the patriarchal hook for a very long time.

Indeed, later, when I was 17, I remember the mixed feelings I went through on giving my father a copy of D. H. Lawrence's *Sons and Lovers*[18] for his Christmas present. It makes emotional sense now to reconstruct that episode as a complicated mixture of vindictive gloating that I'd gone far beyond him intellectually, and a regretful marker of the widening distance between us.

With my mother it was different, of course. Language gave me the means to try to win back my rightful place in the comforting nest of her bed. Language as narcissistic display gave me the glittering appeal to entice her back as my lover rather than his. So I tried to woo her back, please her and gain her approval through language performance.

As a result I took up a promising 'Boy Wonder' role through my language use. I learnt to expect special treatment from my mother for a clever, potential 'Boy Wonder' who would go far. In doing this I also took advantage of the male-supremacist anticipation that privileged any sign of activity and endeavour in the only boy of the family.

Even now my sisters can remember my mother's clear favouring of and pride in me. 'He's the one to watch', she'd say, 'he's up there in his bedroom writing footballing stories, would you believe?'

However, in setting out these interpretative frameworks as apparently separate sections I don't want to lose the relational aspects between them. At all times through my language development there was a competing and conflicting struggle between different frameworks to achieve hegemonic control over each other. The dominant framework wasn't simply embedded within me as a passive object but produced in me out of a series of antagonistic[19] clashes with other frameworks.

Indeed within the patriarchal power-framework there were all kinds of challenges to the prevailing framework. For me, the institutional language practices of the patriarchal family were always a bit wobbly because of the absent centre at the heart of the family organization, although the implied positional and symbolic power of the family head was still very much intact. But at the same time as I learned the language of a privileging one-upmanship to groom me for a future role as breadwinner and head of the table, the assumptions of that kind of language and social relationships were being contested by another way of using language and thinking within an opposing framework of personal disclosure and vulnerability.

I developed a language of intimacy and uncertainty with my mother, and, occasionally, with my sisters. For example, at about the age of five or six I expressed my fear of the strange routines of primary school through the morning ritual of seeking confirmation from my mother about what might happen that day: 'Will I have to take my shoes off for P.E.?' 'How will I tell my right shoe from my left?' 'Will you be there to meet me when I come out of school?' It was like an anxious, repetitive litany and my mother was forced into giving the answer I needed to make me feel safe. If she didn't I quickly dissolved into tears.

Within this framework of personal disclosure I acquired a totally different approach to the pattern of 'communicative competence' that traditionally favoured the interests of male power. Instead of a single-minded focus on making my point as a way of indicating my superiority to the speakers who went before, here I learnt an interactive style based more on reciprocity and exchange. I gradually found out that it was only through the sharing of fear, failure and uncertainty that it was possible to develop the lasting emotional support that was conspicuously lacking in more conventional contexts. But those self-critical insights were only achieved after a great deal of painful struggle.

These struggles were also tied in to varying contexts. My language started to branch apart at the point of transition from one-to-one, loving contacts where the language of intimacy and understanding flowed between us *and* more competitive, public contexts that provoked and joined together my 'Boy Wonder' language habits and the frequent encounters with patriarchal authority (usually 'strong leaders', coordinators, organizers, teachers etc.) that seemed to reactivate that deeply compulsive sparring with my father.

From about grammar school onwards, my language use veered from narcissistic, peacock displays in competitive contexts that cut me off from the other language of reciprocity, to a more fumbling use of words that tried, however inadequately, to face up to my inner uncertainties in the company of friends.

But the dominating position of the patriarchal power framework became intensified by the class dimensions of grammar school and the heightened peer-group language pressures at school and boarding school. And it was at this important stage of development that the alternative frameworks became relatively silenced in the face of an increasingly self-conscious recognition that language performance could bring social rewards for a boy. For a while I basked in the sense that I might turn out to be 'somebody special', a person who commanded attention through a showy language of achievement.

The framework of the grammar school

Grammar school was such an important, formative influence on my language because of the way it brought class relations into close contact with gender relations. And it did so within a context of an all-boys' institution of unrelieved, claustrophobic intensity.

Even though I was a cultural hybrid (with a background of cultural displacement and evacuation to a holiday resort)[20] with no sustained, indigenous roots, I enjoyed playing around with and trying out language. I even remember using an Enid Blyton word 'scrumptious' to mean *delicious* in an 11-plus test. But by then I was vaguely aware of and anxious about the colloquial 'vulgarity' of the choice. I think I can remember asking my mother whether I should have used it. But despite the slight hesitations, I generally revelled in the exuberance of vernacular forms.

[151]

However, the experience of grammar school undermined a large part of this exuberance. The cultural intimidation of the privileged linguistic and cultural capital[21] that I met with in the narrowly academic grammar-school curriculum eroded my confidence in my own language resources. This bred an awareness of class inferiority in me, making me feel ashamed of my own linguistic 'inadequacy' in the face of middle-class cultural authority.

Two examples come to mind; in a boy called Stephen (who exuded the sureness of an economically buoyant, middle-class background) there was no sense of cultural discontinuity between his home background and school performance. He was comfortable in the knowledge that he was a high flier, a destined Oxbridge star, and I was really impressed by the ease with which he was able to handle phrases like, 'Milton's swelling sonorities' in a sixth-form English essay. But I can also remember the sting and smart of the way he put down my language.

I was always using the word 'imply' in a muddled way, and one day he leaned across to me and said: 'Don't you mean "infer"?' That lingering smart sent me off rummaging in the *Oxford English Dictionary*, and deepened a sense of linguistic anxiety in me so that today I still approach possible linguistic pitfalls with extreme wariness.

The other example shows clearly the class conflict and struggle that went on in that school between different languages and knowledges. There was a rigid class hierarchy maintained between the formal, 'objective' knowledges[22] of subject disciplines and the invisible, everyday resources and understandings that working-class students like myself were bringing into the classroom.

My own cultural confidence was sapped by official classroom moments such as when an English teacher, who must have been very insecure himself around this 'objective' knowledge, came in to teach us the social background of the eighteenth century in preparing us for the Oxford Board 'A' level English Literature period paper.

For several hours he gave us dictated notes on the 'rules of neo-classic decorum in eighteenth-century England', not stopping to invite questions but just checking that we copied the notes down accurately. It was such deliberate mystification that as the teacher was leaving the room I asked him why we were doing this. He half-turned towards me at the door and, with a wry smirk on his face said something like: 'We're very flippant today aren't we Jackson? Get the notes down now and you'll find they'll come in very useful in your second year in the sixth form.'

I never looked at the notes again.

It was in this kind of way that I partly learned to distrust my own use of language in home, street and playground. Half-sceptically, I became deferential to middle-class cultural authority. As Harold Rosen says, 'there exists in the working class both an awed reverence for the language of the educated and a deep and justified suspicion that it is used to mystify and exploit them'.[23] This class-based scepticism remained with me all through my grammar-school career and probably formed the basis for the later growth of more critical perspectives in me. What was crucial was the way gender and class relations started to become interwoven within my sense of linguistic distrust, anxiety and 'awed reverence for the language of the educated'.

To fill the illusory gap within myself, the historical product of class-based comparisons not personal failings, the 'Boy Wonder' strivings seemed to become linked with an upwardly mobile aspiration to climb towards the 'language of the educated'. Proving my virility to my father provided the driving force to recuperate a class-based sense of linguistic inadequacy. The collusion between patriarchy/capitalism kept me on its hook through a persistent straining towards an impression of bogus power and authority. And I did this through learning the tricks of a skilled ventriloquist; by mimicking the borrowed phrases of the 'language of the educated'. As a result, my own creative capacity and belief in what I had to say became paralysed. In its place was the anxious search for approval from the confident Stephens of the world.

So I gradually learned to dump any distinguishing traces of home/street talk in official school contexts. I also learned to accept the public/private split in my life and the different kinds of appropriate language that went with that split. I strove for the social prestige and material success tied in to the impersonal, distanced Standard English voice – the dominating voice of malestream discourse. Indeed I wanted that bolstering, authoritative voice of masculine as well as ruling-class power.

Dale Spender criticizes this dualism between public and private spheres within language use as an important part of 'masculine ideology'.[24] She rightly sees it as destructive because it breaks apart the personal/political interrelationship central to a feminist way of perceiving and understanding the total social relations implicit in any world event. She also sees it as a way of perpetuating male power by 'appropriating strength, reason, logic, objectivity' while 'allocating weakness, irrationality, emotion and subjectivity to females.'[25]

Although this is a powerful insight it doesn't do justice to the contextual variety and the fissures and cracks within my own language use. In one-to-one contexts with friends whom I could trust there was still the sometimes baffled language of hurt and uncertainty and the struggle towards some kind of intimacy. In male peer groups (see pp. 168–87) the pressure to be accepted as 'one of the lads' put a high premium on vernacular language forms like swearing, bantering and joking. It's true there was a dominating model of public, classroom language, with its 'plain statement of facts',[26] but what this leaves out is the way I was pulled and tugged between different interactions, uses and contexts.

Within what were traditionally boys' subjects at my grammar school (physics, maths, chemistry etc.) the impersonal language of cool, scientific precision, like writing up experiments, had totally alienated me. There was no place for personal elbow room within that deadening prose. So I turned to the world of cultural sensitivity[27] offered by some aspects of English language and English literature. Amongst the mechanical, formal grammar some feelings could be explored. This appealed to me much more strongly because it allowed me to put into practice my language of narcissistic display, as well as giving me some access to my stifled, emotional side.

I was mesmerized by the sound and flavour of unfamiliar words and often tried them out in English essays. As a result I developed a florid style that drew attention to itself. In 1954 one example of that style was printed in the spring-term edition of the school magazine, *The Totnesian*. It was a forced, stilted piece on 'Racing to school!'[28] that showed the way I tried to cover up my distrust in myself with an anxious search to impress the reader and please the teacher through a use of purple prose.

Over the space of five or six years I picked up the elitist social signals that frowned on the vigorous vernacular of home. Instead I learned to replace that vernacular with middle-class language, using qualification, a more convoluted syntax and a latinate, polysyllabic vocabulary. My classroom language became studied and precious as I strained to emulate the 'elegant style' of middle-class, standard respectability. I dropped my own awkward directness of feeling in order to seek approval in borrowed words.

Two particular incidents seem to sum up the contradictory tensions within my use of language at that time. The first one was the shock of failing 'O' level English language in 1956. This was mostly due to the mismanagement of time under examination conditions (I think I only finished about a third of the paper) but was also related to trying over-hard to impress the examiners with an elaborately wrought essay.

I spent a ridiculous amount of time on getting the essay right (searching for the *bon mot* in the midst of a tortured, long-winded style) and failed to complete the comprehension and formal grammar work. The irony of this was that the certifying system which failed me was also a significant part of that class system of social regulation which had initially produced in me an awareness of my own cultural and linguistic 'inadequacy'. And here, now, in my stumbling 'O' level paper these same examiners were taking these efforts at face value and were judging them as inadequate, 'natural'[29] abilities rather than the class-based results of social inequalities. So instead of directing my anger against the social hierarchy that had produced such damaging inequalities, I carried this personal memory of shame and defeat through the years, only daring to tell my closest friends.

The other incident was from my sixth-form days. The previous head boy, the year before, had dried up while giving the traditional speech of congratulation to the new Lord Mayor in the town's guild hall. The fear of being found out as equally incompetent pushed me to great lengths of preparation and rehearsal. Again, I built up a showy facade that gave an impression of sophistication that I could hide within. Looking back now I can reconstruct the opening of that speech as going something like this:

'In a speech such as this, Lord Mayor, it's very difficult not to sound platitudinous [an impressive sounding word I'd just heard my French teacher using and which seemed to lend me greater power than I actually possessed] but when I take this opportunity of congratulating you, on this important occasion, I'm truly sincere. . .'

[155]

The framework of an all-boys' peer group at school

This section is more fully developed in the next chapter, so here I only briefly sketch in some of the general tendencies in my language use.

In the non-adult public arena, especially from the age of 13 to 17, my language use became much more careful, guarded and defensive. If I didn't watch my back I'd be stabbed with verbal darts before I had time to turn around in some groups and gangs I can remember. The mocking, teasing, ridiculing of anything slightly out of the ordinary (or a physical defect or weakness) was a powerful pressure towards linguistic conformity in becoming 'one of the lads', or rather one of those marginal boys who hovered, uneasily, at the fringes of the group. In fact I can remember several boys from the boarding school who ran away because they couldn't stand the continuing pressure.

I only let my guard drop with one or two close friends whom I knew wouldn't betray me if I risked vulnerability with them. The penalty for not joining in on the endless repartee, wisecracking and banter was to be made the butt of jokes, or to be labelled 'sissy' or 'queer'. That fear of being labelled the odd one out kept me firmly toeing the well-defended, heterosexual line in my language behaviour, throwing in an unnecessary number of swear words (see example (h) in the opening fragments of my language history), boasting and trying to talk tough.

In one sense, 'buddy-boy' language substituted for the public impossibility of physically touching one another. The witty, linguistic sparring was a way of getting closer to another boy, and increasing the solidarity of the bond between the male group, while at the same time appearing to be doing the opposite.

Over the years in the grammar school the defensive armoury of peer-group language habits had a deep effect on me. Although the sharing conversations still went on all the time, on a one-to-one basis, the non-adult public arena was dominated by language routines that taught me to bury the language of personal feeling in order to try and gain acceptance, as a survival strategy, in the 'buddy-boy' network. And over a long period of time those cynically undercutting quips, asides, joking rituals all exerted a

[156]

strong influence on my general inability to value reciprocity above talking for victory.

The framework of educational work

In some ways the movement within me towards a language of masculine control (ordering, asserting, lecturing, advising and debating) was exacerbated by my period of secondary-school English teaching (1963–82) and teacher training.

There were still collisions in my teaching voices between a language of mutuality and negotiation that worked from a positive recognition of how students can build power and confidence in their active, purposeful use of their home/community language varieties *and* ego-tripping language performances from the front of the class. But, overall, I used the job to mask my emotional wobbliness. Immediately after the break-up of my first marriage in 1973 I was emotionally shattered but instead of turning to confront the blockages and the pain I buried myself in the impossible demands of the head of an English department's job[30] in a large comprehensive school outside Nottingham.

Filling up the emotional void in me with a large number of daily jobs, meetings, reading, preparation, marking children's books etc., I made myself feel better through strenuous achievement through work. So I wasn't content to just get through each week, sharing the everyday problems of the department with others. The compulsive, self-validating performances of the 'Boy Wonder' part of me developed into the competitive individualism of the Hero Innovator.

At conferences up and down the country, in editing textbooks and writing articles and books on English teaching and education I evolved a language and style of evangelical fervour with the emotional conviction of the Hero Innovator[31] bringing the Good News to the benighted. Of course, the performance was always fissured with the jagged edge of internal contradiction but for a period of about five years I tried to keep the distress at arm's length through a language of working expertise that expected to command audience attention and respect.

However, the competing framework of intimacy and vulnerability was always there leaking through the Hero Innovator's style

[157]

and the rational, public voice. Every now and again I would sense a huskiness or tightness in my throat even in the most polished performance. The legacy of all that denied emotion was there in the huskiness. What I didn't choose to see then were the male-as-norm assumptions of this public voice which crowded out all the 'minus male'[32] qualities and characteristics of other marginalized or silenced voices. What I was blind to were the insights that showed me that what I unconsciously accepted as a natural, human opportunity to take up the centre stage of each discussion or conference was a part of the invisible, patriarchal structures that favoured my male interests at the expense of more hesitant, self-critical listeners and speakers (often women and more vulnerable men).

Temporarily, I felt dangerously high on the adrenalin-fizz of each talk, performance, conference. I felt that the world was my oyster, that I could bend people's ears in whatever way I wanted. That was the point at which I was most insensitive to the 'communicative competence' needs of other speakers. I often went into groups with the predetermined goal of making my internal agenda the dominating agenda of the whole group rather than building a dialogue slowly by being responsive to the different viewpoints and priorities within the group. I often wanted to grab the limelight, seized turns in conversations, sparred and fenced with others to keep up a sense of pride and superiority in what I had to say. The object of group talk for me seemed to be the competitive race to be a revered speaker rather than somebody who wanted to exchange meanings.

On the other hand, if the context was safe, I could become more fallible and self-critical in my language use. And in other contexts my language energy was used for positive, social purposes rather than narcissistic display. (I don't want to give the wrong impression here; traditional 'masculine' resources, like courage, determination, power etc. can also be used for socialist, anti-sexist purposes if the social relations and context are right. There is an appropriate time for using these resources and hanging on to them. It's learning to judge when the time is right that is really difficult!)

However, what was problematic for me was the context in which a male authority figure appeared to invite me to join in a sparring match. In that situation all my reactivated need to get back at my father came into play with disastrous results. Sometimes I was dimly aware of what I was doing and could control the impulse to clash antlers in language but in situations of great insecurity I quickly got hooked in to the savage cut and thrust, and, sometimes, still do.

From about 1982 I became mostly involved in teacher training, and from 1986–8 I worked as a school tutor, engaged in school-based curriculum-development schemes, in the Division of Education, Sheffield University.

At about this time the world of academia added to my already considerable language anxiety about getting it right in public, especially in the sphere of writing. The climate of academic power-tripping through the pressure to publish, the need to be seen to be up with everything that had been published, the need to appear intellectually adequate – all these pressures, however tangentially I encountered them as a part-time school tutor, contributed to a massive blockage in my writing. A journal entry for 23 September 1987 shows something of what I was going through at that time:

I'm always gripped with fear at the thought of sitting down to write again. That tense ache in my back starts up again. I'm gripped by the effort of trying to get it right, of measuring up, of struggling to gain approval and acceptance in a company of people who appear assured in their settled authority.

That's certainly true of competitive settings like yesterday. A conventional university seminar on change in teacher education. It started with a formal introduction from the Reader in Education, as High Priest, working his way around the circle and announcing each person's credentials and current academic projects.

In these kinds of settings I start to freeze up with the anxiety that I associate with joining in the competitive race again. It's the language of public prestige where all the dislocations between my personal and public worlds are left out. That's what makes me freeze in my writing I think.

When I make a contribution in this kind of situation I hear myself really screeching, 'Pay attention to me. *I* matter!' That's the hidden message of all that clever-clever fencing. That screech takes me right back to my earlier, infantile methods of trying to woo back my mother's approval and love.

I suppose it's something like that as well in conventional writing for publication in academic circles. Leave out the messy bits, the stuttering gaps, the mismatches between what you say you feel and what you feel, the contradictory wedges driven between personal and public voices, emotion and reason, inner and outer, masculine and feminine. In order to be rated sanitize the public voice and make it appear rationally coherent, harmonious and authoritative.

But it doesn't have to be like that. Alternatively I can develop another image of the person I'm writing for – affectionate, unguarded, wanting to make contact through recognizing the fear and the failure, also wanting to change things, wanting to understand me in all my contradictoriness and un-right-on-ness. I hope it makes a difference.

Anti-patriarchal framework

As well as changes in my material circumstances (like living on the breadline in 1984–5 when I temporarily split up from my partner, my physical health breaking down, working part-time, being .self-employed and then unemployed), language played a significant part in helping me to break with the patriarchal/male-as-norm assumptions of conventional, prevailing frameworks.

A challenge to taken-for-granted frameworks developed in me slowly from about 1982 as I began to involve myself with the anti-sexist men's movement and its writing,[33] changing social relations with the men and women around me and especially relating to the feminist perspectives of my partner, therapy and increased involvement in domestic labour.

To understand these grapplings towards change that I'm still messily engaged in, Michel Pecheux's[34] concept of counter-identification (or 'disidentification') is most helpful here. Unconscious and unacknowledged compliance with linguistic, male-as-norm assumptions can be countered. But first these unconscious assumptions have to be critically highlighted, made visible, made open to political struggle and then dismantled through a set of 'disidentification' practices and strategies.

The implicit consent I gave to the patriarchal ordering of the world through language in public contexts and awareness, like in opening example (e) where I partly accepted the 'man as false generic'[35] assumptions in my use of pronouns, can be worked on and against through 'political and ideological practices' cutting back against the received grain of what seems most natural and normal in me.

Pecheux, according to Macdonell,[36] believes in a politicizing process of 'disidentification':

Disidentification, by contrast, comes from another position, one existing antagonistically, with the effect that the identity and identifications set up in dominant ideology, though never escaped entirely, are transformed and displaced. In other words, a disidentification can be brought about by political and ideological practices which work on and against what prevails.

In other words a dissenting, anti-patriarchal discourse, never consistently achieved but struggled towards, can deliberately oppose my 'Boy Wonder'/Hero Innovator use of language. So what do these anti-patriarchal linguistic practices look like for me? Here are some examples that suggest the complexity of these new directions:

(a) A fresh, critical perspective on 'gender-differentiated communicative competence' has been offered to me by working within an anti-patriarchal framework. Now my group priorities are about making contact rather than perpetuating those linguistic, one-upmanship patterns, although there are odd moments when I still revert to 'Boy Wonder' behaviour.

An example of this changing behaviour occurred in a Nottinghamshire 'Gender and Education' group meeting. Although I felt tempted to try and hog the show I deliberately limited my contribution to a single remark made about halfway through the meeting. I noticed that my contribution did attempt to 'transfer the focus of the discussion to my pet issues'[37] but at least I'm becoming more critically aware of what I'm doing in group interactions.

From being tense and speedy in group conversation where I used to blurt out what was on my mind I'm becoming more responsible towards the whole group and as a result limiting my talking time. What it feels like is best summed up in an image of travelling on the M1 motorway I generated in a therapy session. I was used to pushing myself and being pushed when driving on the M1. I became accustomed to a fast-lane, restless surge of 70–5 mph. But I'm now learning to be in the slow lane, hanging back behind a coal wagon as it starts to crawl up one of the M1 inclines. I'm almost stifled by the exhaust fumes, and I'm still gripped by considerable frustration, but I'm hanging in there until I begin to calm down.

(b) I'm breaking my silent collusion with the patriarchal framework by trying to write out of my present state of personal contradictoriness rather than faking it out in that habitually distanced, rational public voice. I'm trying to go public in my uncertainties (and new confidences) as well as in new forms of inner strength.

In doing that I'm attacking the culturally and historically produced splits between the individual and society, subjectivity and objectivity, masculine and feminine etc. that continue to keep up the pretence of the external strength, control and efficiency of public, organizational men.

So in an article in *Achilles Heel* called 'Scoring'[38] I tried to show how the adolescent imagery of conquest, victory and going for the chequered flag estranged me from loving understanding. In keeping the personal/political dynamic going within the article I also attempted to point up the anti-patriarchal implications of the connections between male power and a thrusting, capitalist logic: 'It's as if learning to be male was really about learning which kinds of appropriate activity or performance a leapfrogging society rewarded and gave greatest prestige to.'

(c) Within therapy sessions I found that I could use stumbling, faltering words in a sheltered space. I grew easier around working with some of the silted-up pain of my past, and inventing and reconnecting words with recently rediscovered feelings long repressed.

The radical context of this reinvention was largely up to me, to link unconscious structures with social ones. So I could set, for example, the pre-Oedipal relationship with my mother (see pp. 114–16) and related questions of personal identity within a wider critical frame of patriarchal ideology. I'm not sure how far I've been able to do that but the intention was certainly there.

(d) I'd like to finish this chapter with an example of present-day confusions and contradictions. I'm still very torn between bossy and unsure language uses, but I think I'm moving towards a position where language plays a part in being a force for anti-sexist change in my life.

In late October 1988 the Nottingham Men for Change group (a consciousness-raising group) organized a 'Changing Men' weekend conference. My ambivalent approach to working with other men for inner and outer change was reflected in some of the bewildering experiences of being one of the seven men in the conference planning group.

Except for one other man in his early thirties, all the other members of the group were in their twenties. I was scared of dominating the group because of my age and experience but also sceptical about whether the group could organize itself without a more precise commitment to organization. My ambivalence was expressed through wanting to work collaboratively with other men but also, in the early stages, unconsciously wanting to cling on to a controlling and condescending position within the group to make sure that things got done. This impulse to control was also heightened by the dominating presence of another member of the group who stirred up some of my old, defensive sparring habits.

In terms of 'communicative competence' I hovered between forcing my personal agenda on the others through arguing my case, and withdrawing, sometimes, into an active listener's role or, at others, into a sulky pique. Eventually I began to trust the collaborative working within the group but still my history of tight, professional organization as a teacher and the struggles around the legacies of 'whizz-kid' leadership made me uncomfortable in accepting the more casual and shared styles of organization from the others in the group.

In the end 50 men came to the weekend, the organization worked without too many hiccoughs and I learned a bit more about the patriarchal limitations of my language of masculine control. Next time I hope to relax a bit more around shared leadership, trust more in the group resources and throw away my predetermined agendas.

Notes

1 C. Kramarae and P. Treichler (1985) *A Feminist Dictionary*, London, Pandora.
2 J. Coates (1986) *Women, Men and Language*, London, Longman.
3 W. Labov (1972) *Language in the Inner City*, Philadelphia, University of Pennsylvania Press.
4 Coates, op. cit.
5 B. Kokopeli and G. Lakey (1983) *Off Their Backs. . .and on Our Own Two Feet*, Philadelphia, Society Publishers.
6 C. Weedon (1987) *Feminist Practice and Poststructuralist Theory*, Oxford, Basil Blackwell.
7 Coates, op. cit. This part of the chapter is indebted to Jennifer Coates's book.
8 ibid.
9 ibid.
10 D. Cameron (1985) *Feminism and Linguistic Theory*, London, Macmillan. The whole of this part of the chapter is indebted in its thinking to Deborah Cameron.
11 The concept of 'communicative competence' was first used by Dell Hymes. See D. Hymes (1972) 'On communicative competence', in J. Pride and J. Holmes (eds) *Sociolinguistics*, Harmondsworth, Penguin.
12 See J. Hearn (1987) 'Theorising men and masculinity. Specific problems and diverse approaches', unpublished paper given to the symposium on 'Men's Response to the Feminist Challenge: Relationships of Theory and Practice', July. Third Interdisciplinary International Congress on Women. Held at Trinity College, Dublin, Ireland.
13 See V. Seidler (1988) 'Fathering, authority and masculinity', in R. Chapman and J. Rutherford (eds) *Male Order*, London, Lawrence & Wishart.
14 A definition of discourse is offered by Chris Weedon as: 'Discourse, in Foucault's work, are ways of constituting knowledge, together with the social practices, forms of subjectivity and power relations which inhere in such knowledges and the relations between them'. See Weedon, op. cit.
15 See D. Spender (1985) *Man Made Language*, 2nd edn, London, Routledge & Kegan Paul.
16 See J. Lacan (1982) *Feminine Sexuality*, ed. J. Mitchell and J. Rose, London, Macmillan.
17 A great deal of my thinking here leans upon Cathy Urwin (1984) 'Power relations and the emergence of language', in J. Henriques *et al.*, *Changing the Subject*, London, Methuen.

18   D. H. Lawrence (1913) *Sons and Lovers*, Harmondsworth, Penguin.
19   See D. Macdonell (1986) *Theories of Discourse*, Oxford, Basil Blackwell.
20   See Chapter 4.
21   P. Bourdieu (1976) 'The school as a conservative force: scholastic and cultural inequalities', in R. Dale *et al.*, *Schooling and Capitalism*, London, Routledge & Kegan Paul. By 'cultural capital' Bourdieu means that an elitist culture can have a material force in benefiting and perpetuating the already existing power of the ruling class. He says:

> The culture of the elite is so near to that of school that children (from lower social orders) can acquire only with great effort something which is given to the children of the cultivated classes – style, taste, wit – in short, those attitudes and aptitudes which seem natural in members of the cultivated classes and naturally expected of them precisely because (in the ethnological sense) they are the culture of that class.

22   See M. F. D. Young (1971) *Knowledge and Control*. London, Collier-Macmillan.
23   H. Rosen (1982) 'Language in the education of the working class', *English in Education*, vol. 16, no. 2 (Summer).
24   Spender, op. cit.
25   ibid.
26   A. Easthope (1986) 'Masculine style (1) Clarity', in *What a Man's Gotta Do*, London, Paladin/Grafton.
27   Against the ferociously homophobic climate of the traditional, all boys' school round about that time, any cultural or artistic sensitivity was seen as vaguely 'feminine'. Richard Dyer has commented that, 'In an all-boys' school in the late fifties and early sixties, culture was as peculiar, as "other", as being "queer"'. So, in looking back from my present position, I'm slightly surprised that I risked myself by associating with unmanliness in my choice of a 'feminine' subject. Perhaps that was because English Studies was more formally focused then, than the late 1960s 'personal growth' model of English Studies. See L. Segal (1990) *Slow Motion: Changing Masculinities, Changing Men*, London, p. 145, Virago, p. 145.
28   **Racing to school**
     Records! When you think of records you usually think of various magnificent records such as Neville Duke's bid for the speed record or Emil Zatopek's stamina testing runs in the Olympics. But I am just going to tell you about what may seem a dreary or a rather childish record which interrupts the monotony of going to school every morning from the boarding house. Every morning a long trail of straggling boys swinging cases, satchels, football boots and other necessary equipment, move slowly towards their own personal enemy, school! They look like a marching platoon of soldiers as they trudge their way to town On our way we catch brief glimpses of the railway stretched out before us, disappearing

mysteriously around a distant bend. We might see a colleague or the whole party of boys from Ashburton and Buckfastleigh. They glare at us and sneer but we all try our best to look unperturbed. The aged, crumbling remains of Totnes Castle stands aloof on top of its mound, high above the pale green fields and dreary grey buildings. We see the girls of the County School and either wink at them or blush. Boys of the Secondary Modern School torment us on their way to school, but we have to smother our blows unless the prefects vent their wrath upon us. But finally we trudge up Station Road, trying frantically to see something that will interest ourselves such as a car or arrangement of a garden. We might then see Mr. C–ld–w–ll chugging up on the road on his mini-motor and a mysterious hush suddenly closes down on the queue. As we near the High Street we urge the boys on in front of us; will we beat our record? Faster and faster, the legs of the boys pound on; every second counts. We frantically struggle on towards High Street. Somebody drops their satchel in the mad confusion and quickly gets left in the frothing wake of the tornado. With one last tremendous heave of our legs we reach the busy High Street and utter a thankful sigh of relief; we have beaten our previous record! The solemn hands of the Arch clock send out their joyful message; the time is twenty-one minutes to nine and we have beaten the record of how quickly we can get to school by one, whole, solid, grim minute! The prefects then arrive panting for breath, looking very tired and beaten completely. The queue slackens its pace considerably and makes its way slowly towards school, thinking of the grim things that lie ahead of them in school for the ensuing day.

29 See J. Donald and J. Grealy (1983) 'The unpleasant fact of inequality: standards, literacy and culture' in A. Wolpe and J. Donald (eds) *Is There Anyone Here from Education?* London, Pluto. 'The habit of treating social inequalities as if they were natural differences is clear enough in the old Black Papers.'

30 Something of the flavour of that time is captured in the book I wrote on the work of that department. See D. Jackson (1982) *Continuity in Secondary English*, London, Methuen.

31 N. Georgiades and L. Phillimore *The Myth of the Hero-Innovator and Alternative Strategies for Organisational Change*. 'This then is the myth of the hero-innovator: the idea that you can produce, by training, a knight in shining armour who, loins girded with new technology and beliefs, will assault his organisational fortress and institute changes both in himself and others at a stroke. Such a view is ingenuous.'

32 Spender, op. cit. The 'male' and 'minus male' language relations are explained in this way: 'The semantic rule which has been responsible for the manifestation of sexism in the language can be simply stated: there are two fundamental categories, "male" and "minus male". To be linked with male is to be linked to a range of meanings which

are positive and good: to be linked to minus male is to be linked to the absence of those qualities, that is, to be decidedly negative and usually sexually debased.'

33   See D. Ford and J. Hearn (1988) *Studying Men and Masculinity*, Bradford, School of Applied Social Studies, University of Bradford, particularly the section on 'Anti-Sexist and Men-against-sexism literature'.

34   M. Pecheux (1982) *Language, Semantics and Ideology*, London, Macmillan.

35   See Kramarae and Treichler, op. cit.

36   Macdonell, op. cit.

37   Kokopeli and Lakey, op. cit.

38   *Achilles Heel* (anti-sexist magazine), no. 8 (April 1987), available from PO BOX 142, Sheffield S1 3HG.

CHAPTER 8

'One of the boys': male bonding and masculinities

Boys learn very early that they had better be able to bond. What they learn in order to bond is an elaborate behavioural code of gestures, speech habits and attitudes, which effectively exclude women from the society of men. Male bonding is how men learn from each other that they are entitled under patriarchy to power in the culture. Male bonding is how men get that power, and male bonding is how it is kept. Therefore, men enforce a taboo against unbonding – a taboo which is fundamental to patriarchal society.

(John Stoltenberg)[1]

I have to find some male places, groups that won't be so macho, so he [Daniel – her son] can learn from and be with good men and good boys. But look at the male organizations they've built. They're all unacceptable. Curse them. What should a 'boys' group' be *for*? What might they discover, boys together? Hopefully, not 'bonding' to exclude females, but just the pleasure of being who they are, together, without woman-hating.

(Judith Arcana)[2]

From early adolescence onwards I've been ashamed of my 'unmanliness'. I think I know how that sense of inadequacy was produced in me. I certainly know that my culturally learned view of my own body as 'unmanly' mainly comes from the socially constructed contrasts between ideal, heterosexual norms and a withering sense of my own puniness. But that recently acquired awareness didn't prevent me from feeling inadequate, especially between the ages of about 10 and 16: ashamed of not having to shave until well after most boys had started; ashamed of my breaking voice, seesawing from husky gruffness to a thin, squeaky piping; ashamed of my ridiculous, unboylike hands – smooth, delicate and 'never seen a hard day's work in their lives'; ashamed of my 'half-pint'[3] body, relatively undersized for most of that time; ashamed of being a short-sighted, 'specky four-eyes' who couldn't sit in the back row with the troublemakers with my glasses off because I couldn't see the blackboard.

At a more unconscious level that sense of 'unmanliness' also came from a deep-seated ambivalence over my gender identi-fication. Problems over separation and individuation[4] from my mother left me confused over the boundary division between my 'masculinity' and 'femininity'. I felt constantly in-between those restrictive categories; partly learning that the privileged activities of boys were rewarded in a male-supremacist culture and that I could benefit in the same kind of way, but also vaguely aware of the dangerous pleasures of a range of feelings, affections and aesthetic responses that couldn't be choked into the starched-collar category of 'masculinity'.

For instance, discovering embroidery at primary school. I liked the rhythmic movement of weaving coloured wool threads back and forth through a canvas latticework. I enjoyed slowly building up the cross-stitches into a decorative design. At that time it was a relatively unmoulded me, fluidly moving back and forth across given categories and fixed boundaries, acknowledging a broader spread of myself before the shutters came down.

They came down soon enough in the form of a male teacher who made a special point of reminding me that I couldn't opt for needlework in next term's programme of work. 'Boys do handicraft', he pointed out. That's when I realized I had to conform, like other boys, to the social/institutional meanings of what is manly/unmanly. Needlework was sissyish girls' work and any healthy, self-respecting boy should shun it with all his might. I learnt that to be accepted in the male club I had to turn my back on that uncomfortable bundle of feelings, pleasures and desires and begin to rehearse the defensive practices – Stoltenberg's 'code of gestures, speech, habits and attitudes' – of male bonding. In my case it was certainly my sense of personal precariousness, existing within a social network of male power, that made me so susceptible to the conventional norms of male bonding.

But why did male bonding gain such a grip over me? To explain that I need to explore the origins of male bonding. Heterosexual masculinity, aware of its precarious formation in confusion, ambivalence and self-doubt, defines itself in opposition to the 'other' (women, homosexuals). It strengthens and buttresses its internally cracked condition through jeering at what it most fears, and takes refuge in the solidarity and support of other heterosexual men in groups and organizations.

It's important here to emphasize the power relations between different versions of masculinity as well as between men and women. Hierarchical heterosexual culture achieves its dominating position through its social construction of contrasted, deviant cultures that 'normalize' and consolidate its own position.

As Jonathan Dollimore[5] puts it, 'the demonised abnormal other' (in other words, the socially powerless, contrasting cultures of women, gays, bisexuals, unbonding men, etc.), 'whose alienness reinforces through contrast the rightness of normality'. That's why outsiders/'deviants' are treated with such aggressive bullying, mocking and ridiculing. Through focusing scorn on those who are outside the male bond, the male club overcomes internal tensions and fears (like my fears of 'unmanliness') and, in so doing, unites separate individuals into an undifferentiated pack, who can hide within the pack membership while putting pressure on outsiders to join up as well.

So male bonding is not just about group dynamics. It's a political process because it viciously exploits men's internal contradictions and uses these to sustain patriarchal power over other people. I actively sought the reassuring badge of belonging to the male club because of my shaky grip on my masculine identity. I was in a continuous state of fear that my 'girlishness' would be discovered and publicly ridiculed, and so, to survive, I learned to consent to the accepted codes and conventions of heterosexual masculinity (that dominating version of masculinity) that made up the rules of the male club.

The tightly organized network of male bonding represents an important institutional force for regulating women and powerless masculinities. It effectively polices the boundaries of what counts as masculinity through 'norm–enforcing mechanisms'[6] (like joking, bantering and swearing), and the dominant cultural features of boys' and men's groups and organizations.

Here I want to limit myself to:

(a) looking at joking, bantering and swearing; and
(b) looking at some examples of boys'/men's groups and their specific cultures and atmospheres.

Joking, swearing and bantering

In primary school and at an all-boys' grammar and boarding school I half belonged and half didn't belong to the dominant peer-group pack. I was pulled between a class identification with the piss-taking, joking banter of the 'lads' and their rejection of the middle-class, upwardly mobile educational ideals of the school, and an inner unease at the aggressive, brutalizing culture that the 'lads' celebrated and were victims of. To save my own skin, particularly in the boarding school, I had to appear as 'one of the lads'. To compensate for my vulnerable manner and size, I went out of my way to prove my masculine virility through successful sporting activities (see pp. 207–22) and through my acceptance of the mock bravado and swagger of a joking, peer-group culture. Hovering on the edge of the group, I wasn't any good at wisecracking one-liners and smart repartee. But I tried to joke, swore and horseplayed with the rest of them, and vied for the label of 'clown of the class'.

This unofficial competition to be the 'clown of the class' was always a strong temptation to play to the gallery, get one over on the teacher and grab the limelight through being laughed at. One incident that happened to a friend of mine was when 'Chippy' Carpenter, a hopelessly inadequate supply teacher, came to teach us maths.[7]

One of Chippy's unfortunate habits was that flecks of spit used to form in the corners of his mouth and these flecks used to spatter my friend and other pupils sitting in the front desks. Fed up with this and wanting to gain star attention for himself my friend appeared in class, sitting in the front row seat directly in front of the teacher's desk, with a navy-blue mac pulled over his head. Chippy fell for it and asked him what he thought he was doing in a maths class. 'Keeping myself dry from your spit!' fired back my friend in a flash.

We made constant jokes about 'browners' and 'queers', and were always on the look out for any unguarded hint of effeminacy in each others' gestures and behaviour to deflect the focus of attention from ourselves. Any slight diffidences, stuttering oddness, weakness was seized upon by the rest of the group, held up for public inspection and devastatingly ridiculed. The wrong colour or style of vest revealed while undressing in the changing room, writing a letter to your sister during the weekend compulsory letter-writing session, or wearing slippers around the dormitory that were suspiciously furry – all these associations with a culture that wasn't ferociously heterosexual were ruthlessly put down.

As one of the men in David Collinson's investigation of masculinity and joking in shopfloor culture[8] comments, the pressure to conform through joining in the humour acts as a regulatory mechanism to keep the imbalance of power between the sexes, and the conflict between different forms of masculinity, intact and unchanging: 'You've got to give it or go under. It's a form of survival, you insult first before they get one back. The more you get embarrassed, the more they do it, so you have to fight back. It can hurt you deep down, although you don't show it.'

While you're busy protecting yourself against any sign of vulnerability in yourself, and dishing out the ritual insults, any possibility of challenge to the patriarchal system of male bonding is lost, along with any chance to develop closeness and emotional support with other boys and men. Indeed, the emotional structure of the male bond, as I've mentioned already, is one of defensive confirmation through the use of joking and jeering at the expense of feared others.[9] It not only puts down women through sexist innuendo and at times through brashly overt misogyny but it also reduces men's emotional range to a crippling, self-alienating narrowness.

Stoltenberg's 'taboo against unbonding' as an institutional way of sustaining patriarchal power was very real for me in my own life history. I complied with the *status quo* (with unease and discomfort, admittedly) through my fear of being shut out of the male club of 'normal men', and made the butt of their insults and teasing. The humour did help me to make a V sign against the middle-class, cultural authority of grammar school but it also kept me toeing the line of heterosexual masculinity. The contradictory nature of this joking, brutalized culture always prevented it from gaining the more purposeful cultural resistance attributed to it by Paul Willis.[10] In joining in on the joking and back-slapping, it only made me more firmly entrenched within the assumptions of a male-supremacist culture.

In particular I remember a moment of joking that demonstrates this contradictoriness. Every lunchtime in the grammar-school dinner queue we had to wait out in the cold, patrolled by prefects. We were supposed to be totally regimented and silent in this queue. I was secretly joking with a couple of my dormitory friends, at the end of the queue, about the supposed dangers of too much masturbation. The joke might have gone something like this:

'It's supposed to send you blind, isn't it, if you go at it too hard?' whispered Chris.

'Don't be daft!' I replied, 'but it's true that there's a white ring left on your skin between your thumb and your first finger if you wank more than four times a week.'

'Oh, go on!' Chris protested, furtively glancing at his own hand.

The repeated 'Made you look!' joke went up and down the queue of waiting boys, with murmurs, glances and laughter that was hushed down by the prefects, several times.

The joke was certainly a way of challenging the boredom of queueing and waiting, and the authoritarian control of the school regime. But it was also, at the same time, a joke that negotiated[11] inner fears and tensions about developing male sexuality. I was laughing at what I was scared of – dangerous, illegitimate sexuality was being publicly recognized and acknowledged through the 'made you look' tactic. The joking form allowed me to negotiate my contradictory feelings of guilt and uncertainty at possibly deviant sexual practices ('wanking more than four times a week'), and my almost fetishistic fascination with my own sexuality. While the joke explores the boundaries of 'normal' and 'abnormal' male sexuality it does it through shared laughter that reaffirms the safety and solidarity of the male bond. So that the 'rightness of normality' within the male club is further cemented because it's been able to strengthen itself in contrast to these dangerously 'deviant' sexual habits.

Swearing was another peer-group/male-bonding badge that I frequently displayed to seek acceptance from the group. (Indeed now, in certain contexts where I need to assert my class origins, and possibly release pent-up feelings, I catch myself throwing in a few 'fucks' – see Chapter 7).

Jennifer Coates[12] remarks that there's a 'high correlation between peer group status and use of non-standard language' like swearing. So that swearing in my experience was a norm-enforcing mechanism in that to gain approval and status in the male, peer group you had to sound tough, aggressive and cocksure. Intensely aware of my 'unmanliness' I unsuccessfully strained to build an impression of virile sophistication and everyday swearing was one of the building blocks I used.

My attempt to gain approval through a deliberately vernacular language form like swearing was done at the expense of women, and other, 'deviant', masculinities. Sexist slang and swearing is about the linguistic dismemberment of women's bodies through words like 'fuck', 'tits', 'arse' (like 'she's got a lovely arse on her!'). And I joined in the swearing with elaborate gusto just to show the other lads that I was one of them.

Masculinity is founded upon its denial and exclusion of the potential for being bisexual. But even in the most swaggering performances these hidden fears and anxieties are always implicitly there. Similarly, banter appears on the surface to be insulting and aggressive but often carries with it a repressed homosexual element. In my personal history mock punching and banter ('You old bastard! What have you been up to then?') gave me an acceptably aggressive form within which I could express some of my frustrated need physically to touch other male friends. I would often put my arm around other boys' necks, thump a friend's shoulder, wrestle and even have 'friendly fights' when, unconsciously perhaps, I wanted to hug and be affectionate. Also with much older boys I used to try and gain a higher peer-group status by exploiting this ambivalence within bantering. I used to humorously insult, tease and mock them knowing that I wouldn't have to pay the full price for my insults; in fact, knowing that I could get away with it. The older boys put up with my antics, perhaps recognizing that they couldn't be seen to use their full force against an irritating gnat like me.

According to Antony Easthope[13] male bantering is a 'way of affirming the bond of love between men while appearing to deny it'. Certainly male bonding becomes a more intensely addictive

[174]

process because of these repressed homosexual elements implied within it. But bantering has more forms than Easthope suggests and can be more viciously wounding while still working within the bonding process.

An example from my time as a dormitory prefect in the boarding school shows what I mean. The housemaster had occasional difficulty in finding suitable leaders among the boys, and it was very much as a last resort that he chose me in the fifth form to become a dormitory prefect. I was supposedly in charge of eight other boys in the dormitory. But I was nervously aware that I was smaller than several of the third and fourth formers there.

Every night, lights-out time, with an official ban on talking, was a traumatic moment for me because I was always put into a contradictory position between whether to side with the boys (who wanted to go on talking and giggling all night) or traditional authority (with which I had some class reservations). I usually compromised and we went on talking until I suggested that we'd better go to sleep. Most of the boys accepted that except for one fourth former who merely saw me as a hostile representative of the system of authority at school and in the school house that he was dedicated to undermining.

This fourth former used to spend all his inventiveness in mocking me through banter and other forms. I tried to keep my temper and ignore his needling. I wanted to talk about what was going on. He wanted to keep me at a distance and objectify me as the Enemy.

We used to keep our Sunday suits (worn only for the compulsory church service) in a wardrobe in one of the dormitory corners. And I remember the moment when, with a great deal of pain, I took my suit out one Sunday and found this note in one of my pockets: '*Jackson* – you're a sawn off runt'. As Easthope says, 'banter depends on a close, intimate and personal understanding of the person who is the butt of the attack'. I knew, without thinking, that the note was from the fourth former. He was the only person in the dormitory who had the motivation and perverted ingenuity to understand and play on my insecurities as an 'unmanly' prefect. His understanding of my castration anxiety ('sawn off') and my hang-up about being undersized ('runt', the smallest, weakest pig in a litter) was clearly targeted. He sensed minutely and intimately what would eat away at my belief in my masculine identity, and he succeeded. He drew closer to me, through his detailed observation of my weakness and knowing how to really get at me, and in my rising hatred of what he had done I became more closely bonded to him.

Boys'/men's groups

An all boys' dormitory in a boarding school

Boys-only boarding schools, like sporting teams, certain pub cultures, working men's clubs, military training establishments etc., provide the social organizations[14] where patriarchal power can be produced and reproduced through the institutional routines of a vicious form of male bonding.

Except for the time at around five or six when my Dad came home from the AFS[15] there was no more powerfully shaping influence on my masculinity than those years boarding at school. I was never so ruthlessly exposed, night and day, to so many contexts and pressures to mask the full range of my feelings, desires and interests and to buy into the dormitory framework of a strutting, heterosexual culture. Behind the scenes I had my own one-to-one relationships which kept me relatively sane but the public arena was taken over by a bullying, misogynistic culture that was defined in brutal opposition to anything vaguely associated with women and homosexuality. Many sensitive and gentle masculinities were trampled in the rush to define themselves in opposition to women that entitled them to entry to the masculine club. Nowhere was this psychological violence more keenly felt than in two dormitory scenes from my childhood.

The cohesion of the male pack in the dormitory was achieved by isolating and victimizing any boys who in their weakness, oddness or awkwardness they could connect to a despised culture of effeminacy. One of the boys constantly picked on, a boy called Martin, was an outsider like me – sensitive, a mummy's boy, son of a squadron leader down Plymouth way, and self-consciously aware of his own gangling awkwardness. He had a fatal habit of blushing deep red (which in the pack's warped imagination was always linked with the imagined embarrassment of young girls) on hearing anything that was rude and offensive to him. The pack immediately latched on to his blushing and kept on at him, night and day, with endlessly repetitive, mocking comments that were intended to make him blush. Gaining a blush from Mart (like a severed scalp) earned a pack member greater status and made Mart even more hunted.

After one weekend when the rest of the dormitory pack had caught a glimpse of Martin's mother – elegant, smart, well-turned out – while bringing Martin back from Plymouth, we gave him hell. (Notice here how I've become a part of the 'we'. I couldn't afford to take Martin's side against the pack as I would have been turned on as well. To survive I had to keep silent *within* the pack.) 'Does your mother shag then, Martin?' suggested one of the pack. It was painful to watch Mart writhing in embarrassed confusion but we knew if we didn't join in it would be our turn next.

Martin tried to duck the question and offered the pack leaders some cake he had brought back with him from the weekend. They took his cake, recognizing a soft touch when they saw one, but persisted, obsessively, with their taunts. 'I bet you watched them shagging together didn't you Mart?' Martin fumbled with his cake tin and locker door and tried to defend himself in a voice that was trembling on the edge of tears. Underneath what he was saying you could feel him pleading with the pack to let him go. But they didn't. They had him in a corner and the scent of blood was in their nostrils. A voice of victory suddenly rang out: 'What are you blushing for Mart?' and was chorused by the pack together, *'What are you blushing for Mart?'*

And there it was – a deep, reddening flush burning across his cheeks. Mart just wanted the floor to open up and bury him, to hide his blushes. But the pack had sniffed blood and pursued and harried him until well after lights out. 'Are you crying Mart?' And then, later, on hearing somebody's bed creaking:

'Stop wanking Cornhill!'

This represented just one night in two years of misery (day and night) for Martin, when he had no place to hide away or be comforted by anybody. After a botched attempt to run away in the third year Martin was taken away and sent to a school much nearer home where he didn't have to board.

The dormitory is painted cream with brown institutional lino on the floor, and nine iron beds are crammed in around the walls. I stand at the centre of a grinning ring of faces. I've a hollow sinking feeling beginning to spread from the pit of my stomach.

[177]

I look down at the polished brown lino, knowing I mustn't cry but feeling my nose start to twitch with tears.

For the second night running they've pinched my pyjamas from under my pillow. My supposed friends, even Martin, have vanished into the anonymity of the grinning ring. They know that if they don't act with the mind of the pack it will be their turn next. Even Chris, who had his pyjamas taken last week, is there now within the ring of faces, mocking and calling me. The pack hunts down any outsiders, and forces them to forget their own contradictory resistances, and teaches them to snarl, like the rest.

The pack leader ambles up to me and pushes the stolen pyjamas right under my nose. Steady now! Keep your cool! I know that I mustn't rise to the temptation of snatching. I know the pack want to goad me into chasing them. I look, mock-casually up at the plaster frieze on the ceiling, pretend to look away and then I suddenly lunge forward to grab the pyjamas. At that very moment the pack leader whisks them away to another boy within the circle.

I can't help myself now. I know I'm trapped within the rules of the game. I haven't got a choice anymore. I have to become part of the action. I flail this way, that way, arms outspread, trying to intercept the flung pyjamas.

I'm openly sobbing with anger now and with injured pride. They've got me on the run and they know it. I hear myself pleading with them to give my pyjamas back. Mucus and tears are dribbling down my chin. I half-intercept the flying bundle but two pack members land on top of me just as I am about to get my hands on the pyjamas.

The throwing gets more hysterical. I'm shrieking at them now. One of the pack makes a mistake and drops the pyjamas. I get a hand to my pyjama jacket sleeve while the pack seize hold of the other, and I tug with all my might. Two other boys drop on me from behind and try to pull me away. The jacket sleeve is ripped off. The pack stops in alarm.

I hurl abuse at them between my sobs. I grab up the torn remnants and slam off to lock myself in the toilet for half an hour. For the next week I go around in hurt silence hoping the pack will forget my pyjamas and move on to some other victim for next week. But they don't. It's always there in the banter, the incessant jibes and the repetitively brutalizing actions. I've shown the pack that 'I can't take a joke', that I'm easily hurt and offended (like Martin) and I've cried like a girl, and that's the kind of person the pack likes to hunt. The barbaric system of male bonding is achieved at the expense of all those other forms and varieties of masculinity – the misfits and the vulnerable ones like me – that are choked off in their infancy without ever having a proper chance to develop and grow in a more gentle and openly emotional way.

The changing room

The rituals of male solidarity were most clearly seen in that most private and most intimidating place – the sport's changing room as a male preserve.[16] It was one of those male places that held power over regulating 'deviant' masculinities through fear of being publicly teased and ridiculed as 'girlish', 'unmanly' or physically inadequate. I was always half-fearful in those kinds of places, fearful that I would be exposed and jeered at because I was wearing an unconventional vest, socks or underpants. It was there that I learned to measure negatively my own physical qualities, like the size of my penis and relative absence of body hair, in relation to those ideal, heterosexual, bodily norms. I didn't have much hair where it counted; my pubic hair seemed to be a bit sparse and I had a desperate need of a chest wig! Hairiness, an 'insignia of power'[17] and masculine virility, was conspicuously absent on my body. That's one of the reasons why, when I became head of English in a tough comprehensive school in Lancashire, later in life, I grew a straggly beard and then a moustache.

A desire for physical closeness with other boys expressed itself through raucous horseplay in such places. Boys were always chasing each other, trying to flick each other with the edge of their wet towels, catching the other person off guard. Practical jokers thrived in such surroundings. Underpants were always getting nicked, shoelaces tied together, ties losing their expert knots. Sexual innuendoes about the liniment rub, 'Fiery Jack!' or 'Zambuk', flew around, and jokes about putting bromide[18] in the aftermatch tea when we were playing the Royal Engineers' apprentices just outside Newton Abbot.

The showers were the most terrifying places for 'unmanly' boys like me. I used to position myself in the most secret corner of the changing room, protecting myself from being ogled or ridiculed. And frequently I used to skip the shower, hiding my muddy knees, and waiting till I got back to the boarding school when I could scrape the mud off my legs in a wash basin without exposing the rest of my body to the public gaze. But the teachers were always on the lookout for boys like me, and often forced me to have a shower before I could go.

There was also a forced male camaraderie that made me squirm, such as the communal team baths after rugby matches with the Royal Naval College, Dartmouth. On the field the opposing scrum half had been full of solidarity, with hearty phrases like 'Coming in starboard, ship!' just as he was placing the ball at the centre of the scrum. And, inside, in their changing rooms the same kind of pressure towards team spirit had been planned for us by the building of enormous communal baths that a whole team could sit in together. I think I can remember the steamy haze after the match, and the echoing shouts and yells as a member of the team was got by the others, debagged and flung into the bath.

I was lucky that day. My team members ignored me but I had to give in to the pressure to join the rest of the team in the coiling vapours of the bath. And I have to admit that after the bleakness of a raw, November afternoon such warmth was welcome. I just lay back in that steaming, muddy liquid and felt my bones start to melt and dissolve in the heat. And then there was the obligatory round of dirty rugby songs, 'Balls to Mr Banglestein, dirty old man', and 'Oh, Sir Jasper do not touch me!'[19]

The wolf cub pack
Male-bonding processes were explicitly encouraged by boys-only organizations like the Boy Scout/Wolf Cub movement in Britain. From 1948 to 1950 I was a member of a wolf cub pack, meeting every week in a church hall, that sexually segregated boys into a group-bonding process and organized them into sub-groups of 'sixes'. The pack was led by an 'Akela', a young woman who we were all in love with, and the evenings were very tightly regimented and repetitive.

Obedience to authority was instilled through the wearing of a military-type uniform and weekly routines and rituals. I remember wearing an itchy blue jersey, a green cap, and a neckerchief held together at the front by a leather woggle. And this uniform was inspected every week.

The evening had the opening and ending ritual of the Grand Howl. Even between the ages of 8 and 10 I smelt something fishy about this strained, worked up, ceremony. While saluting Akela with two fingers held up to the ear, the pack chanted:

'Akela. We will do our best.
Dib. Dib. Dib. Dib.
We will do our best.
Dob. Dob. Dob. Dob.'

The ideals of the Scouting movement were the 'robust, muscular, Christian ideals'[20] of Charles Kingsley and Thomas Hughes, linked to Baden Powell's imperialist notions of manliness[21] – physical courage, determination, adventurous action and resourcefulness – with an emphasis on military drill and discipline. These ideals came through to me, every week, in the form of wildly rowdy, muscular games like 'Clear the decks' and 'British bulldog' (a Scouting game but played by our wolf pack in 1949).

'Clear the decks' was a deliberately rowdy game to help cubs to let off steam before the more purposeful work of the evening. When Akela shouted 'Clear the decks!' you had to make a mad dash to the stage end of the church hall and leap up onto the stage, getting your body off the ground. The last cub was out. Then there were other commands: 'Man the boats!' (reach the refuge of chairs arranged in the shape of a boat), 'Boom coming over!' (hurl yourself flat on the floor), 'Admiral coming aboard!' (stand to stiff attention and salute), and 'Freeze!' (become a totally unmoving statue).

As well as careering around like wild things, we were also learning obedience to military authority, respect for hierarchy, and deference to commands. 'British bulldog', with its Churchillian emphasis on strength and assertiveness, usually ended up with somebody being hurt, either with a nosebleed or an injured knee or leg.

Victory in this game always went to the most 'red-blooded', muscularly built cub. As there was no chance to show skill or intelligence I normally went through the motions in this game, making myself inconspicuous in the main pack and watching out for possible injury.

The game went something like this. Most of the cubs were gathered down one end of the hall and had to charge their way to the other end. The only obstacle to their charge was one cub in the middle of the room who had to try and capture a cub by stopping him in his charge, often holding him down on the floor, and then lifting him off the ground, yelling, 'British bulldog!'.

At times the cub in the middle was humiliated by not being able to capture one boy, and quickly labelled 'weakling!' by the others, but usually somebody was caught and hauled off the ground. And then there were two in the middle, then three, four. . . until the tables were turned – the whole wolf pack was trying to stop and capture the last rogue elephant. And that's when boys got hurt. The last cub to get captured was always the largest, toughest, most muscular member of the pack and he always went down with a really ferocious fight, lashing out, kicking and yelling like a cornered beast. Sometimes we all had to sit on him, pinioning him down to the floor and blocking his way, before we were able to get a grip of his legs and arms and lift him off the ground.

The rest of the cub business was always an anticlimax after that. The 'difficult arts and practices' of the 'backwoodsman, explorers, and frontiersmen' that Baden Powell explicitly recommended[22] – like learning to tie knots like reef, sheep bend, clovehitch and bowline and understand compass points – left me a bit cold. The only things I found to be practically useful, and that I could see some point in, were telling the time and tying up my shoelaces properly by myself.

All that talk about badges for collecting, naturalist, gardener, athlete, swimmer, artist, book reader, etc., made me an ardent badge collector. It was very much a contrived set of decontextualized tasks that had to be checked out by an impartial adult in order to be able to persuade your mother or your sister to sew on your new badge on your jersey shoulder. Like the 'house orderly' badge for example: to be worthy of the badge you had to wash your neckerchief and iron it; sweep and dust a room; cook a meal like sausages and bacon; make your bed; and sew on a button. But it never made me any better at contributing to the daily domestic labour in my own home.[23]

Linked to these concerns was the value of a simple and spartan life away from the debilitating materialism of the city and in response to the natural challenges of the rural and colonial frontier.[24]

[182]

Baden Powell was always praising the special importance of the outdoor life (camping, hiking, tracking etc.) in the training of young boys. Those values certainly filtered down to our wolf cub pack in St Paul's Church, Preston, Paignton. For some time between 1948 and 1950 the pack went for a week's camp back up the Devon coast, close to Combe-in-Teignhead, and I went with them.

It was a very traumatic time for me because it was the first time I had been away from home and I was very homesick. Two episodes stand out for me from that week of dullness and grey drizzle.

The first incident was tent inspection. Every morning we had to prepare for a military-style inspection by folding the groundsheet and blankets very neatly, in straight lines, and displaying them outside the tent, if weather permitted, together with any spare kit we had brought, such as our toilet bags (with my soap in a bakelite soap dish), shoes, towel, torch, etc.

I remember that I was so anxious with homesickness (another moment of withdrawal from my mother's body?) that I wet the bed (meaning the sleeping bag, blankets right through to the groundsheet). I guiltily tried to dry them all by hanging them over the tent but they seemed to get wetter because of the rain from the night before.

When Akela came round on her tour of inspection with other adult helpers there was nothing to see from my tent. I just hung my head in shame, tears welled up in my eyes, and I wanted, desperately, to go home.

The other episode was on one of the afternoons, about halfway through the week, when my mother and two sisters came to visit me. I struggled really hard not to show them how homesick I really was. I sensed how much they wanted their son and brother to be bright, cheerful and energetic, and 'having a really good time' like some of the other cubs appeared to be doing. But the desperation was clearly written all over my face, and, on seeing them, I quickly dissolved into tears.

My mother wanted to take me back with her, but I knew I had to stick it out for her sake. The pressure not to be one of those blubbering sissies was already so intense within the pack, and in my wolf cub group (my 'six'), that I learnt my first lesson in how to toughen up. During the daytime I tried to busy myself in robust action, sport, joking, and it was only at night that I was haunted by my mother's face.

Drinking and pubs

An early training in conformity to the norms of the dominant, heterosexual peer group prepared me for a later entry into the informal, patriarchal network of men's organizations, like the pub and the football terrace.

In my later teens, drinking talk, like sexual-bravado talk, was an important way of proving that I was 'one of the lads'. In fact talking about drink, before and after the event, in a supposedly tough, sophisticated manner was often more significant that the actual drinking itself. [25]

Again the irony was that the more the illicit drinking went on as a form of cultural resistance against middle-class school authority the more we made ourselves susceptible to the routines and practices of patriarchal power. From the moment of dangerous pleasure when we smuggled in bottles of brown ale to drink after lights out when I was about 16 the central question about drink was: could we prove that we were 'real men' by taking our drink?

Drinking always presented a test of my virility and masculine identity; could I drink deeply without puking up? Could I prove that I was 'one of the lads' by holding my drink? But I soon proved that I couldn't. For a short time at university I got the nickname of 'Puker Jackson'. It happened like this.

It was student rag week in 1959, and in the all-men's hall where I spent my first year all the talk was of the yearly 'giant piss-up' on Saturday night. It was designed to be a pub crawl of as many city-centre pubs as we could take in during the evening. I drifted into this contest, anxious for group approval and acceptance, but not really taking in the implications of this pub crawl.

By then I knew about my tendency to be sick through drinking more than four pints but I didn't want to be left out of that hearty, shoulder-thumping, joking atmosphere of the male peer group. I even took precautions by drinking half a pint of milk before we set off, to line my stomach. But, in the end, it didn't do much good.

We started off quite cautiously by sipping half pints of mild in the first two or three pubs but then I got caught up in the climate of cheery adolescent abandonment. I started to feel queasy after the next two or three pints, and then I lost count of the mixture of shorts (vodka, rum, whisky) and half pints we got down between us. In the end the night became a swirling blur of constant laughter, piss-taking and violent vomiting.

I puked up first out on the street, and then I spent the whole night crouching over a metal bucket in the student common room, groaning and puking. And there I stayed for the whole of Sunday stretched out on a brown horsehair sofa with a blanket flung over me, and promising myself, 'Never! I'll never do this again!'

I gained the male club's attention through my feats of puking. There was a tinge of contempt for my not being able to hold my drink in their label 'Puker', but, temporarily, I grabbed the limelight through the repeated stories about my night of puking and was granted temporary club membership.

As well as male bonding processes exploiting men's ambivalent identities, male places like the pub are patriarchal institutions in the way they generate social and cultural relations that 'exclude, fragment and abuse the female sex'.[26]

One example from my life history illustrates the point I want to make. Sometimes on Friday evenings between 1968 and 1972, when I was working in a Lancashire comprehensive school in Whitworth, outside Rochdale, I used to stay on at school to play five-a-side football and other sporting activities. Usually, afterwards, a geography teacher called Harry used to suggest a drink and then would drive me to Rochdale station.

I was dimly aware that I ought to have refused and got home to help my ex-wife feed and get to bed our three kids. But the cosy fug of the pub was too much of a lure for me. It was a place where I could escape from my family responsibilities and assert an illusion of independence in a male club atmosphere (all the early evening drinkers were always men). And I knew what I was avoiding by sitting there for another hour – that exhausting, hectic time between six and seven in the evening when the kids had to be sorted out, read to and put into their pyjamas. It was never as explicitly worked out as this, but a general sense of fatigue, cosiness and beer kept me rooted to the seat.

The pub's atmosphere, and its joking culture of misogyny, was not only built on the exclusion of women, but on their segregated position in the traditional, sexual division of labour. My leisure time in the pub was bought at the cost of my ex-wife's domestic labour, preparing meals and nurturing my kids back at home. And whereas my official labour as a teacher was paid, my ex-wife's domestic work went unnoticed and unpaid. The pub presented me with a bolt-hole, an exclusively privileged territory, a retreat from the world of domestic responsibilities.

Viewed from the perspective of the late 1980s I regret very much how I benefited from such a taken-for-granted, patriarchal network of men's organizations and male bonding interactions. But I also regret how that barbaric system was able to regulate men like me into putting fear of our exclusion from the male club before our personal commitments to other people.

Notes

1 J. Stoltenberg (1977) 'Toward Gender Justice', in J. Snodgrass (ed.) *For Men Against Sexism*, New York, Times Change Press.
2 J. Arcana (1983) *Every Mother's Son*, London, Women's Press.
3 A bantering term of abuse that was used by the gang to put me down.
4 See N. Chodorow (1978) *The Reproduction of Mothering*, Berkeley, Calif., University of California Press.
5 J. Dollimore (1986) 'Homophobia and sexual difference', *Oxford Literary Review*, vol. 8, nos. 1–2. Much of the argument here is indebted to Dollimore's essay.
6 See J. Coates (1986) *Women, Men and Language*, London, Longman, and her use of social network theory which is to be found in L. Milroy (1980) *Language and Social Networks*, Oxford, Basil Blackwell.
7 See P. Willis (1977) *Learning to Labour*, London, Saxon House.
8 D. Collinson (1988) 'Engineering humour! Masculinity, joking and conflict in shopfloor relations', *Organisation Studies*, vol. 9, no. 2.
9 See P. Lyman (1987) 'The fraternal bond as a joking relationship' in M. Kimmel (ed.) *Changing Men*, London, Sage.
10 Willis, op. cit.
11 See Lyman, op. cit.
12 Coates, op. cit.
13 A. Easthope (1986) *What a Man's Gotta Do*, London, Paladin.
14 See B. Rogers (1988) *Men Only*, London, Pandora.
15 Auxiliary Fire Service set up as Second World War firefighting organization..
16 See E. Dunning (1986) 'Sports as a male preserve', *Theory, Culture and Society*, vol. 3, no. 1.
17 See E. Reynaud (1983) *Holy Virility* London Pluto: 'to be a man you must sport the insignia of power on your arms, legs, armpits and pubis as early as possible. Beach, swimming pool and shower can

thus become such a nightmare for the adolescent whose virginal skin is still hairless that he often helps nature along in the privacy of the bathroom'.

18 See D. Morgan (1987) *It Will Make a Man of You: Notes on National Service, Masculinity and Autobiography*, Manchester Sociology Department, University of Manchester. For a similar bromide in the tea folk story.
19 On the significance of rugby songs see Dunning, op. cit.
20 Compare Morgan, op. cit.
21 See V. Hey (1986) *Patriarchy and Pub Culture*, London, Tavistock.
22 ibid.
23 J. Springhall (1987) 'Building character in the British boy: the attempt to extend Christian manliness to working-class adolescents, 1880–1914, in J. Mangan and J. Walvin (eds) *Manliness and Morality*, Manchester, Manchester University Press.
24 A. Warren (1987) 'Popular manliness: Baden-Power, scouting, and the development of manly character', in J. Mangan and J. Walvin (eds) *Manliness and Morality*, Manchester, Manchester University Press.
25 In R. S. Baden-Powell (1963) *Scouting for Boys*, London, Pearson.
26 I'm deeply indebted to Mona KcKenzie for detailed information about the Wolf-Cub movement.

CHAPTER 9

Everyday violence and life in an all-boys' secondary school

Patriarchal power, of men *over* women, of dominant, heterosexual men *over* vulnerable men, is often sustained by violence, and a related culture of aggressive competitiveness, as I experienced from 1951 to 1959 while attending King Edward VI Grammar School for Boys, Totnes, Devon. In this chapter, because of the limiting circumstances of an all-boys' school, I want to concentrate on the violence that boys and men do to each other.

First, let's clear up some popular misunderstandings about male violence. Violence isn't a 'natural' expression of men's innate, warrior/hunter instincts. Instead, violent practices are a part of the social processes that produce masculinity within a male-dominated society.[1] And a very significant part of these processes is the regularly repeated, institutional violence met with in places like my secondary school.

Through this chapter I want to investigate how violence, in all its many forms, became an accepted, almost invisible, part of my secondary-school life.[2] Some of the most important of these threads were:

(a) Violence was a central part of the processes of masculine identification ('the male cult of toughness'),[3] defining itself in fierce opposition to women and homosexuals.

(b) Daily beatings, fights, psychological violence etc. in secondary-school life were institutionally naturalized and taken for granted as part of normal life.

(c) Ideologies of masculinity buttressed aggressive ways of relating to other boys and 'put a premium on toughness and force'.[4]

[188]

Of course none of this happened as straightforward brainwashing. There was much more resilience in the way that I, as an inadequate fighter, parodied and deflected the culture of brutalized toughness. But more about that in a minute.

Links between society and my grammar-school education (1951–9)

In difficult times it is tempting to avert the gaze from problems whose remedy will require a profound reorganisation of social and economic life and to fasten one's eyes, instead, on the promise that the continuity of things as they are can be somehow enforced by the imposition of social order and discipline 'from above'.

(Stuart Hall)[5]

The early 1950s, with the election of a Tory government and an ideological retreat to traditional certainties, was a time of enormous tension between the social upheavals/reconstructions which had developed since the Second World War *and* a pressure from above to conceal those changes and divisions in an appearance of stable order and social harmony. (Indeed, later on in the 1950s, the myths of affluence, 'You've never had it so good!' can be usefully seen as an attempt to disguise those social rifts).

Some of the most threatening dislocations facing the new Tory government in 1951 were the decline of imperial greatness with its racist assumptions of superiority about English culture, language and everyday life. This resulted in a defensive, backward looking clinging on to a narrowly exclusive national identity. Another was the new, egalitarian spirit (often more a rhetorical gesture than a concrete reality) to be found in the wartime and immediately postwar social policies and legislation (Beveridge, Butler, etc.) that unsettled established patterns of class privilege and inequality. Finally there was the emergence of a rebellious youth culture, with its own music (Bill Haley and the Comets, Elvis Presley), clothes (Teddy Boy culture), hairstyles, etc. that threatened adult authority and social discipline.

With this background of unsettling forces threatening to disrupt their old way of life the headmaster and many of the teachers of

[189]

the grammar school that I attended chose to avert their gaze from the problems that would have involved them in the difficulties of reorganization and gained reassurance from the promise that the continuity of things as they are could somehow be enforced by the imposition of social order and discipline 'from above'.

With the decline of deference for adult authority at home (and performers like James Dean and Elvis Presley were key figures in this new symbolism of dissent) and a great flow of working-class children expected to come to the grammar schools after the Butler Education Act, grammar schools like mine intensified their grip on a policy of authoritarian certainty. (The great flow never materialized but according to Michael Sanderson[6] there was a relative increase.)

Instead of struggling for redesigned curricula for the new social intake to increase motivation and purpose in unfamiliar students, the headmaster clung to established standards and a middle-class cultural authority and imposed this on his new students through a mixture of force and competitiveness.

The widening gap between the academic curriculum and the increasing diversity of the cultural and social worlds of the students bred restless discontent amongst the students and was only kept down by firm discipline and an enforced respect for adults.

This resulted in my everyday school life from 1951 to 1959 being governed by an elaborate repertoire of official and unofficial punishment, discipline routines and constraints; canings, cuffs around the ear, masters' detentions, extra school for inadequate homework, order marks for bad behaviour in class (two order marks lost you your 'free' Wednesday afternoon) and prefects' detentions; each half-term's work was measured by a listed form order where each subject was assessed and two NSs ('Not Satisfactory') would lose you the Saturday morning of your half-term holiday. As a result of this you were given a position within the form (like 26th out of 30) and that position directed the choice of where you sat within the form room for the next term.

It's also important to notice that in the imposition of social discipline and control from above, class and gender relations came together. The male cult of toughness (shown both by teachers and students) within a patriarchal institution like my grammar school also joined together with an aggressive competitiveness within a pyramidal, class-based organization that was structured around the interests of a privileged few (through streaming, examining, the privileging of a middle-class cultural background etc.). So masculine assertiveness was socially condoned within the hierarchical logic of getting ahead, scrambling for marks, and for positions in half-termly form orders.

Forms of institutional violence

We are not just talking of physical violence (corporal punishment) in my experience of school but other, subtler forms of coercion and violence,[7] like emotional and psychological violence and verbal violence. So here I'd like to show you something of the range and variety of the violent practices that went on everyday for eight years of schooling, and how they affected me personally.

The habitual climate of violence and fear that I lived in at that time is best shown by an incident in French when I was 11. The classroom was made up of ordered rows of desks on iron runners facing the front and the blackboard. The French teacher was a young teacher from Lancashire, insecure about his rawness, accent and his class origins. (I can always remember myself and others taking the mickey out of his unfamiliar pronounciation of vowels, behind his back. '*Leuk* at this *beuk!*' we used to parody). It was probably that insecurity that made him so vehement in his putting down of any cheek or dissent. In a way he was trapped by the authoritarian norms of the school of keeping order in the classroom. He wanted to be seen by us as a 'proper' teacher and the only way he saw of doing that was being as hard as the other teachers.

One day, in the first weeks of a strange new school, while I was sitting in the back row of the classroom, I got into terrible trouble for doing nothing at all. I started to whisper something behind a cupped hand about what we were supposed to be doing to the person who was sharing the desk with me. An uneasy silence suddenly fell on me. When I started to look up I found that the French teacher had suddenly broken off from the lesson, had picked up the wooden board-duster and had hurled it, with the whole of his force, straight at my head.

Luckily it just missed me. The board-duster smacked into the wall just above my head, leaving me trembly at the knees. No

[191]

explanation, no preliminary warning, but just a berserk shriek and *Wham*! I looked behind me to find a chalk dust imprint on the green wall behind my head. And then the teacher exploded into a torrent of abuse about me talking in class and interrupting his lesson. Looking back on it now from my present position I think one of the reasons why I felt so dazed and bewildered about what happened was the disproportionate relationship between my actions and the teacher's response. It was as if he was using me as a warning to every other boy in the class not to cross him.

In any event, this French teacher succeeded in physically intimidating me. It left me a sullen mute in that subject. From then on all my innocent curiosity about the subject was gone. I used my energy up in making myself inconspicuous, lying low, hiding behind the sheltering back of another pupil, scared out of my mind that the teacher would ask me a direct question or hurl something else at me. Right up to the 'O' level forms I was afraid to open my mouth in that subject again, to ask a question, ask for help, admit a blockage, or even enter into the forced, conversational exchanges of that subject.

The French teacher obviously forgot the incident and misinterpreted my fear as a lack of ability, and decided not to enter me for 'O' level French at 16-plus. It was only when I started to find my voice again in the sixth form, when relationships between teachers and students became much more informal and personalized, that I gathered my courage to challenge him about this put-down. He didn't seem to know what I was talking about but gave in to my pressure and entered me for the exam at 17-plus. I passed the formal exam easily enough but hadn't generated enough confidence over the six years to utter a meaningful word of French in the outside world.

As I became used to the daily, weekly pattern of institutional violences, the acts of aggression from both teachers and boys lost their shocking novelty and became part of a taken-for-granted, normal way of life. The daily beatings, the clips and slaps around the head, the slow lifting and tugging of a single hair from a boy's head – all these increased as students' resistances increased. There was a tense, hostile, 'them-and-us' atmosphere among the boys, grumbling and moaning secretly and getting their own back in small ways, like wearing lime green socks to school, cultivating a rebellious hairstyle (long hair, 'combed into a "D-A" with a boston neck-line, sideburns and a quiff'),[8] or wearing thick-creped suede shoes, narrow, drainpipe trousers or a school tie that was tied with a Windsor knot, or pulled narrow and thin to imitate a bootlace tie.

Doing particular subjects, like geography, were so bound up with brutal coercion that I almost became emotionally numb to the physical beatings that happened every lesson. Fear of intimidation, fear of being shown up in front of everybody else, saving your own skin, got in the way of learning or understanding the subject. And what was left were the obsessive, militaristic rituals of maintaining a disciplined order and obedience in the classroom.

The geography teacher, particularly, regulated what went on in his domain with a Montgomery-like[9] efficiency and fussy precision. He was always lecturing us about the rules for lining up and waiting, in total silence, outside his geography room. You were supposed to wait in meek submission (of course we always failed to do this) in a neat queue for the previous class to file out. But there was never enough space along those crowded, cramped corridors. Elbows were stuck out, one boy flicked another one who was passing, jokes were muttered, 'Gandhi'[10] (the geography teacher) was sent up. Then there would be hell to pay with Gandhi reading the riot act for almost half the lesson, and the offenders wheedled out and brutally beaten on Gandhi's dais in front of the blackboard. That's where the real lesson went on, underneath the coloured, distorted maps that showed the British Empire in pink, and in direct conflict to the official geography lesson.

At the end of his lesson you had to stand in rows, again in silence, and wait for each row to be dismissed. No running or talking were ever permitted through all this parade ground ceremony, so when you did get out into the jostling corridor again, you always wanted to shout at the top of your voice, or kick somebody, just to let off steam.

Inside the geography classroom 'Gandhi' officiated over a reign of terror. He orchestrated a deep hush of fearful deference through the black and silver conductor's baton that he regularly used for pummelling arses and prodding inattentive boys. Any pretence of learning through inquiry, questioning, analysis was given up in the pressure towards conformity, and keeping in Gandhi's good books.

Another significant aspect of physical violence was the way the beatings were responded to, and this was closely tied in to masculine identity. 'Did he take it like a *real* man?' or 'Did he snivel like a sissy' was the unheard question that every boy asked themselves inside their heads in their race towards virility and peer-group acceptance.

A clear example of this comes from one of the beatings that went on repeatedly in the boarding house attached to the grammar school. Gandhi, the geography teacher, was also in charge of the house and he tried to maintain the same reign of terror that he organized in his geography classroom, although slightly modified by the presence of his wife and two gentle sons.

As the boys became more truculent and rebellious in their opposition to his disciplined regime, as the decade wore on, Gandhi, fearing massive disruption of his regime, struck out even more savagely. He tightened up the rules for boarders going about the town independently. In the morning we had to queue up outside his study to get an 'Exeat' that gave us formal permission to move about the town to the barber's, the chemist, the newsagent.

As Judith Okely comments about boarding education for girls, boarders in my experience were severely regulated almost every minute of the day through 'limitations on the [students'] movement in space and time, and on their sounds and speech'.[11] So in the morning we had to have bed inspection, and then parcelling up our laundry on Thursday morning. We then walked to school in a formal 'crocodile' overlooked by boarding prefects. After we got back from school we had tea, then supervised 'prep'. On Sundays we had organized letter-writing time, a compulsory visit to church, a supervised walk in the afternoon. So it went on, day after day.

The time that Gandhi couldn't control very easily was after lights out in the dormitory, when over the years boys escaped for night walks, meetings with girls, jaunts, adventures, breathers away from constant restriction and supervision. It was an important time for boys to remind themselves of what time away from Gandhi's stifling control was like.

However, Gandhi caught two boys coming back from a night jaunt, and that provoked a general clampdown of liberties and free movement. One of Gandhi's pet hates was talking after lights out. It wasn't just the trivial event but the flaunting of his authority that he couldn't stand. So the night he caught four of us yarning on after lights out stays with me.

I think I can remember Gandhi's sudden step outside the dormitory door, the light snapped on and the detailed inquisition of who was talking. After some threats the four of us owned up and he immediately flew into a temper, launched into a long harangue of us, and had us down outside his study to cane us, one by one.

I've forgotten the exact words that Gandhi used but what I remember was the pressure to be seen to take the punishment like a man. As I waited outside his study in pyjamas I was trembling with fear inside but knew that I had to hide my emotions, at all costs. Instead what I had to do was to appear jokey, grinning and unconcerned in front of the others.

I was the last to go in. Each time the door closed the vicious sound of the cane jolted right through me. He didn't stop at four. There were six whacks. Each time the door reopened I asked the red-eyed face what it was like. Two of them couldn't reply. They were near to blubbering themselves. The other one gritted out something like, 'Oh. . . it's not too bad', while he hugged himself to keep himself together.

Gandhi was using the same black and silver conductor's baton that he used at school. He asked me to bend over in my pyjamas. And then the blows came, cutting into my bottom with a force that took my breath away. I don't know how I stayed there taking this assault. But I just managed to control myself till the sixth stroke fell. Then I stood up, quickly (I wasn't going to let him see my face) with my whole body howling out with pain, and went straight to the toilets where I let the tears come, with nobody around.

They were tears of intense distress mixed with real anger at the absurd injustice of the lack of proportion in the punishment. My whole body felt queasily sick after the violent shock of the beating. When the sting started to cool down a little, I washed my face and checked in the mirror to see if the others could see that I had been crying.

When I re-entered the dormitory a few minutes later, all the other boys wanted to know what it was like. I just shrugged and muttered something incoherent. In my fantasies I wish I had said something brave and defiant like, 'Gandhi's a vicious, little bastard, and one day I'm going to break his cane in two and shove both pieces up his arse!' but I didn't. With my body still on fire, it was almost more than I could do to drag myself into bed. I put on my dressing gown, and curled myself up into a foetal hug in bed. And it was in that position that I stayed till morning.

A few days later the four of us were looked up to as 'Hard Cases' in dormitory gossip. In the evening just before lights out groups of admirers used to gather in the toilets to view the purple welts on our bums as tangible evidence of what we'd been through.

I dropped my pyjamas and proudly displayed those angrily scowling bruises[12] as a badge of masculine honour, almost like a rite of passage from boyhood to manhood. But by then I had conveniently repressed the memory of the wrenching hurt and my tears wetting my cheeks in the wash basins.

Although the atmosphere of classroom life was poisoned by the fearful anticipation of frequent physical violence, its customary mood was more subtle and less dramatic. The peculiar tone of a rigidly authoritarian, all-boys' grammar school in the 1950s was one of mock ridicule, of teachers habitually using emotional or psychological violence to show up the weak, inadequate, defiant or deviant through a heavy-handed sarcasm. Indeed I suspect that many students feared being held up to ridicule in front of the whole class much more than a straight physical beating.

For example, our history teacher, a very dedicated and talented man in other respects who could make his subject come alive through dramatic improvisation in the classroom, used to carry around with him a very frayed carpet slipper, regularly stuffed into one pocket of his tweed jacket. What stands out in my memories isn't his very infrequent use of the slipper, but his tone of mock-humorous intimacy used to refer to his 'flapper' (called that because it used to 'flap' boys' bottoms). A homo-erotic suggestiveness and threat was constantly linked to the supposedly playful rituals used to keep the class in order, like: 'Now 2A you're getting a bit rowdy again! Hands up all those boys who would like a little taste of Flapper this morning? Well?' and 'Jackson – you're really asking to get acquainted with Flapper, aren't you? If you keep twanging that ruler under that desk lid, you and Flapper will end up as really close friends!'

The violence here, though wearing a supposedly humorous, playful exterior, was full of a twisted, sexual innuendo, useful in throwing the spotlight on a few boys who were taunted and ridiculed unmercifully in front of the class:

'Jones? How many children has your mother got?'
'Three, Sir.'
'She will only have two by four o'clock.'

The boys who were picked out from the others for this kind of psychological violence often had in common a number of broadly related class characteristics, as Colin Lacey has pointed out.[13] The incident from his field notes concerning a boy called Thornton is so striking that it deserves to be quoted in full:

> The following examples are highly selective. They are incidents which highlight the point I wish to demonstrate: that teacher behaviour, conditioned by the reputation of the pupil, is one of the central factors producing differentiation. The first concerns a boy, Thornton, whose behaviour was neither difficult nor unruly but was handicapped by a number of class characteristics. He had a broad accent, his manner when addressing teachers was negative and a little surly. He mumbled. His poor reputation, however, was based mainly on his poor work and unreliability: he rarely did his homework.
>
> Mr Bradley was demonstrating the substitution of minus numbers into equations to a bottom stream. A number of boys had failed to grasp the idea, and as he questioned round the class, getting more and more wrong answers, he became more and more irritable. Eventually, he arrived at Thornton, who was quite unable to give the correct answer. The master persevered, but the boy slipped further and further into the mire. The class groaned at his mistakes, some flung up their hands in order to answer correctly. Thornton went pale as the master, despairing of ever getting the point across, let fly. 'We've been at this now for six weeks, Thornton! My God, you're driving me up the wall. I could have taught a fox terrier more than this in six weeks. You know, Thornton, you're the stupidest boy I've ever met. Lord knows how you ever got into this school!'
>
> Bradley calmed himself, and then followed a further attempt at explanation, step by step, with thinly veiled irritation. At each stage he asked the boy the answer and, at last, Thornton made another mistake. The master burst out, 'Now look

[197]

here, Thornton, I've had enough of this. If you give me another wrong answer, I'll thrash you. I'll murder you. If you can't. . .' Thornton gave the correct answer and with obvious relief the class subsided.

The tension this incident generated was such that the boy had obviously stopped thinking about the task long before the final stages. He was so worked up that he was incapable of concentrating. In three consecutive lessons this master erupted in a similarly violent way at four boys. Their positions in class at the last examinations were twenty-fourth, twenty-sixth, twenty-seventh and thirtieth. On each occasion he could have chosen several others, but he lighted on these because they were particularly appropriate for this sort of treatment (i.e. they had the appropriate reputation).

Imagine yourself on the receiving end of such emotional and verbal bullying. Remember your own anxiety and fear, as under a nagging pressure from an authority figure, your mind has gone blank and your whole body is seized by panic. Many boys, including myself, were caught squirming like Thornton in this example as the full glare of classroom attention and the full beam of the teacher's perverted wit are used to strip away any positive self-esteem their students possessed. Surely a clear example of mental cruelty!

Also notice the verbal violence used to intimidate Thornton. Masquerading as humour, mutilating phrases like, 'I could have taught a fox terrier more than this in six weeks', and 'Thornton, you're the stupidest boy I've ever met', 'I'll thrash you. I'll murder you' are used with barbed effect.

Similarly, I remember a maths teacher flattening any self-respect I might have had in his subject through the laboriously facetious ridicule of his comments on my work. Handing my maths exercise book back to me after a homework gave him wonderful opportunity to humiliate me in public: 'Jackson – out of the deep generosity of my heart I'm going to give you one out of twenty for trying – *very trying!*'

This was said in a very loud, world-weary voice that brought ripples of contemptuous titters from the rest of the class. The '*very trying!*' ending was uttered with great relish as he played to the classroom gallery, his voice positively dripping with ironic delight at his own punning. And I was left, like a wounded insect wriggling on my back, unable to look anybody straight in the eye.

Some cultural clashes between the world of the school and the world of the students

As I've indicated already the students weren't beaten into a state of passive submission to the school's cultural norms (middle-class/patriarchal authority). Instead there was a much more contradictory series of cultural struggles involving teachers as well as students. For example there was the biology teacher who refused to wear a gown while teaching, and who refused to join in the physical violence. And there was the young teacher who opposed the habitual brutality of the boarding house and was eventually chucked out.

In saying this I want to guard against an over-determined, monolithic view of a clash between a dominating culture and a subordinated culture. The living dynamic that I experienced was much more complex with inconsistencies, challenges and contradictions on *both* sides.[14] There were teachers like the ones above who never laid a finger on us who were also struggling, in their own ways, against the authoritarian climate they found themselves in, as well as students who refused to give consent to the dominating framework through their own languages of subcultural resistance. But here, for obvious reasons, I want to focus on the students' dissent.

Dick Hebdige[15] defines subculture as a way of challenging the dominant culture. In doing this he uses Gramsci's theory of hegemony.[16] This is that the ruling class cannot keep its dominating position simply through the use of physical force but must gain the consent of the subordinated classes through various political, ideological and cultural forms of leadership.

In this process of winning spontaneous consent from an oppressed group there is always the concept of counter-hegemony or resistance to established power and authority. And counter-hegemony today is usually found in the forms of opposition a rebellious youth culture produces in its struggles against a dominating culture.

Hebdige goes on to say: 'However, the challenge to hegemony which subcultures represent is not issued directly by them. Rather

[199]

it is expressed obliquely, in style. The objections are lodged, the contradictions displayed. . .at the profoundly superficial level of appearances.'

So in my grammar-school experiences the main challenges to a middle-class/patriarchal authority were similarly through the way we dressed, our physical appearance, the music we listened to and our verbal wit (dealt with in Chapters 7 and 8).

The use of the school cap offers a clear example of how these student challenges to authority worked. Whenever we went outside the school gates into the street, school caps had to be worn. On one level they symbolically represented our tacit conformity to school authority and acceptance of the hierarchical ordering of that authority (in the displaying of prefects' badges on the front of the cap).

From the school's point of view the caps also gave an opportunity to stress the hierarchical power relations between the teachers and the taught, and students' overt deference to that authority. When a student passed a teacher in the street the boy should, as a mark of respect, touch the peak of his cap. I suppose it was a compromised form of doffing the cap, of raising the cap right off the head as the teacher passed, passed down from nineteenth-century public-school behaviour.

Some younger teachers were embarrassed or amused by it but teachers like Gandhi were always ranting on about boys being seen out in the street without their caps, or the insolence of boys not touching their caps as teachers passed. The important point was that most working-class students tried implicitly to ridicule the obligation of wearing the cap. The most frequent way was through perching the cap right at the back of the head with bustling hair sprouting out at the front so that the whole appearance was sent up as absurd. Indeed prefects and teachers were waging a losing battle about wearing caps and lectures about tucking the carefully groomed hairstyle under the cap went in one ear and out of the other.

Other boys deliberately bent the cardboard peak of the cap into a stylish curve at the front. Others deliberately 'lost' their caps for weeks on end. And always, at the end of the school year, there was the ritual throwing away of other boys' school caps, often through the bus window as the school made its way back to Paignton, again a symbolic gesture of 'Go and get lost! You can't alter my way of life!' to the school authority.

Hairstyles were also an important part of getting our own back. My own hair went through a period of being so wild and bushy (in the third and fourth forms) that all its curly straggles could nev·r be contained under a school cap, until Gandhi insisted that I get it cut. Then I went up to Mendham's, the barbers, and deliberately had my hair shaved off into a defiant crew cut, all stiff and hedgehog bristly. My mates went round calling me 'Convict' for several weeks afterwards. Gandhi glowered at me but couldn't say anything.

The invention of the social category of teenager in the 1950s was mainly announced through music. We were allowed to play music in the student common room at the boarding house (except on Sundays). So our defiance against the petty stupidity of house discipline, rules and regulations was expressed through turning Elvis Presley's 'Hound Dog' or 'Blue Suede Shoes' up to full volume. The raw, sexual energy of the new music (Elvis Presley, Little Richard, Tommy Steele, Bill Haley and the Comets) seemed to promise a future time of freedom of movement and a stunning explosion of our own bottled-up desires.

The only problem with this oppositional youth culture was that in defying middle-class cultural norms it also strengthened the 'Hard Case' culture of the lads against authority (and also perpetuated brutal relations between the bullying gang and group leaders and other, more vulnerable boys).[17]

I was caught in the middle of these contradictions: in one way tugged towards joining in the lads' piss-taking and challenging of the middle-class authority of school, but in another way shocked by the brutality of the lads and afraid of their jeering, joking and bantering.

In the end I suppose I settled for survival (of accepting and joining in many male bonding activities) but also allowed myself, very occasionally, a gentle parody of macho culture. One brief example comes to mind.

Knowing very early on that I couldn't and didn't want to be a respected part of a fighting culture (a primary-school hammering by a boy called Bill Warburton convinced me of that) I drifted into a mock fighting exchange at grammar school that seemed to parody the 'tough guy' pretensions of a macho culture. Particularly between the ages of 11 and 13 I used to go up to large, beefy lads and pretend to challenge them to a fight.

[201]

I knew they wouldn't want to be seen taking me on (an insignificant shrimp) in public because of the humiliating abuse they would have got from their mates. So I often went up to them at break and suddenly ruffled their hair, or aimed mock blows at their stomach. I got the reputation of being a 'cheeky chappie' that improved my status in my own circles. I also quietly sent up the rituals of a belligerent culture, and gained several important protectors in the senior forms who sometimes came to my rescue when I was about to be bullied. (Despite their protection, and my sporting skills, I was bullied in the early years at grammar school and the memory of that misery and fear stays with me still. For a fuller treatment of bullying see the two dormitory scenes in Chapter 8).

Student/student violence

In that climate of daily acts of aggression, an ideology of masculinity flowered. This ideology operated through the 'commonsense' assumptions which boys held about what qualities go into the making of 'real' manliness – the qualities of force, strength, hardness, toughness and a cool indifference of style. And these qualities were defined, as usual, in strict opposition to the supposed vulnerability, passivity and incompetence of women and homosexuals.

So some boys, in their daily contacts with each other, although often engaged in the contradictory struggles outlined above, strained for a physical superiority and mastery over others to achieve the status-laden badges of masculinity. They were also often influenced by the brutalized culture of violence and aggressive competitiveness they found themselves in, and took their cues from what they saw around them, in the most coercive teachers' behaviour.

Acting hard and talking tough were the main ways boys proved their masculinity in school, largely at the expense of the marginal students who couldn't or didn't want to confirm their identity in that way. The line of conventional masculinity led straight from the brutalizing behaviour of certain teachers like Gandhi to the swaggering, bullying behaviour of the 'cocks of the class'.

Sometimes this aggressive behaviour led to school fights down the lane at break time. Shouts would go up, 'Fight! Fight! Fight!'. A crowd of boys would immediately block the lane (a narrow pathway leading down to the toilets) but there would usually be a last-minute fizzling out as teachers or prefects stopped the fight before anything really serious could develop. Although I do remember one grudge fight between a sixth former and a fifth-year lad called Collins that developed into a real warrior clash with bloodied noses and grazed knuckles.

But, generally, the violence that went on between students was a niggling, less dramatic kind of bullying aggression that had become normalized as a routine part of classroom life. (Of course there was also an emotional and psychological violence as well as a verbal violence, but see Chapters 7 and 8 for a description of that).

As an example of this, I can remember an egghead friend of mine called Mike, who wore very thick-lensed glasses, always being picked on as an everyday part of school life. His cleverness and keenness, or middle-class conformity (his mother was a teacher), grated on the nerves of the 'cocks' in the class. Mike was just a little too well turned out for his own good. He always had the compasses, set square, rubber and crayons that the 'cock' had come without. Or he was always being treated by the teachers as a privileged 'insider', always being handed notes from teachers to pass on to his teacher mother. So the 'cocks' raided his store of school equipment, 'borrowing' his rubber, appropriating his compasses, relying upon him for a spare pen and not giving it back.

Tubby Sloman wasn't one of the accepted 'cocks of the class' (he was too podgy and cowardly for that) but one of the sniggering hangers-on who circulated within the protected orbit of one of the most brutal 'cocks', picking up crumbs from his table, flattering him and doing his errands when needed. Tubby used to sit next to Mike and sponge off him, pretending to be his friend when there was something in it for him, but, occasionally, betraying Mike's intimate secrets to the 'cock' when he needed to gain the 'cock's' favour.

I think I can remember the moment when Mike brought a Christmas present of a brand-new geometry set to school. It was full of equipment like protractors and set squares, and all in plastic. Tubby Sloman immediately sucked up to Mike so that he could borrow the foot-long plastic ruler that he needed to carry out the measurements in his own work.

When Tubby had used it Mike asked for it back but Tubby, wanting to tease a bit, hung on to it, repeatedly twanging it along the ridges of the radiator. A mock struggle broke out with Tubby fending off Mike's attempts to snatch the ruler back. The 'cock' and his other cronies egged on Tubby while jeering at Mike.

Suddenly seeing red, Mike lunged out to try and grab his ruler back. But, in trying to retain his grip on the ruler, Tubby leant his full weight back down on it as it was still stuck under the desk lid. You could hear the brittle crack all over the classroom as the ruler snapped in two. I don't think Tubby did it on purpose. It was a semi-accident, but it was the kind of everyday intimidation and use of physical force that was going on unnoticed in most classrooms, right under the teachers' noses, for all of the eight years that I went to that school.

What this school culture of everyday violence meant to me

I was one of those marginal boys who just about survived the eight years of having to live on the fringes of a climate of fear, intimidation and violence from both teachers and some 'Hard Case' bully boys.

I didn't just passively accept the warping values of a schoolboy culture with its stress on toughness, pugnacity and aggressive competitiveness. As an 'effeminate' boy, I knew my own devious ways of getting round those aggressive models of masculinity, and even, sometimes, sending them up, but nevertheless those brutalizing values left their mark on me. Perhaps not in the way you would expect, but they certainly scarred me for life.

I learned to survive in that hostile climate by hiding my emotional life and playing up those aspects of my character that might gain me credibility in the suspicious eyes of the bully boys so that they would keep their fists off me. As a result, I strained for approval and acceptance from them by emphasizing the robust, energetically active, competitive parts of myself at the expense of other suppressed areas (I knew I could never gain acceptance through toughness or my fighting ability so I had to make the most of what I had).

In this way the 'Hard Case' bully-boy culture not only physically intimidated but pressurized me into being partly positioned by the dominant framework of masculine identification that it

[204]

represented. The harshly authoritarian classroom discipline, and the often vicious relations between teachers and pupils (both physically and psychologically) also contributed to me toeing the line defined by the dominant, heterosexual culture. In a way, I was terrorized into giving my public approval to a model of masculinity that effectively stole away my emotional self.

The emotional scars that this left me with are still with me today. I had to murder a large part of myself in order to get through in the daily classroom world and the day and night world of the boarding house. The resulting suppression of my emotions, the bottling up of my grief, and the long dislocation between my reason and emotion, between the public and private areas of myself, has only now started to heal over after a continuing struggle involving therapy and counselling.

Tied in to this coerced emotional suppression was the personal denial of those parts of me that would have made me more supportive and caring within relationships. But because these nurturing/succouring elements were always associated, within the schoolboy culture, with a polarized culture of effeminacy, I also learned to look down on them. What that has left me with is a self-hatred, and a destructive habit of despising the emotional, vulnerable aspects of myself. Only now, 35 years later, have I begun to come to grips with the devastating effects of those eight years of daily beatings, psychological cruelty, bullying, cuffs around the ear on boys like myself.

Given the emotional needs of my early personal history, it is difficult to count the emotional and social costs of that time of having to 'act hard and talk tough'. I was deprived of affection, any kind of tenderness, stroking, hugging, caressing, softness. What I received in its place wasn't the necessary toughening up process needed for character-building, but the vicious pummelling and battering of a savagely disturbed, bully-boy culture. I will never forget the damage it did me and thousands of other vulnerable, marginal boys who grew up in the 1950s.

Notes

1 R. W. Connell (1985) 'A new man', in *The English Curriculum: Gender*, London, ILEA English Centre.

2   The whole of this chapter is indebted to D. Morgan (1987) 'Masculinity and violence', in J. Hanmer and M. Maynard (eds) *Women, Violence and Social Control*, London, Macmillan. On a broader level, it's also important to acknowledge the background of feminist research, analysis, campaigning and practice in challenging men's violence that informs this chapter and David Morgan's own chapter. What I'm referring to is the way those 'naturally' aggressive assumptions of dominant, heterosexual boys and men have been explicitly named, analysed and called into question.

Examples of this context of feminist practice and research are to be found in the other essays in *Women, Violence and Social Control*, and it is clearly summarized in an overview of second-wave feminist theory and practice in Britain in relation to sexual violence in L. Kelly (1989) 'Our issues, our analysis: two decades of work on sexual violence' in C. Jones and P. Mahony (eds) *Learning Our Lines: Sexuality and Social Control in Education*, London, Women's Press.

3   See P. Strange (1983) *It'll Make a Man of You*. . . Peace News/Mushroom Bookshop. Nottingham.

4   R. W. Connell (1987) *Gender and Power*, Cambridge, Polity.

5   S. Hall (1980) *Drifting into a Law and Order Society*, London, Cobden Trust.

6   M. Sanderson (1987) *Educational Opportunity and Social Change in England*, London, Faber & Faber.

7   Morgan, op. cit.

8   See S. Hall and T. Jefferson (1976) *Resistance Through Rituals* (and especially 'Cultural responses of the teds'), London, Hutchinson.

9   Second World War British general especially famous for his part in the desert campaign against Rommel.

10 A racist reference to the geography teacher's slight physical resemblance to the leader of Indian independence from British colonial rule.

11 J. Okely (1987) 'Privileged, schooled and finished: boarding education for girls', in G. Weiner and M. Arnot (eds) *Gender Under Scrutiny*, London, Hutchinson Education/Open University Press.

12 A few years later public awareness of savage physical beatings in boarding schools and other institutions had grown so much that I think I remember public outrage being expressed at a Sunday newspaper photograph of similar 'purple welts' on the buttocks.

13 C. Lacey (1970) *Hightown Grammar*, Manchester, University of Manchester Press.

14 See R. W. Connell (1983) *The Porpoise and the Elephant:* [Birmingham on class, culture and education] in *Which Way is Up?* Sydney, Allen & Unwin (Australia).

15 D. Hebdige (1979) *Subculture: The Meaning of Style*, London, Methuen.

16 See section 4, 'Class, culture, and hegemony', in T. Bennett *et al.* (1981) *Culture, Ideology and Social Process*, London, Batsford.

17 P. Willis (1977) *Learning to Labour*, London Saxon House.

CHAPTER 10

Sporting activities and masculinities

At first sight sport seems an innocent leisure pursuit, a casual letting off of steam at the margins of one's life. But looked at more critically sporting practices represent one of those apparently trivial but significant lifetime sites where masculinity is constructed and confirmed. Through regular, everyday actions, institutional practices, language, images, daydream and night-time fantasies and definitions, masculinity was actively produced in my body and my head. Of course, that process was not without its tensions and conflicts but more about that in a moment.

All through my childhood I hardened my body through everyday sporting practice. Sometimes, while my sisters were doing the washing up, shopping, cleaning, I was developing my footballing skills and my throwing arm. There were intermittent grumbles about being late for mealtimes from my parents but generally it was accepted that I could spend most of my spare time out with my mates kicking balls, bunging things, playing Subbuteo when it was wet whereas my sisters' movements were much more severely constrained and regulated.

Occasionally I used to dribble a balding tennis ball along the pavement all the one and a half miles to school, learning to play wall-passes, selling dummies to lamp-posts, or sending the ball round one way and going the other way with my body.

Then at primary school and later at grammar school I used to join in the rushing mêlée of playground football in boys-only yards, rarely connecting with the ball but hacking, lunging and swiping at it as it whizzed past. In the evenings I used to spend solitary hours kicking a ball against a garage door and learning to trap the rebound, bring the ball down under control and send it back against the door or a neighbouring brick wall.

During the holidays, and particularly the long summer one, whole days were spent playing 'three and in' (so-called because if you scored three goals you automatically became the next goal-keeper), with piled up jumpers and coats as make-do goalposts down on the seafront green. Down there we used to play with an air-filled plastic ball lofting it high up into the goalmouth from the wings and then pelting in very hard after it to leap and shoulder charge the goalie, with the remote chance that we might be able to head the ball in. We learnt delicate touches with the ball as well as brute force. One of these subtleties was to hit the ball with the outside of your foot so that it wouldn't follow the line of the foot but would swerve off at a tangent to the expected direction. Very rarely we accomplished this and foxed the goalie. But not often.

What seemed like innate physical superiority to girls in sporting matters like learning to throw balls becomes critically exposed as the result of very different social practices and power rela-tionships.

From where I am now, I can reconstruct something of that experience of exasperation when playing French cricket with my sisters down on the sands. I inwardly groaned at their puny, underarm attempts to throw the ball back at my shins. They never seemed able to exercise any control over the direction of their throws. They flapped around the ball and lobbed it back erratically, sometimes even back over their heads.

But none of this ought to have surprised me. Whereas my sisters had been trained for domestic labour, childcare, homemaking and servicing other people (including me), with very little opportunity, time, positive context and motivation for the sporting activities I took for granted almost every day of my life, I had learned to throw with concentrated strength and accuracy through hundreds of hours of informal practice.

I developed the muscles in my throwing arm through frequent games of cricket up on the Bumps (the grassy headland sticking out between the beaches near where I lived) and mastering the quick, deadly throw at the stumps (only we used a wastepaper basket or chalk marks on an old air-raid shelter wall).

Looking back now from my very different vantage point I can reconstruct one brief moment of my life, somewhere between the ages of eight and ten, as a time of compulsive stone-throwing. It seems to me now that I had to have a stone in my hand, firing away at road signs, advertising hoardings, even occasionally blackbirds fussing away in a nearby hedge. On the beach it was the same; with my mates I arranged a constant stone-throwing target practice. We searched the beach for adequate targets like old Brasso tins propped up on a pile of stones, then spent a furious quarter of an hour bombarding the target with specially chosen stones, until we got tired of putting the can back on top after a direct hit. At other times we found an empty pop bottle and chucked it out to sea as a floating target. Then we hurled away at it until we broke it up.

Despite the physical exhilaration at that time while being caught up in the furious action, I can now see other implications of what I was doing. What all this target practice added up to was an ever-increasing dissociation between my throwing hand and the results of my actions (the smashed pop bottle). These sporting activities contributed to my accepting a destructive relationship to my own body, to other people and the world around me. It's as if my 'throwing arm' and 'scoring legs' became mechanically detached from the humanizing web of emotional connections and social commitments in the process of striving for sporting success and achievement.

It seems to me, looking back, that I was particularly susceptible to these destructive approaches to my own body because I was unhappy with it. Measuring my body (with my delicate, 'girlish' hands and frail, undersized[1] frame against the ideal male body – 'the "muscle-man" type body characterized by well developed chest and arm muscles tapering down to a narrow waist'[2] – and finding it wanting, made me prepared to try and take on some of the tough facade of the Tarzan/Johnny Weissmuller type of male. Because of my culturally learned view of my body as inadequate, I urgently wanted to see it in a new way – as a potential 'instrument of power' – and to develop a virile physical presence that would help me to hold my own in the street and playground. So I was ready to strive for a swaggering physical presence and put in hours and hours of routine practice to try and achieve such an end.

Trying to develop power in my body and the symbolic 'promise of power'[3] created a set of social relations that not only objectified my rival within the game but also objectified me. I allowed my body to become a thing at the point of 'going for goal' or, in today's terms, 'going for it'[4] in all kinds of sporting and then later in working and sexual activities. What 'going for goal' felt like was an obsessively thrilling single-mindedness in being able to shut out all questions of the other person (and how I was brutalizing myself) in the drive for success and performance. As Michael Messner[5] comments: 'the successful athlete (or sportsperson) must develop a highly goal-orientated personality that encourages him to view his body as a tool, a machine, or even a weapon utilised to defeat an objectified opponent'.

From my present standpoint I can now see that these brutalized and brutalizing social relations become naturalized in the male body through years and years of exercise, practice and habitual relations. The assumption of superior strength, aggressive force and competitiveness in some men seems to be a 'natural' expression of warrior instincts until we attend more closely to the social processes that have embedded[6] this compulsive masculinity within the body itself and our taken-for-granted ways of relating to it, and other people's. But these social processes themselves are not without inner tension and contradiction.

The shaky psychological foundations of many masculinities were very clearly in evidence within my own white, working-class, Western upbringing. From about the age of seven to twelve sporting activities partly acted as masculinizing practices and played a part in developing my 'masculine' identity against a background of great personal insecurity. In my case the usually problematic process of separation and individuation[7] from my mother was made worse by an over-close attachment to her and the prolonged absence of my father. So I was all at sea within my gender identification. My ambivalence about wanting to gain independence from my mother to model myself on my father was shown in the way that, although I partly wanted to be accepted by an actively virile schoolboy culture that stressed the values of physical toughness, aggression, honour and daring at the expense of 'girlish' softness and physical incompetence,[8] another part of me felt extremely uncomfortable within conventional masculine behaviour and that part was able to use sport to express a number of choked, contradictory feelings and qualities like a sense of grace, sensuality, poise, passion and, sometimes, even delicacy.

Living in a society that overvalued physical strength in the ideal male image, I developed my ball-playing skills, probably as some kind of compensation. When I was in goal in the 'Three and in' games it wasn't enough to just keep the ball out of the goal but I had to do it with a self-dramatizing sense of burlesque style and grace (or so I thought at the time). Much influenced by comic heroic fantasies I used to jump, dive, pirouette, more like a ballet dancer than a footballer, partly mocking them, partly believing in them, fanatically. I used to try and tip the ball over the non-existent bar, fling myself sideways, wrap myself around the ball, flap and wave my hands demonstratively. The climax of all this miniature theatre was the diving save, hurling myself full-length to try and bring about a finger-tip save. Football has always been the arena for the releasing of a great deal of frustrated, bottled-up passion for me. The only problem with that is that it's also been a displacement activity as well. It seems easier, even now, to roar and shout with the crowd than to risk awkward emotional honesty with a friend.

In cricket it's not the moments when I tried to hammer the ball out of the ground (there weren't many of those) that still intrigue me, as I turn them over in my memory, but the rare moments of fluent spin-bowling. It was the undulating rhythm of leg-break bowling that gave me a glimpse of what unclenched, unlaboured movement could be like in sport. I can never remember officially learning how to bowl leg-breaks. The skills seemed to grow out of playful experimentation and some sense of close connection with the slow, looping rhythm of the action.

I used to shuffle in from behind the umpire, keeping my body sideways to the batsman, and corkscrew the ball out of the back of my hand with a flick that felt as if it came from the unwinding of my whole body and not from a gripped, competitive will. Usually the ball was over-pitched and clobbered off to the nearest boundary but occasionally I could bowl on a length. Then I sensed the brief satisfaction of being able to deceive the batsman through the floating twist of the ball through the air and not just through speed or crude power.

That's why today I can still re-experience some of that same movement in spin-serves in table tennis or through playing flat-green bowls. It's as if the curve of my body and my hand get into the arc of the bowl's line as it slows down and moves towards the jack. That sensation takes me straight back to my leg-break bowling days. I know all this talk of balls and jacks sounds like yet another example of cultural and sexual goal-getting, but the experience was much more mixed and contradictory than that.

[211]

It was a sense of graceful pleasure inextricably caught up with a much tougher pressure to compete and win at all costs.

These playful yet confusing dimensions of sport were savaged by my entry into the much more harshly competitive world of grammar-school sport in 1951. The historical and geographical specificity is important here. The Butler[9] Education Act of 1944, with its egalitarian rhetoric (and less radical actions) had unsettled old, established grammar schools like the King Edward VI School which I went to in Totnes, South Devon. In a region far removed from any of the institutions and organizations of an industrialized labour movement, and with a tourist industry close at hand and beginning to find its feet after the Second World War, the threat of coping with a greater number of working-class boys (a threat that was always more of a rhetorical gesture than a concrete reality) had intensified the school's grip on the traditional certainties.

In the area of sports this meant clinging on to a watered down but still powerful public-school ethos of manliness. The historical origins of this are to be traced back to the second half of the nineteenth century when the 'English, middle class, Anglican ideal of Christian manliness',[10] associated with Charles Kingsley and Thomas Hughes, was popularized through the cult of games in the public schools. Over the years the moral and spiritual ideals lost some of their potency, leaving behind a contract between masculinity, sport, nationality and imperialism. As a contributor to the '*Boy's Own Paper*' explained in 1892:

> One thing is certain, and may as well be at once admitted, that as long as England wishes to maintain her supremacy and reputation as a great nation, our boys must be trained in those games which develop physical strength, endurance, skill, and courage.[11]

Character-building in schoolboys and the future development of the Empire were generated, so the public-school ethos goes, through competitive sports. Above all team games like rugby and cricket were seen as the most significant shaping forces in building a manly ideal as well as team spirit, corporate loyalty and deference to a tightly rule-governed authority.

In 1951, at a time of social change, crisis and dislocation (and the decline of Britain as a great power becoming an everyday

[212]

reality) my grammar-school headteacher, a minor-public-school man himself, seemed to want to create a reaffirming framework of stability and certainty through the 'invented tradition'[12] of the public-school ethos of manliness, nationalism and honourable character-building. I can certainly remember the hollowly elaborate fuss over the Queen's Coronation, the compulsory Commonwealth essay-writing prize, the yearly civic ritual of the head boy congratulating the new mayor in the ancient guild hall and the speeches at the Old Boys' reunion dinner after the school versus the Old Boys' rugby and cricket matches. But the routines of weekly sporting activities are inescapable because they were so repetitively frequent.

The weekly school programme was organized around the centrality of sport and sports training. So training went on every lunchtime and after school on every weekday, and we had Wednesday afternoons 'off' to make time for school games (under 14s, under 15s, second eleven and first eleven) and house matches (junior and senior elevens). Saturday morning acted as a replacement school time for the lost Wednesday afternoon.

Playful enjoyment of my body was mainly gone, and in its place was the gladiatorial imagery of a military-type[13] discourse. From the ages of 11 to 19 the continual assembly talk of cups, results, trophies, winning, school colours, and the hothouse rivalry between teams, players and houses constructed a symbolic imagery of combat, tactics, battles and conquest, defending the honour of the school against the enemy. The clash and collison of boy against boy, the values of aggressive competitiveness, physical toughness and honour, were applauded and encouraged every day by obsessive housemasters and by the familiar hectoring of the headteacher from the dais. Every house practice after school, every net practice, every crosscountry run, usually in grim weather, was solemnly and religiously approved of. They were precisely executed hardship rituals, as found in military training,[14] which seemed to be about preparing one for a toughened-up, future masculinity.

I was coaxed, cajoled, bullied into joining these warrior's initiation rites, at first with some resistance, especially in those activities that demanded physical endurance, strength and size. But, later, the ball-playing team sports became a forum where I could grab the limelight and compete for approval and applause.

[213]

The narrative incident that seems to sum up that particular moment of my life is the time when I gained my school colours for playing scrum-half in the first fifteen rugby team.

I had always turned up my nose at the prospect of playing school rugby. I wasn't built for battling in the scrum, or leaping and winning balls in the line out, and besides I was much more involved in playing soccer in one of the local leagues outside school.

But one year the school rugby team had been cleaned out of its key players and, on entering the lower sixth at the age of 17, enormous pressure was put on me to try out the vacant scrum-half position. I half protested but gave in after a great deal of flattery and subtle coercion from teachers and the team captain. Gradually I began to enjoy the dramatic position of displaying my ball-playing skills in that position (catching, kicking, passing although I didn't run very far with the ball before getting squashed) and the histrionics of the dive pass, launching myself into body-stretching space from line out or scrum and then belly-flopping into mud.

The conflict between the crumbling public-school ethos, with its established, middle-class preference for rugby as the dominant winter sport, and the more informal, working-class preference for soccer came to a head one weekend halfway through the rugby term. (The compromised school position was to play rugby in the longer autumn term and soccer in the spring term.) One Saturday afternoon both the town and school teams put pressure on me to turn out for them.

I wanted to play for my home soccer team in the Torbay league but came under extraordinary exhortation and bribery 'not to let the school team down'. In fact it was made very clear to me that if I did play for my home team then I would never play for a school team again. So I caved in under that kind of pressure and played rugby.

The most significant incident in that match, in terms of my present purposes, was a crazy moment of self-destructiveness. Our opponents' forwards were much stronger than us that day and I remember their pack breaking through our defence with the ball at their feet. For a brief moment the ball broke loose and I fell on it, curling my body around it so that only my own forwards could get at it. It was a really daft thing to do and nothing to do with courage. I just unthinkingly conformed to the warrior norms of the game. That's what you were supposed to do when playing school rugby, wasn't it? At all costs, you had to defend the citadel against invaders. You had to detach your body from your head and feelings to be heeled and brutalized. To save the team, the platoon, the male club you had to pretend that all that bruising didn't hurt. Or that you had to pretend it only hurt a bit, but you could bear it. That was the name of the game, wasn't it?

The opposing side's forwards tore at me, screwing their boot studs down into my buttocks, trying to kick me off the ball but I clung on to it till my own team mates had got back behind me and managed to scramble the ball into touch. The warrior ethos – displaying courage and bravery, and not deserting my post, while under heavy enemy fire – only became clear to me much later.

For that action, and other performances that season, I was publicly complimented by the headteacher (the general mentioning me in dispatches?) for team loyalty, and later awarded my school colours for rugby, almost as a bribe. (Colours were the gold letters XV or XI that you could emblazon your school blazer with, just under the school badge.) These competitive matters of whether or not so-and-so was going to get the honours this year were endlessly gossiped and speculated over by the boys in the fifth and sixth forms. The public celebration of walking up through the central aisle at morning assembly with the stuffed caribou head, presented by an ex-pupil, the Governor of Newfoundland, looking down on you, and receiving your colours from the headteacher with clapping thundering in your ears was like receiving the Victoria Cross for bravery in battle. The mystique worked like a symbolic ritual, initiating me into the hierarchical priesthood of some religious order, or the Freemasons.

Because there was such an obsessive emphasis on competitive performance and winning, the related moments of failure and put-down burned into my consciousness with a special intensity and stayed with me for a considerable time. I was hopeless at crosscountry running. I lacked the strength, stamina and the motivation to do well in it. More importantly, like athletics, it seemed to me then to deny me any opportunities for skill and subtlety, although I'm sure a crosscountry specialist would tell me that tactics require considerable shrewdness and intelligence.

House practices after school in the autumn term were a long, slogging graft for me. After a tiring day at school we had to go out in all kinds of weather and run for two miles in a bunched pack

[215]

along the main Newton Abbot road to a place called the Chateau Belle Vue. I can remember the searing and bubbling in my lungs as I fought for air, pulling myself up that hill, then the miles over ploughed fields on the brow of the hill, pushing through brambles in the rutted, often flooded lanes, and then the long slosh back through the River Dart marshes.

The school closed down for one afternoon in November so that everybody, except the chronically asthmatic, the sick, or the boys with legs in plaster, could compete against each other in the four rival houses, at junior and senior levels.

The most memorable day of failure was probably in 1954 when I had just entered the fourth year and was competing for the first time in the senior school run. The day was raw grey and bitter cold. Because I knew I was likely to be shown up at the end of the day I developed a counter-humour that gently mocked some of the rituals of the occasion. In this instance it was the wearing of grey, woolly gloves to stop my hands from turning into ice-blocks. Also in a mood of irritation I made a pact with some friends of mine to all come in together at the very end of the race, almost like a non-competitive protest for boys who couldn't run.

Of course that was the declared intention but it never happened like that. As soon as the games master fired the starting pistol we all forgot about our promises, rushed off and got caught up in the race. Flickering impressions stay with me from that race; the sobbing pain in my chest as the haul towards the Chateau Belle Vue began; the sense of legs and arms passing me all the time; the frequent stopping with a stitch in my side; the iron-hard earth ridges across the ploughed fields. Some of the more liberal teachers thought this military emphasis on crosscountry running a bit of an anachronism and showed me where they stood in response to my gloves. 'Trying to keep warm then Jackson?' one of them teased as I dragged myself over the field gate at his checkpoint, halfway round the course.

Groggily, coming back across the marshes, I could hear the roars and cheers, and hoots of derision. I came in 83rd out of about a hundred competitors and I remember the jeers when the spectators and finished runners clustering around the finish noticed my woolly gloves. I tried to look as if I didn't care as I entered the roped-off funnel leading to the finishing line. My mates were nowhere. They'd all come in before me. So I tried to show I was a non-competitor in the way I approached the line. But I was so dog-tired I couldn't even raise a grin. Somebody yelled out, 'Didn't you go fast enough to get a steam up then, Jacko?'

The fear of public failure has stayed with me ever since, formed from events like this one, and other humiliating put-downs.

Sporting activities in my life history certainly played a significant part in producing and reproducing in me a masculinity that was a part of the social power network of patriarchy. My learned physical occupation of space, my stuttering attempts to achieve a swaggering, confident physical presence, my embodiment of strength, determination and competence (however imperfect and contradictory inside) were all founded on the systematic subordination of women; my mother's and sister's domestic servicing of me, and their blocked opportunities to get out of the house, allowed the extra, privileged time to work up my own physical strength.

But as I've indicated in the incidents and episodes of my personal history, this was never a fixed, monolithic and inevitable process. There were also continuing cultural struggles going on, like the home/school and class divide in the rugby story, the woolly gloves, and the leg-break bowling. The grim stoicism of the public-school ethos of manliness as seen in the yearly crosscountry ritual wasn't just passively accepted and reproduced in me, in an overdetermined and mechanistic way. The headteacher's definition of the meaning of the crosscountry run was constantly being interrogated, cheeked, mocked and very occasionally subverted. Some boys skipped crosscountry practice, many boys stayed away on the day of the race, skived off in the middle of the practice or the race, achieved a group 'go-slow' policy in practice, wore bizarre clothing while running, carved mocking grafitti about the head into the school toilet door, or just simply refused to comply with the school rules and conventions.

These other cultural struggles for me centred around such things as the fantasy imagery of sporting success. As Richard Dyer says, 'Sport is the most common contemporary source of male imagery',[15] and I was certainly affected by the availability and force of such imagery. Because of my own sense of physical inferiority and powerlessness, fantasy images such as this offered compensatory confirmation and mastery. Sunday newspapers like the *Sunday Pictorial* used to cover their back pages with the

[217]

tangled bodies of footballers being muscularly active. With their fierce striving for goal the players presented me with a view of thrusting masculinity that I was supposed to admire and accept as normative. In this way they became a powerful source of daydream and night-time dream fodder.

Indeed my early attempts at being an acrobatic goalkeeper in the 'Three and in' games down on the seafront were constantly influenced by my daydream fantasies of imitating Bert Williams, the Wolves and England goalkeeper, nicknamed 'The Cat'. I had a scrapbook with one page full of newspaper pictures of him full of agile daring, backwards somersaulting as he stretched for an unexpected shot, pouncing at forwards' feet. It was a complex fantasizing; the denied areas of myself certainly responded to his agility and grace but that was all interwoven into a haunting, adolescent imagery of spotlight-grabbing activity, strength and competitive performance that seemed to offer me the illusion of greater physical force. At an early age these opposing tendencies were allowed to co-exist but from about 13 upwards fantasy images of conquest, achievement and mastery started to blot out the more fluid images of balletic movement.

This imagery of power and control in sporting activities (as well as sexual ones) was strongly influenced by the narrative codes and conventions of the male romance.[16] That is to say that my memory processes, dreaming and moments of perception were organized and structured, to some degree, by the narrative forms of male romance that I was meeting, everyday, in newspaper stories, and particularly footballing and sporting stories from comics like, the *Rover, Hotspur* and *Wizard*, and reading *Biggles*.

These narrative forms were derived from long-established epic codes of heterosexual male honour and virility being proved and defended through a test of competitive rivalry or combat. In the form I experienced them, heroes like Wilson, Cannonball Kidd or Alf Tupper were faced by apparently impossible dilemmas but battled their way through, in the climax of physical combat, to defend their status, honour and masculinity.

My fantasy dream narratives were frequently organized around similar images of chequered-flag moments of victory and triumph. One of my favourite ones was in the last minute of the FA Cup Final at Wembley stadium where I used regularly to dribble past six or seven bewildered defenders, draw the goalkeeper out from the net, body-swerve past him and push the ball into the empty goal just as the referee whistled for full time.

Another was based on the actual moment from the 1951 Cup Final when Newcastle United were playing Blackpool. Ernie Taylor, inside forward for Newcastle, back-heeled the ball into space for Jackie Milburn to hit a 30-yard 'screamer'[17] past the 'flabbergasted' George Farm in the Blackpool goal.

My own memory processes were structured in the same kind of way. No images of shy touching, of loving reciprocity, but blatant moments of banners, cups, glory and scoring, like the one when I scored in playground football at primary school. Occasionally I get a flickering impression of the moment when I connected flush with my instep (in open-toed Clark's sandals too!) and the ball flew half the playground and whacked high up on the opponents' painted air-raid-shelter goal.

Another was the incident at grammar school when I played for the first eleven soccer team against Sutton High School at Plymouth. I usually had difficulties in lifting a water-drenched football but the exact moment surfaces, every now and again, in my dreams when another member of my team rolled a free kick in front of me and I ran forward a few steps to bend the ball a full 20 yards into the top right-hand corner of the goal. Cannonball Kidd, Jackie Milburn and my FA Cup Final narratives are all focused together as ghosts just behind my own life-story narratives, looming up and arranging them in particular directions.

But all these dream narratives were constantly coming into conflict with everyday realities. Frequent failures like the crosscountry example often shattered these dream bubbles and brought them down to earth. This meant that I was always stuck, half in and half out, of these false promises and never completely taken over. That also meant that occasionally I was able to refuse fitting in to the enticements of masculine glory and romance.

Also the contradictory impulses within my approach to sport still existed to complicate the image of the callously hardened body with the steely purpose. The incongruous elements of artistry and skill always existed within the dream image to modify the main thrust towards forceful conquest, so that the FA Cup Final images were conflicted; on one hand I looked up to Jackie Milburn's 'rocket' shot from 30 yards out, but on the other my own invented dream fantasy was mainly to do with a Stanley Matthews-like tricky ball-play that allowed me to dribble past seven opponents and to mesmerize them with a demonstration of skill.

In a way the imagery of conquest was at its worst when it acted as a compensatory, buttressing structure at times of immediate insecurity. But it could never remain as a continuously sustaining purpose because its controlling priorities were always at odds with the everyday world of failure/imperfection, and an opposing narrative of change and ironic subversion.

Over the years, sporting relations have produced in me a partly destructive relationship to my own body and the world outside. Although I have also used sport to express a number of choked, contradictory feelings and qualities inside me, my unsuccessful but driven attempts to develop a virile physical presence and power in my body have severed emotional and social commitments and responsibilities from my physical actions.

Thrusting for goal over the years has shaped my body in a particular way. It has taught me to impose my will on my body and other people, rather than listening to it and learning to acknowledge its needs. I have a tendency to treat my body as an external machine that carries out my clenched determination to achieve through work and, particularly, intellectual work. In this way, one specific version of masculinity – dominant heterosexuality – has become naturalized in my bodily relations. The clenched legacies of my past determination to win or achieve or score are there in the rigid way I tense and hold my body.

This has also led to an emotional paralysis about my bodily relations with the world outside. While my body has been used to pushing, driving, thrusting, being goal-oriented in a physical and sexual way, I've been able to shut out the personal and emotional consequences of these mutilating relations through an addictive absorption in useless facts, statistics, odd details about sporting activities.

Indeed, I often turn first to the sports page in the daily newspaper, concerning myself with the raw material for endless non-emotional non-conversations with other men, material like sporting results, league table positions, team names, transfer deals, that protects me and helps me to avoid facing up to the uncomfortable world news, or the emotional consequences of any physical relations. It's almost as if the daily dose of useless sporting facts anaesthetizes me to what's going on in the world, like my relation to personal knowledge – why, for instance, so many women die of cervical cancer each year.

My physical breakdown has at last taught me the necessity to set my own physical limits, take responsibility for my bodily relations, and start changing my daily physical relations with myself and the outside world. I've understood that the physical striving for goal is not only damaging to other people but also played a significant part in my collapse. So now I'm learning, with great difficulty, to slow down, and not to impose my will on my body but to bring my feelings back into sync with it. It's certainly not easy but there are signs that I'm beginning to move in the world in a different way.

Notes

1 It seems to me that physical size (and the lack of it in my case) has been largely ignored in the discussion about the social and cultural forces that shape masculinities. My crushing sense of being inferior to how I should have been as a 'proper' boy was culturally learned, but it did have some solid basis in my being short for my age. In fact I was still being asked my age (18 was the minimum age for entry to British pubs) in pubs when I was 25 and married!

2 From M. Mishkind et al. (1987) 'The embodiment of masculinity', in M. Kimmel (ed.) Changing Men, London, Sage.

3 J. Berger (1972) Ways of Seeing, Harmondsworth, Penguin.

4 A slogan used by a Worthington advertising campaign, September 1988.

5 M. Messner (1987) 'The meaning of success: the athletic experience and the development of male identity', in H. Brod (ed.) The Making of Masculinities, London, Allen & Unwin.

6 The whole of this 'physical embedding of masculinity' argument is indebted to R. W. Connell (1983) Which Way is Up? Sydney, Allen & Unwin (Australia), in a chapter called 'Men's bodies'.

7 See N. Chodorow (1978) The Reproduction of Mothering, Berkeley, Calif., University of California Press.

8 B. Kidd (1987) 'Sports and masculinity', in M. Kaufman (ed.) Beyond Patriarchy. OUP (Canada). Toronto.

9 See R. Johnson (1981) Unpopular Education, London, Hutchinson.

10 J. Springhall (1987) 'Building character in the British boy: the attempt to extend Christian manliness to working-class adolescents, 1880–1914', in J. Mangan and J. Walvin (eds) Manliness and Morality, Manchester, Manchester University Press.

11 ibid.
12 By 'invented tradition' I refer to Eric Hobsbawm's definition of 'a set of practices, normally governed by overtly or tacitly accepted rules and of a ritual or symbolic nature, which seek to inculcate certain values and norms of behaviour by repetition, which automatically implies continuity with the past'. From E. Hobsbawm and T. Ranger (1983) *The Invention of Tradition*, Cambridge, Cambridge University Press.
13 I'm indebted to J. A. Hargreaves (1986) 'Where's the virtue? Where's the grace? A discussion of the social production of gender through sport', *Theory, Culture and Society*, vol. 3, no. 1, for a great deal of this argument.
14 See W. Arkin and L. Dobrofsky (1978) 'Military socialization and masculinity, *Journal of Social Issues*, vol. 34, no. 1.
15 R. Dyer (1982) 'Don't look now', *Screen*, vol. 23, nos. 3/4.
16 'The genre of "romance" is, in its historical origins, didactic, aristocratic and predominantly masculine. The common meaning of the "romance" comes from the later [seventeenth–nineteenth-century] popularisation and feminisation of romance.' From J. Batsleer *et al.* (1985) *Rewriting English*, London, Methuen.
17 These words in inverted commas are echoes of popular journalese at the time.

CHAPTER 11

Boys' comics: reading the Rover, Hotspur and Wizard, 1948–50

As well as through social practices and relations, masculinity is produced through cultural and ideological struggles over meaning. In my own life, boys' comics, in particular, played a small but significant part in the ideological construction of my masculinity.

Between the ages of eight and ten I went through an obsessive phase when I collected, hoarded and read the *Hotspur, Rover* and *Wizard* in what seemed like most of my leisure time, when I wasn't playing football. (Remember, those were the days when most homes, especially working-class ones, didn't have television.)[1] These comics,[2] with their brightly coloured covers, seemed to have a potent and striking 'reality', much more than my everyday living. Propping the comic up on the back of the Puffed Wheat box I used to sit at one end of the kitchen table, as if in a mesmerized trance and deaf to the demands of my parents and sisters, and vanish into the world of the story. Or lying belly-down on the rug, I used to become completely absorbed in the continuing stories of Wilson, Cannonball Kidd and Alf Tupper, the 'tough of the track'.

Every Thursday morning, when these comics were delivered with the morning paper, I remember racing my sisters to the door when I heard them rattling through the letterbox. For about two years, tuppenny comics were part of my personal world, in a special way that marked off what I did as *me* from the other world of adults at home or at school, and helped me to develop a separate sense of personal esteem from how I was seen by parents and teachers. This felt like a kind of mental breaking away from what I ought to be doing in that adult-regulated world that had, up to then, kept me tightly in rein, within its boundaries. Mental breaking away was like generating through my own efforts, and through working on my own popular literature, a personal and social space (within that space there was also a safety and security that comforted me when I was up against it) which couldn't be colonized or taken over by interfering adults. I think I did this by occupying a mental territory that was suspended between the imaginary and the real, with an ability to move in and out of fantasy escape and everyday reality in a way that protected me from confining adult categories and false dualisms.

For long stretches of time I was able to hide myself away in this 'play space',[3] keeping the adult world with all its demands at bay, and also preserving my integrity. So in the house I would take comics to the lavatory with me and spend long periods of rapt absorption in there until my sisters nearly kicked the door down in their frustration. I also took comics to school with me, sneaked glances at them under the desk when a lesson was particularly boring, and found them comforting when school was too alien and impersonal.

The pleasure I took in reading comics was heightened by the official disapproval of them amongst most schoolteachers. The more they disapproved of them, the more I seemed to identify myself through my personal closeness with these rebellious comic worlds and favourite characters.

Of course this sense of closeness and personal identification could also act as a trap. Later in this chapter I'd like to investigate how this personal identification also sometimes made me more prepared to buy in to sexist ideologies.

Rereading boys' comics like a struggling, anti-sexist man

The process of reading and rereading comics is a dynamic process of collaboration and dialogue between the codes and conventions of the comic story, and the particular personal and social history of the reader (a mixture of gender, race, class, age, location etc.). Readers don't just internalize the comic's hidden message in a docile, powerless manner but actively interact with the comic to produce a variety of meanings and pleasures.

Meaning for the reader isn't just locked inside the text, in a static, predetermined way, but is actively constructed through a complex negotiation between the reader's social frameworks of understanding, the context and relations within which the reading takes place, and the structures of the text. And often this process of negotiation is a very contradictory one, involving fantasy projections and illusions as well as half-formed, fragmentary ideas that vary from context to context, and change in different periods of life.

In terms of my own specific social history as a reader, I grew up slightly out of sync with the dominant culture. Culturally and socially displaced (with my grandfather's history of immigration from northern Italy, with a semi-evacuee's consciousness, class-damaged and uneasy in my masculinity), I didn't slot neatly into the dominant ideology. This upbringing kept me slightly at a distance from the usual habits of thinking around me. I suspect that the embryonic roots of my later critical perspectives developed out of that early watchfulness from the margins, of not being totally a part of the club. But it was an extremely complex process. On one level I didn't swallow wholeheartedly the aggressive, virile posturing of the traditional diet of patriarchal culture, but, on another, to survive I needed to be seen as joining in with the male club.

Also to complicate matters still further, the period of my life from eight to ten was a time when I was particularly susceptible to the way that certain fantasy stories, like Wilson in the *Wizard* (see later section), connected to my unconscious desires. During this period comics seemed to exercise an obsessive grip over me. It was a distinct phase in my development which offered an intense, temporary engagement for me as a reader, and then had faded away by the age of 11.

Therefore as a reader then, at the age of eight to ten, I think I read in a much more fluid way than now, both half in and half outside the stories. I was partly gripped at a level of fantasy and desire, but also, occasionally, partly sceptical, watchful, aware that these stories were escapist entertainment. Certainly I didn't judge them less worthy because of that. It was just that some stories enticed me into a relation of reader/writer where I had to give them my full attention, and others I could just skim through, perfunctorily, without stopping.

Rereading now, as a man struggling to become anti-sexist, those latent critical perspectives experienced as a child have become the

[225]

foundations of a movement towards an anti-patriarchal critical practice. As a reader I have lost that early fluidity and intensity of engagement, but have gained a more coherent critical edge to my reading. The danger about that adult coherence is that it should become a merely rational, abstracting device to hold the real contradictoriness at bay.

In rereading now in 1989 I will present my reconstructed version of the complex reading relations when I was eight or ten, and make explicit my present critical standpoint. Clearly, reading at that young age has been reconstructed in the light of my present critical values and priorities of being a struggling, anti-sexist male reader now.

Those present critical values began in the process of unlearning the hidden images and norms of a dominant, heterosexual culture. By standing back from my present, invisible situation of unexamined privilege, I learned to bring my taken-for-granted masculine assumptions into critical visibility. And through this process I gradually made those assumptions open to the possibility of critical reconstruction, rereading and political choice.

Exposing the false universality[4] and imaginary unity of dominant white, middle-class, heterosexual experience lies at the heart of an anti-patriarchal critical approach. It involves demonstrating that the dominating, universal definition of 'masculine experience = human experience' acts as a system of male power that is achieved at the expense of women's perspectives; and that also large areas of powerless and vulnerable male experience have been ignored and silenced because they have been concealed by that imaginary unity, organized in the traditional interests of white, middle-class heterosexual men.

The critical approach of men's studies to rereading comics is to delve deeply beneath the surface features of the text to reveal the ideological construction of masculinity through attending to the distortions, omissions and misrepresentations of the text.

Instead of a 'masculine' mode of reading[5] (a single-minded, concentrated focus from a 'centred'[6] reading subject) working on a 'masculine' narrative (a narrative involving a fixed closure with a singular point of view and single plot) an anti-patriarchal approach would want to change the customary reading relations offered by the text. Then, gradually, male readers like myself can grapple with the shared movement towards more open, interrogative readings of problematized, more plural texts. As Catherine Belsey comments:

> Composed of contradictions, the text is no longer restricted to a single, harmonious and authoritative reading. Instead it becomes plural, open to re-reading, no longer an object for passive consumption but an object of work by the reader to produce meaning.[7]

Rereading 'Cannonball Kidd' from the Hotspur (30 April 1949)

The first thing I want to point out is the different reading levels of attention and engagement that I gave comic stories. With 'Cannonball Kidd' I used to enjoy coasting through the very predictable story line, not needing to give my full attention to what was happening, almost as if I was keeping half of myself ironically detached from the story.

What kept me turning the pages week after week, I suspect, was the way the writer coaxed me into an easy identification with Cannonball Kidd, the single, all-powerful, super-hero character of the story. The character was deliberately aimed at young boys' fantasies about achieving a fully-formed masculinity through physical strength and competitive performance. As John Fiske suggests, super-heroes like this are 'particularly popular with boys at the age at which they have learnt that their masculinity requires them to be dominant, but who have neither the physical strength nor the social position to meet this requirement'.[8]

At that specific moment of my growing up, between eight and ten, my shaky grip on my masculinity, both socially and psychologically, needed compensatory fantasy and symbolic ways of reassuring myself that I might be as competent as that in the future. With a half sceptical mocking at and yet, at the same time, powerful connection with the fantasy promise of strength and force, I read the Hotspur mainly for the Cannonball Kidd stories.

The figure of Cannonball Kidd spoke to me because of his combination of youthfulness (the 'Kidd' part of him, 'the school-boy centre-forward' that I urgently wanted to emulate) and his physical embodiment of forceful activity (his 'blockbuster' shot in football – his 'Cannonball' aspect.) In this episode his 'activity' is established through the intensely energetic verbs always associated with him. Cannonball 'slammed', 'streaked', 'flashed', 'blazed', 'slashed', 'flushed', 'rammed', and 'sizzled', scored two goals to win the FA Cup for his team, and successfully sorted out the sly 'swank', Jack Bowers and his pompous headmaster, Mr Brasser.

This particular episode, 'Cannonball Kidd for the Cup' is slightly different from the traditional, single-plot focus of masculine narrative. It employs a main and a sub-plot. The main story features Redvale Blades' (a Third Division football club) preparation for the FA Cup Final against 'mighty Crayford Arsenal', and their eventual 2–1 win in the final, after being 0–1 down at half-time.

The sub-plot is there to give an unexpected twist to the routine main plot. It involves an eccentric character called Roughneck Jake, who like Cannonball Kidd is an expert 'marksman' but this time with guns. Roughneck, one of Redvale Blades' supporters, has travelled all the way from Alaska to see the Cup Final but hasn't got a ticket. Initially Cannonball Kidd tries to get another ticket for Roughneck from Mr Brasser his headmaster (and manager of nearby Greyport Rovers!). But the ticket is conned from Mr Brasser by Jack Bowers. Cannonball gets his own back on Bowers and retrieves the ticket by challenging and beating him in a three-shot penalty contest where Roughneck (as the goalkeeper) literally shoots down the three penalty kicks.

During the Cup Final the Grayford Arsenal winger sends over a dangerous cross but the ball bursts. The triumphant end of the match is interrupted by the accusation from Bowers and Brasser that Roughneck shot down the ball. The reader is left in suspense until Roughneck states that he couldn't have shot the ball down because he left his gun back at his hotel, safe from pickpockets. The story ends in triumph for Redvale Blades, Cannonball Kidd and Roughneck Jake.

Cannonball Kidd bridges the two plots together through his successful activity in the main plot (scoring the two goals for Redvale Blades) and his ingenious activity in the sub-plot in helping another 'wonderful shot' to get in to watch the match (through the penalty contest), and helping him to clear his name at the end of the match.

Despite the two plots, the general effect is still of a tightly closed story, organized around a main controlling figure with whom the reader can identify.[9] This serves to close down the range of possible interpretations, and to deny the reader the chance of multiple identification or the possibility of seeing the events from different viewpoints. As such, it's very much a 'masculine' narrative.

Whereas 'feminine' narratives like soap operas on television stress the process of personal relationships, close sharing of emotion, problem-solving together, 'masculine' ones, like the 'Cannonball Kidd' story, resolve dilemmas, like Roughneck Jake not having a Cup Final ticket, through strong actions and few words; and all their events take place in the public arena rather than in a more personal sphere.

The movement of this 'masculine' narrative structure is very much an ejaculatory one. Moving from the opening disruption of a stable order (the introduction of Roughneck Jake without a ticket) and the surprise of a lowly Third Division side getting into the Cup Final with 'mighty Crayford Arsenal', it builds up inevitably to the grand climax of the ending. The rhythm of this story development concentrates on a goal-oriented focus (literally and metaphorically), at the expense of relationships and emotional process.

The triumphant ending (of winning at all costs) is supposed to justify the drabness of some of these stories' middles. Fame, glory and success are achieved through spectacular, dramatic feats of physical competence and strength. Cannonball Kidd's 30-yard drive, directly from the Cup Final kick-off, nearly scores. But then after the predictable set-back at half-time (a sure sign that everything's going to turn out fine in the end!), Cannonball scores twice in the second half to win the Cup for Redvale Blades. This is the description of Cannonball's first goal:

> Cannonball had speed up. His sudden terrific dash took him brushing past Renfrew. Grosvenor was in front. On the space of a doormat Cannonball turned, went a yard to the side and slashed at the ball. It flashed past the centre-half and went into the net just inside the upright.

He has power and pace, but also skill and poise ('on the space of a doormat'). A completely rounded super-hero and only a schoolboy! What more could I desire to model myself upon?

Here it's interesting to point out how the ejaculatory 'masculine' narrative structure of sports stories in boys' comics has persisted through the years. Picking up a boys' picture sports' comic, *Roy of the Rovers*, in early March 1989, I find the 'Terrible Twins' winning a Cup Final through dramatic, personal feats (bicycle kicks and heading ability), *after being 2–1 down at half-time*! The same narrative logic is there, even though in a vastly different format because of the influence of television etc. And the sub-plot involves the minor comedy of their eccentric manager, Victor Boskovic, who drops the FA Cup on his foot. Roughneck Jake = Victor Boskovic. Nothing seems to have changed very much!

Each of these boys' sports comic stories masquerades as authentic 'realism' but they're all dressed up fantasies really. Initially, I think I was lured into the world of the stories through the surface appearance of authentic details (as in this story of a cup team in training, with the player-manager giving advice to young footballers: 'be sharp in the tackle. Don't hang back!'), but my willingness to get really involved at a deeper level was always related to their fantasy grip on my unconscious desires. The odd thing was that if the surface details of these sports stories were obviously phoney and unconvincing then I had great difficulty in giving myself, totally, to the fantasy elements.

Here, in Cannonball Kidd, because the background details are so cardboard (the eccentricity of Roughneck Jake so extreme, and the pompous headmaster and the sly villain, Jack Bowers, so crudely drawn) I was always on the margins of the story. I was partly grabbed by the fantasy identification with Cannonball Kidd but only half awake, flicking over the other details with some impatience to get at the expected performance feats at the end of the story.

Rereading 'The Tough of the Track' from the Rover (18 June 1949)

The pleasures of reading about the sporting triumphs of the long-distance runner, Alf Tupper, the 'tough of the track' (see the complete story printed at the end of this chapter) were tied into the way the social details of working-class culture carried me into the

[230]

heart of the fantasy elements as well. Unlike the 'Cannonball Kidd' story where I lost interest because of the unconvincing background details, the authentically gritty social conditions of the Alf Tupper story immediately grabbed me.

It was the anti-heroic spirit of setting the story firmly in a northern, industrial working-class context that marked this story off from conventional, minor-public-school ones like Rockfist Rogan in the *Champion*, and hooked me into the story so easily. A great deal of that background was unknown to me; with Alf sleeping on a mattress under the archway in a railway viaduct, working as a welding-shop apprentice, only getting 25 shillings a week, pawning his running prizes and living off fish and chip suppers. But I was able to make imaginative connections with it, in my own head.

Although some of the writing hovers on the edge of caricature, I felt a deep class affinity with the deprivation of the social background ('somebody else who regarded being hard-up as the normal state of existence'), and I understood the power relations between the 'hooligans' and the 'swanks' in the story.

Certainly the anti-snobbery theme was not an original theme in boys' comics; Orwell in his essay on 'Boys' weeklies'[10] had pointed out the long tradition of scholarship-boy stories in the *Magnet*. And the calculation of shrewd publishers and writers, in using the gritty elements of working-class experiences to widen the class base of their readership, and to domesticate the oppositional potential of those working-class elements,[11] certainly can be seen here. But that's only partially true.

The full reconstructed complexity of how I might have read this comic was, initially, about being gradually lured into it by the gritty texture of the story, but what really engrossed me was Alf's cheeky, answering-back tone. It was the personal recognition of finding a mode of talking and behaving that made sense of my own social powerlessness in a constructive way.

Alf Tupper's gruff voice of independent integrity ('I'm not letting the [swanks] laugh at me') establishes him as the working-class rebel, the 'lone wolf' and the misfit all combined in one character. There are two main strands to his rebellion; the first is his 'anti-authoritarian populism'[12] that connects him with children's fun comic characters like Dennis the Menace[13] in the *Beano*, and the second, his anti-bureaucratic approach.

[231]

All through this story of the trip to the Brussels meeting and his 10,000-metre race, the 'tough of the track' is involved in an antagonistic struggle with the Granton Hall 'swanks', and especially their official voice, Commander Churcher. Churcher represents the dominant ruling-class voice of British athletics that usually silences ignored voices like Alf Tupper's. In the newspaper Alf reads Churcher's respected judgement that 'it would be two years before Britain would be able to challenge the Continental runners for the 10,000 metres title'. And later on in the story, when he hears that Alf will be racing in the 10,000-metre race, Churcher's imperialistic viewpoint is made clearer: 'It will be bad from the international point of view for the crowd to see a Britisher hopelessly beaten.'

I tuned in to Alf's challenging of Churcher's class-based put-downs. The points of connection were all those similar moments in my own life when my own personal worth had also been under-valued; moments like my father not believing that I was capable of passing the 11-plus and asking for verification and, much later, the grammar-school headteacher wanting to dissuade me from entering for a county scholarship grant for a university place.

The class relations of the 'hooligan' versus 'swank' conflict is what riveted me to the pages, week after week. Here in this story it's there in the sharply contrasted journeys that Alf and the Granton Hall athletes make to Brussels. While Alf just about makes it by travelling rough, via the ferry, a lorry, walking, bicycling, and on the tailgate of another lorry, the 'swanks' of Granton Hall have a privileged journey on an 'airliner that flew smoothly over them on the same course'. And in the racing stadium itself Alf's 'brown paper package', containing his racing gear, is set against the Granton contingent in 'dark red blazers and white flannel trousers'.

The second strand of anti-bureaucratic dissent[14] is entwined with the class relations of this anti-authoritarian approach. Alf openly shows his contempt for the agencies of social control in the story, like Commander Churcher and the Belgian policeman, Gendarme Roothert. His lone-wolf independence and unconventionality are constantly at odds with the principles of doing it by the book, and official respectability. So he deliberately ignores Churcher's advice and jointly wins the race, and fights back against Roothert's officiousness by throwing a blanket over his head, locking him in

[232]

a prison cell and gaining his freedom through his own actions. At the end of the story Alf, through his determination and courage, wins a joint victory not only literally in the 10,000-metre race, but metaphorically against the forces of bureaucratic custom when Captain Mercier tears up the summons for Alf's arrest.

Alf's irreverent undermining of middle-class cultural authority also comes through in his use of language. His jaunty, vernacular use of language with its curt, clipped asides, quick retorts and quips brings the standard correctness of Commander Churcher rapidly down to earth. Indeed, his colloquial cheek ('snapped', 'growled', 'chipped', 'grunted' etc.) works as an affront to official, established authority throughout the story.

Although the story sets out to create an impression of verisimilitude (through the Olympic Games images of the visual title sequence put side by side with the 'tough of the track' image, and the starkly 'real' working-class background), its powerful grip on my imagination came through a sense of connection with these weekly fantasies of defiance against established authority.

At a time when my daily social experience, at school and to a much lesser degree at home, was often one of passivity and obedience, I needed these substitute fantasies of sticking up for myself, of answering back, of sticking out my tongue at authority, and even protesting and rebelling. In some part of my hidden self I was secretly nurtured by these stories of working-class dissent to dream of getting my own back against those adults, at home and at school, who kept putting me down. And in those first stirrings of a sense of personal injustice there might have been the origins of a later challenging of a class system that also tried to reduce my sense of personal and social worth.

The real problem with all this is that these constructive elements of working-class opposition in 'Tough of the Track' also trapped[15] boys like myself into accepting the ideological construction of masculinity that went along with it. The comic not only offered me a fantasy of class defiance of and opposition to established authority, but it also promised me the fantasy of redressing wrongs through superhuman drive, physical strength and thrust.

The experience of having a body that was weak and relatively undersized (and also socially powerless within the family and school) at nine years of age, existing within the cultural expectations of a men-on-top society, produced a disturbing mismatch

[233]

for me between the material reality of my immediate conditions and the symbolic need for a controlling dominance. The ideology of masculinity provided me with a way of negotiating this mismatch by constructing confirming fantasies of compensatory strength and power. These ideologies gave me the reassuring framework of how a 'real' boy/man like Alf Tupper should behave, what it is he should be thinking, what it is he likes, and how he *ought* to be acting in the real world.

That's why I was so susceptible to the influence of Alf Tupper's rugged masculinity. I admired his stubborn individualism and his independence, never pausing to admit his emotional needs or looking for a close relationship. Alf seemed to hold out the possibility for me of making my own way in life through my own grit and courage. He remained cheerful while living in appalling conditions. He never whined like me, or revealed his uncertainties, but got on with the job. (He didn't seem to have an inner world. His whole focus was on public actions in the public domain.)

I assumed that all 'proper' men should be like Alf, stoically clinging on to his desire to win at all costs. Indeed something he says in the episode might stand for his epitaph:

I'm sticking to it till I come in first.

Here patriarchal values are summed up in a nutshell; a dogged determination to strive at what you're doing and to succeed replaces all feelings and social relationships that might have made you more aware of the personal and social costs of what you were doing.

Also the narrative structure similarly embodies that determination to succeed. In this story the habitual, ejaculatory narrative rhythm gains an almost hallucinatory quality. As Alf flogs himself on, everything becomes 'misty and blurred'. It doesn't matter how much his body suffers, or that the stone jabs deeper into his foot. All that matters is the single-minded concentration of focus on the goal of coming in first through the performance/climax.

The climax of the tie between Clemmsen and Alf is a combination of independent, muscular integrity and dramatic heightening. When the pain in his foot becomes too much Alf flings his running shoes off (how much real time would that have taken?) and gains a superhuman quality by running on in his bare feet. But just in case the superhuman strength distances the reader

[234]

too much from the story's hero, Alf's physical suffering is made much of:

> He was *staggering* towards the tape just ahead of the Swede.
> Alf *tottered*. A yard from the line he *fell* on to his knees. On his knees he *crawled* over the line while above him Clemmsen broke the tape. (my emphasis)

Alf jointly wins because of his dogged determination to succeed – the height of masculine achievement. It was these kinds of assumed, masculine qualities that I strained for in sporting, sexual and work relations, later on in my life. As I say in Chapter 10, 'What "going for goal" felt like was an obsessive single-mindedness in being able to shut out all questions of the other person (and how I was brutalizing myself) in the drive for success.'

Rereading 'The Man Named Wilson' in the Wizard (15 October 1949)

> a work is tied to ideology not so much by what it says as by what it does not say. It is in the significant *silences* of a text, in its gaps and absences, that the presence of ideology can be most positively felt.
>
> (Macherey)[16]

The sustained and significant absence in all of the boys' comics I read between 1948 and 1950 was women. The ideological construction of masculinity, produced through all those competitive clashes, trials of strength, and mental and physical conflicts, was achieved through the exclusion of those repressed 'feminine' elements in itself that it most feared. The illusion of flawless manhood is kept going in these stories through the silencing of the potentially threatening voices of the 'feminine'.

For many boys and men, who have been constructed within the false binary system, of 'masculinity'/'femininity', the 'feminine' is only acceptable as a totally separate, dichotomized element that doesn't confront the illusions and fantasies of their world. The ideological values of girls' comics – romance and an emphasis on

[235]

personal and domestic life – are there to complement implicitly (but not to challenge) the superiority of boys' values – activity, force, endurance, achievement – and clearly play their part in producing and reproducing the imbalance of power between the sexes.

In these 'The Man Named Wilson' stories from the *Wizard* the unconscious assumptions about the superiority of masculine experience are very much there. They assume a false universality for masculine experience through emphasizing its normative features. As it says in the story, '*men* could be almost as gods if they only trained themselves to give forth their best'.

This story doesn't go through the motions of pretending to be 'real' because it's not operating within the genre conventions of the sports story. Its deliberately exotic setting (in the Dalai Lama's monastery in Tibet) helps to foreground its fantasy/irrational elements. Here's a summary of the story.

Wilson is the leader of an expedition which wants to climb Mount Everest. He is accompanied by a journalist called Webb who tells the story. In trying to persuade the Dalai Lama in Tibet to grant his group permission to climb the mountain, Wilson flies with Webb to Tibet and then has to undergo many preliminary tests of his strength and endurance before the expedition can be considered.

This particular episode focuses on the hostility of the scheming Tibetan monk called Lha-Chu, who is worried because he feels his control over the boy Dalai Lama is being undermined by Wilson. A grand contest of mental and physical strength is organized by Lha-Chu between a yogi called Nang-Yam and Wilson. The test is about who can control his body and best stand cold in sub-zero temperatures.

The test takes place on the monastery roof where the yogi is slowly encased in ice from many buckets of water being flung over him. Nang-Yam survives this ordeal through 'using his will to prevent loss of heat', and 'keeping vital organs warm'. Wilson is finally triumphant in this contest with the yogi by not only surviving the trial but also generating enough body-heat to melt the ice around his body.

Unknown to the Dalai Lama, Webb and Wilson are thrown into a rock-chamber prison where an intimidating future vision of Wilson's defeat and death on Mount Everest is projected onto their imaginations. Wilson remains unmoved through all of this and is more concerned with helping his friend Webb overcome a drugged drink that creates a feverish drying out of both their throats. Wilson leaps across a ravine and back ('as good as a world-record long jump') to collect snow to relieve his friend's fever.

The story ends with Webb going to sleep with every blanket piled on top of him, and is contrasted to Wilson sleeping comfortably on the stone floor.

I was engrossed in these Wilson stories because they spoke to my conscious and unconscious desires[17] at that age. Indeed the very unreality of the stories, within this different genre, invited an engagement with those wish-fulfilment longings that were so important to me between eight and ten.

Materially and psychologically it was a time of great insecurity for me. I was unsure of my grip on masculine identity and powerless in the home. I was disappointed in the comparative frailty of my body. I knew that it didn't measure up to what a boy's body ought to look like. It lacked the height, the size, the muscularity, the toughness of a body like Bill Warburton's. He was the boy who hammered me into shameful tears on the way back from primary school. It was the way he had me on my back, and pinioned me down by his great, hulking knees squashing down into my shoulders and the top of my arms, that afterwards made me cringe with humiliation and a need for revenge.

But the only way I could take my revenge was through the fantasy solutions of stories like Wilson. I partly read the stories with a wry sense of fun but the other half was compulsively immersed in fantasy longings for that same kind of unruffled assurance and power that Wilson possessed, and that would have made Bill Warburton whine and plead for mercy. The stories offered me a different 'imaginary relationship' to those shaky and often humiliating material conditions. They beckoned me with the false promise that I could become as toughly masculine as Wilson if only I was prepared to strive with all my force to achieve that exalted state. Of course that future promise of achieved masculinity was hollow. The significant thing was that the processes of striving to appear more manly were the ideal circumstances within which a capitalist society could prepare young boys to accept their given place within the workforce, and within the gendered division of labour.

The character of Wilson resolved my inner conflicts and contradictions in a beguiling fantasy of omnipotence. Perhaps I could also conquer and control the physical environment like Wilson? In contrast to my shameful tears over the Bill Warburton fight, Wilson is unafraid (unafraid of Lha-Chu and the intimidating vision) and totally at ease in every threatening circumstance. He is bare to the waist, wears sandals and is 'serenely unconscious' of the intense cold in Tibet.

We first meet him in this story 'Standing before the [Dalai Lama's] throne, with folded arms and looking completely at ease'. He is self-assured and calm, totally in charge of the situation. In this strange, unsettling monastery, Wilson establishes his authority at once in being able to influence the Dalai Lama through his command of the Tibetan language and his strong arguments.

In the contest between himself and Nang-Yam, Wilson is removed from the realm of human fallibility. He endures the physical hard ship with the unflappability of an unmoving or unmoved 'statue':

> Once again men with buckets of ice water approached and began to empty them over Wilson's head. Even at the impact of the first icy shower he did not tremble or even wince. I did not see a muscle move. He might have been a bronze statue, for his skin was dark against the background of white snow.

He didn't whinge like me, but offered the bolstering, reassuring hope of an iron self-discipline and physical toughness and endurance.

In his controlling drive and emphasis on physical strength and activity, Wilson offers all young boys the alluring but tantalizing mirage of patriarchal authority: 'Given sufficient bodily force, and sufficient will to drive him, few things are impossible to man'.

But he also has miraculous powers that intrigued and engaged readers like me. Wilson often slept in the open, living off herbs on the Yorkshire moors. His age is unknown but he is very ancient. As in this story, his body has magical powers, with the capability of leaping ravines, and generating enough inner heat to melt his ice prison. This is what gives the Wilson stories their compelling dreams of bodily competence and authority.

The narrative structure of this Wilson story is the traditional, questing pattern of masculine romance.[18] The autonomous hero's bid to reach the top of Mount Everest (a patriarchal/imperialist dream soon to be realized by Hillary and Tensing in 1953) is challenged through rivalry with Lha-Chu, and the ritual contest or trial of his mental and physical strength. In winning through, the hero displays and proves his masculine honour and bravery. In this patterning the story stays very close to the Homeric code of adventure, quest, trial and the affirming or reaffirming of masculine honour. Wilson proves himself descended from an established line of epic warrior-heroes. The only slight departure from the traditional trajectory of the lonely hero's quest, trial and victory is the bonding with the journalist Webb in this particular Wilson story. Wilson's obsessive quest for fame and honour doesn't totally blind him to the human needs of his friend Webb. Wilson worries about Webb's sensitivity to cold, and then puts Webb's condition of a feverish burning throat before his own when they drink the drugged liquid from the stone jar.

However this behaviour isn't inconsistent with certain kinds of caring warrior-heroes, in the epic tradition, who have practised restraint and responsibility, rather than aggression.[19]

And here in this story those same kind of complexities exist. Wilson wins the contest with Nang-Yam by the use of *inner* resources and not by *outer* aggression and violence. He is a hero with not only superhuman physical strength but also a hero who exercises moderation, self-discipline and responsibility.

Conclusion

Boys' comics, at a particularly susceptible period of my life, played a small but significant part in securing my consent to a future gendered organization of labour. Despite the complexities and contradictions of that process, the stories of Cannonball Kidd, Wilson and Alf Tupper acted on me as an ideological preparation for future work (and the social relations to perpetuate that gendered organization). However I don't want to exaggerate their importance. They *contributed* to an ideology of masculinity. Other significant influences were at work as well.

The complementarity of that gendered division of labour was clear to see: whereas girls' comics and magazines offered incitements to girls to accept making themselves physically attractive (in male-defined terms) to a future husband, prepared them to accept being a mother, having a family and becoming a housewife, and generally softened them up to accept passivity, so boys' comics prepared the way for a 'natural' acceptance of a striving, individualist energy and a single-minded determination to win at all costs that was necessary for the fuelling of a capitalist social order.

So my fixation as a secondary-school English teacher on ego-bolstering performance and a strenuous commitment to achievement as a pioneering hero-innovator fitted very easily into the necessary drive needed to lubricate the male breadwinner ethos (during the 11 years I was married to my first wife) and my blind acceptance of the 'invisible' support I received from her unequal role as child carer and homemaker.

The boy and then later the man soon learn that the production of that 'drive' is rewarded socially in a male-dominated society, and that distinct economic benefits are connected to going along with the conventional striving towards manhood. As Bob Connell puts it: 'The overall gender organisation of labour concentrates economic benefits in one direction, economic losses in another, and on a scale sufficient to produce a dynamic of accumulation in its own right.'[20] Therefore profit, within a patriarchal/capitalist society, is made on the backs of women who are 'invisibly' supporting the male commitment to identifying themselves through fantasy imaginings related to success and achievement at work.

But how did these ideologies work in the lives of boys like me? In reading these comics I was offered a chance to negotiate my real material conditions (of social powerlessness and obedience) in a way that took into account my unconscious desires and fantasies. These desires and fantasies weren't free-floating but worked in me as a series of invitations to fit myself into the unconscious categories and frameworks through which I made sense of the material relations and circumstances in which I lived.

Those dominant frameworks (capitalist/patriarchal in orientation) partly defined and controlled what it was possible for me to think of or imagine as a young boy, and offered me dominant codes of what is acceptable masculine behaviour and what is effeminate.

Although I read in an occasionally distanced, ironic way, these interpretative frameworks powerfully influenced my customary way of perceiving myself in relation to my actual, material conditions. Through my fantasy identification with the worlds of Wilson

[240]

and Alf Tupper I entered into a set of 'imaginary relations'[21] with my material conditions of existence that, occasionally, allowed me to half-engage myself in the striving towards achievement, winning and success as a suitable future model of masculinity. That later contributed to a commitment to those social practices and relations that might secure me full membership in the 'tough-guy' club.

The other crucial consideration that this chapter throws up is the point that 'Narrative imitates life, life imitates narrative'.[22] In a men-on-top society that privileges 'going for goal' over caring, my memory process, dreaming, ability to perceive experience, were organized and structured by forms of masculine narrative codes and conventions.

As we have already seen in the boys' comics the traditional movement of this masculine narrative convention is very much a mounting, goal-focused, ejaculatory one. From sporting, chequered-flag narrative moments in dreams and newspaper reports of football matches through to the structuring of 'sexual-conquest' life stories (a step-by-step escalation of sexual-invasion techniques from the 'less-serious' zones to the 'really serious', as described in Chapter 6), masculine narrative structure works as an important part of those interpretative frameworks that *actively* produce, as well as reproduce, the social relations needed for a patriarchal culture.

By this I mean that the inevitable process of straining to accomplish the performance climax of achievement in masculine narrative lends a spurious validity to the life-history incident (or gives point and purpose to the overall life journey) in men's lives but also blinds many men to the different priorities and values of personal relationships, collaborative working and emotional process. Regular habits of proving their dignity through 'going for goal' in sport, sex and work reduce many men to a narrow, individualized egotism that makes a different kind of narrative and life organization, like a circular or spiral arrangement, almost impossible for them to imagine.

The crowd loves a thrilling finish to a race. Alf Tupper brings the spectators to their feet in a storming burst at the end of the 10,000 metres !

The TOUGH of the TRACK

In the 5000 metres final at the Olympic Games in 1932, Lauri Lehtinen, of Finland, and Ralph Hill, U.S.A., were thought to have run a dead heat. It was later established by photo that Lehtinen had won by inches.

The finish of the 100 metres sprint final at last year's Olympic Games was so close that Barney Ewell, of U.S.A., did a dance of victory, thinking he had won. The photo finish proved that Dillard, of U.S.A., had really won, Ewell being second.

Miss Maureen Gardner, Britain, and Mrs Blankers-Koen, of Holland, both broke the world's record in the 80 metres hurdles' final in the Olympic Games last year. Both returned the same time of 11.2 sec., though Mrs Blankers-Koen won by a foot.

'The tough of the track'

The Brussels meeting

Alf Tupper, the welding-shop apprentice whose one great interest in life was athletics, put a sack down on the counter of the pawnshop. He took out a chiming clock and two big cabinets of fish knives and forks.

'How did you get hold of these?' asked Dan Sherwin, the pawnbroker.

'If you think I pinched 'em you're wrong,' snapped Alf. 'They're all prizes I've won for running. I want six quid on them.'

'I can't advance you six quid,' said Sherwin.

'I want six quid and don't go selling them either because I'll be back for 'em when I've earned the money,' growled Alf.

Sherwin nodded.

'Okay,' he said. 'I'll loan you the cash if I'm going to get it back.'

Alf hurried from the shop with six pounds in his threadbare jacket. He kept his hand in his pocket, for six pounds felt like a fortune to him. His pay as an apprentice to Ike Smith was only twenty-five shillings a week.

His next call was in the small, backstreet shop of Fred Green, the newsagent, who was his only pal in Greystone. Alf had fallen out with the only local athletic club, the Greystone Harriers. He was regarded as a hooligan at Granton Hall, the Athletics Centre that had been started for the improvement of British athletics.

'Whato, Fred,' chirped Alf. 'Dan Sherwin came across with the six quid. Now fill in the papers for me.'

'It beats me why you want to go to Brussels,' said Green. 'Forget the Five Thousand Metres—'

'No!' retorted Alf. 'I haven't won a distance race on the track yet, pal, and I'm sticking to it till I come in first.'

They both studied the papers that had to be filled in for Alf's week-end visit to the Continent. The fact that Alf's entry had been accepted had been of assistance in putting things through.

Alf left Green to fill in the forms. He saw a copy of an athletics paper on the counter. He picked it up and read:–

'Athletes from ten Continental countries will assemble at Brussels on Saturday for the big International Meeting.

'Following on Clem Gatacre's win at Wembley, there is hope that the Granton Hall runner will carry the British colours to victory in the 5000 Metres Track event. He will again be opposed by Vurmi, the Flying Finn, and the opposition will be strengthened if Igar Clemmsen, of Sweden, takes part in the race. Clemmsen has not yet decided whether to run in the 5000 or 10,000 Metres event.

'Britain has not a representative in the longer race. Interviewed on this subject Commander Harold Churcher, Warden of Granton Hall, stated that in his opinion, it would be two years before Britain would be able to challenge the Continental runners for the 10,000 Metres title.'

Alf glanced up.

'Ten thousand blooming metres! That must be over six miles,' he grunted. 'Whew, what a race! Five thousand just about cooks me. Have you finished filling in these forms yet, Fred?'

'Yes, but you'll have to do the signing,' said the newsagent. 'You're leaving it late, Alf, going over on the Friday afternoon boat.' I was reading that the Granton Hall lot are flying over by special plane on Thursday.'

Alf shrugged.

'I've a week's work to do first,' he said.

'Where are you training this week?' Green asked.

'Where d'you think?' scoffed Alf. 'I'll be out on the road, same as usual.'

Alf slept – on a mattress placed on the draughty floor – under the archway in a railway viaduct where Ike Smith had his welding shop. He was already at work when his employer walked in next morning. Ike was in his grimy overalls and had not stopped to shave.

'Good-afternoon,' growled Alf, sarcastically.

'None of your lip,' muttered Ike. 'Who's boss here?'

'That's easy to answer,' Alf retorted. 'If I was boss you'd soon be out on your blooming ear.'

Ike took this calmly.

'Take the hand-cart along to the City football ground,' he said. 'They're overhauling the heating apparatus, and there are some broken parts to be fetched down here for welding.'

Alf trundled out the battered old hand-cart and went off down the alley. It was a two-miles' trek to the Greystone City football ground.

The gates were opened and Alf pushed the hand-cart up against the stand. After a search he found a door that opened, and muffled thumping led him to the boiler-room. Two men were dismantling the pipes connected to the boiler.

'Ike sent me along for the pieces that want welding,' Alf said.

'You'll have to wait a bit,' was the answer he received. 'We haven't shifted them yet.'

'Suits me,' replied Alf.

Alf went down the passage and came out on to the pitch. It looked strange without any goalposts.

A gleam came into his eyes. Here was a track he had forgotten. A wide cinder path encircled the grass.

'Gosh, this is a bit of luck,' muttered Alf. 'I'm having a go on this.'

Alf tossed off his jacket and took off his boots.

Off he went, padding in his bare feet over the grit. He did a jog and slowed to a walk, another slow jog and a second walk. By the time he had made a complete circuit of the track he was warmed up.

Alf increased his pace and settled down into his racing stride.

When running, he gave the impression that he was butting his way along. His head seemed hunched into his shoulders, and his arm movements looked jerky. Still, it was his natural style and he felt comfortably relaxed.

Alf guessed that the circuit was more than the usual 440 yards. He aimed at lapping a dozen times and kept count.

Ben Sanders, the old groundsman, came out with a spade over his shoulder. He stared at Alf and then shouted as the runner approached.

'I'm waiting for the bust pipes,' Alf called out as he padded past.

Sanders scratched his head.

'That's a funny way of waiting,' he muttered.

Alf was frowning.

'Now I've lost count,' he thought. 'Was I finishing the ninth lap – or starting it? I can't remember. It doesn't matter, I'm feeling fine. I'll keep going till I'm tired.'

It was after mid-day that Ike heard a clanging from the alley. Alf arrived panting and he had to shove hard to get the loaded hand-cart into the shop.

'You've taken your time about it,' Ike complained.

'I bet you haven't been over-working,' retorted Alf. 'I had to wait for my load, anyway, and I'll have to go again to-morrow.'

'Haven't you brought all the stuff?' asked Ike.

'No, it's a big job,' replied Alf. 'I'll be making four or five trips before I've fetched all the bits and pieces away.'

Alf made five trips altogether and each time he lapped the track at least a dozen times and usually more, adding a few more circuits for luck.

On Friday morning, he left Greystone by train for Dover and the boat for Ostend.

The suspicious gendarme

A deck-hand glanced at Alf's face.

Alf's complexion was a sickly green.

The sea was choppy and the cross-channel steamer was making a rocky crossing. Alf was not feeling very good.

'How much more of this is there, mister?' gulped Alf.

'We're about halfway now,' said the sailor.

'Only halfway?' groaned Alf.

'We'll be in Ostend in a couple of hours,' the deck-hand remarked.

'If I'm still alive it'll be a miracle,' muttered Alf, and stared up enviously at an air-liner that flew smoothly over them on the same course.

The steamer docked in the early evening, but it was an hour before all the formalities were completed and Alf found himself on foreign soil.

He was standing on the quay wondering which way to turn, the brown paper parcel containing his running kit under his arm, when a luggage porter in a peaked cap and smock came along.

'I don't suppose you speak a bit of English, mate?' said Alf.

The porter grinned.

'I was four years in ze Pioneer Corps,' he replied.

Alf cheered up at finding a foreigner who could understand him.

'How do I get to Brussels?' he asked.

'Zat is ze way to ze station,' said the porter. 'You must run. Ze boat express for Brussels is about to depart.'

'I'm not going by train, pal,' stated Alf. 'I want the bit of money I've got left for grub. How far's Brussels?'

'It is about eighty miles,' was the answer. 'Why are you going to Brussels?'

'I'm running in the races to-morrow,' replied Alf.

'There is a special coach on ze express for ze athletes,' the porter told him.

'Ay, but they'll have tickets,' said Alf.

He had found a pal, somebody else who regarded being hard-up as the normal state of existence. The porter said he would be knocking off work as soon as the ship was cleared and that he would try to find a lift for Alf on a lorry.

Alf hung about until the porter was ready. He led the way to a small cafe near the docks. Alf said he would like some fish and chips, and was surprised when he got them.

The porter called over a short thick-set man who wore his cap back to front, and who turned out to be the driver of a heavy lorry. The driver said that he was going as far as Ghent, which was on the way to Brussels.

The lorry was a vast vehicle with a trailer. As soon as the lorry started, Alf got in the back and settled down for a nap.

The driver put him down in Ghent. From that big town, Alf tramped out along the road to Brussels. It was a warm, moonlight night and the road stretched out white and dusty ahead.

Every time a car or a lorry came along, Alf turned and held up a thumb hopefully. The good luck he had met with at Ostend was not repeated and none of the vehicles stopped.

He must have walked about four miles when a policeman riding a bicycle appeared.

The bicycle stopped and the policeman challenged Alf in a language that sounded like nothing he had heard in his life before, but which, in fact, was Flemish.

'Try English, mate,' said Alf, but this Belgian policeman did not speak English.

He turned the cycle lamp on Alf and looked him up and down suspiciously. He was a big, fat man with a big moustache.

The policeman was big, but he was quick. His hand shot out and clutched Alf's arm.

'Gosh,' gasped Alf, as he was marched along. 'I've been pinched.'

The gendarme held on to Alf with one hand and pushed the cycle with the other. In this fashion they reached a village, and the police officer steered his prisoner towards a small square stone building.

Evidently of an economical frame of mind, the policeman turned out his cycle lamp before marching Alf into a room with a desk, a chair and a calendar for 1947 hanging on the wall.

Alf was made to turn out his pockets. He put his passport, his return steamer ticket and his competitor's ticket on the desk.

Speech between them was impossible, but he was hoping that the documents would prove that he was up to no harm, and that he would be released. Clouds of suspicion, however, did not clear from Gendarme Roothert's face as he thumbed through the papers. He had found a stranger tramping along the highroad at midnight and, being a man whose suspicions were easily aroused, he was not satisfied by the mere production of documents.

Several minutes passed while the gendarme breathed heavily and re-read each paper. He then pointed to the brown paper package that Alf had under his arm. As the spiked shoes, the running vest with the wolf's head badge, and Alf's pants, were shaken out of the parcel he studied them as if they were the clues in a murder case.

Gendarme Roothert shook his head solemnly. He opened another door and took Alf again by the arm. He led him down a short passage to a cell and pushed him in. The door clanged shut and the policeman turned the key.

The only light was provided by a gas jet that burned in the corridor, but by its light Alf saw that the cell had a bunk and a blanket.

Alf sat on the edge of the bunk and pulled the boots off his aching feet.

'This is better than sleeping under a blooming hedge,' he muttered before he rolled on to the bunk, pulled the blanket over his shoulders and shut his eyes.

Daylight was streaming in through the small, barred window when the rattle of the grille woke Alf up. As he rubbed his eyes, Gendarme Roothert entered the cell. He held a plate on which there was a long roll of bread and a piece of butter. In his other hand was a mug of coffee.

Alf scrambled from the bunk. He pointed at the doorway. The gendarme shook his head emphatically.

'Here, mister, I've got to get to Brussels,' exclaimed Alf. 'You can't keep me shut up in here.'

Gendarme Roothert wasted no words. He walked out, banged the grille and turned the key.

Alf glared through the grille, but food had been brought for him and he was ravenous. He wolfed the bread and butter, washing it down with the hot sweet coffee.

When he had finished every crumb, Alf put on his boots and laced them up. He started to pace up and down the cell like a caged lion. He heard a church clock strike eight o'clock.

Not until nine o'clock did the gendarme reappear. He unlocked the cell. Alf stepped forward eagerly. Roothert waved him back. He had merely come to fetch the plate and mug. Then he noticed the rumpled blanket on the bunk and gestured to his prisoner to fold it neatly.

Alf picked up the blanket and shook it loose. Then, swiftly, unexpectedly, he flung it over the gendarme's head and twisted the ends round his neck.

Roothert tore at the blanket and, mistaking his sense of direction, rushed heavily into the wall. Alf leapt out of the cell. He slammed the grille. The gendarme had left his bunch of keys in the lock and Alf turned the key just as the officer got rid of the blanket.

He roared furiously at Alf and shook at the grille in his fury. His anger increased when he saw his keys taken away.

Alf hurried into the office and shut the door behind him. The desk drawers were locked, but he found the keys to open them. He threw the papers the drawers contained on to the floor till he found his passport and his tickets. His running kit was in a cupboard.

There was a pile of ashes in the grate, and Alf buried the keys in the cinders.

He then went to the outer door and looked out cautiously.

A big dog pulling a milkman's little cart padded past, but, startling as was this sight to Alf, another thing interested him more. The gendarme's bicycle was leaning against the wall.

Alf nipped down the steps, jumped on the cycle and pedalled off. The saddle was too high for him and he had to stand on his toes to make the creaking pedals go round. About a mile from the village the road forked. One arm of the sign-post was inscribed 'Bruxelles.'

A farm-hand leading a horse was approaching. In the hope that he, too, might be a former member of the Free Belgian Army, Alf addressed him.

'Can you tell me the way to Brussels, mate?' he asked.

To Alf's surprise, Bruxelles was apparently Brussels, for the farm-hand pointed down that road.

Secretarial error

Before arriving at the next town on his route, Alf left the cycle against a telegraph pole and hurried along on foot. It was here that he got a lift on a lorry. The driver did not invite him, but by a bit of quick work, Alf managed to jump on to the tail-board. There he squatted for the last twenty kilometres into the capital.

Alf was lucky enough to spot a cafe with the notice, 'The English is spoken here,' in the window. It was then eleven o'clock and he went in and ate a good meal.

He was told in the cafe where to queue for the buses to the stadium. The crush was terrific. If he had not been good at using his elbows he would have been continually pushed to the back, but he managed to get on about the fifth bus that came along. There, wedged in so tightly that there was no need to strap-hang, he travelled to the stadium.

Many gendarmes were on duty. Alf kept out of their way on his way to the entrances. He showed his ticket and was admitted. Before reporting his arrival he had a glimpse of the great bowl, of the fluttering flags and the track.

'Well, I've got here,' muttered Alf. 'It's been a bit rough, but I've made it.'

Interpreters were on duty and one of them told him that he had to see the Competitors' Secretary to receive his number card and instructions. He was shown to an office where the Secretary, Monsieur Raveneau, with the assistance of a large staff of under-secretaries, was dealing with a group of Italian athletes.

Alf's turn came, and Raveneau, an alert, beared man, looked at him inquiringly.

'I'm Alf Tupper,' stated Alf, and showed his tickets. 'I'm running in the Five Thousand Metres.'

Raveneau threw up his hands.

'I am looking for you,' he began.

'Well, I'm here,' grunted Alf.

'I am looking for you as there an error has been in the correspondence,' said the official.

'What?' roared Alf. 'Don't tell me I've come all this way for nothing.'

'Your entry for the Five Thousand Metres made its arrival too late for you to be in the race,' replied Raveneau. 'The number of runners is made up, but you have been put in the Ten Thousand Metres contest. Is that, what you say all right?'

Alf stood silently and stared hard at the secretary. All his experience of distance racing on the track had been in the 5000 metres. All his lapping practice had been for the 5000 metres. Now he was being asked to run in a race of double the distance, a race of nearly six and a quarter miles.

More competitors had come into the office and were waiting impatiently. Alf shrugged.

'I haven't come all this way for nothing, mister. I'll have a go,' he said. 'What's my number? Gosh, I've clicked for thirteen again.'

Alf was handed the big cardboard number and a pin to fasten it on to the back of his vest. He was shown the way to the dressing-rooms.

'I guess I'm a sucker,' he muttered, as he plodded down the corridor. 'If anyone gets messed about, it's always me—'

He stopped. A group of figures in dark red blazers and white flannel trousers had appeared in the passage. The Granton Hall contingent had arrived. In addition to Clem Gatacre in the 5000 metres, they had representatives in the 100 metres, the hurdles and the jumps.

Alf watched which dressing-room they went into. He turned into the one next door.

A stack of programmes was on the table. He took one and sat down. He turned to the 10,000 Metres Race and the first name he spotted in the list of runners was that of Igar Clemmsen, Sweden. Under it came Vestro, Italy; Jacques, France; Hemmal, Luxemburg, and Talon, Belgium. His name was printed in the list and in brackets behind it 'Grande Bretagne.'

Alf shoved the programme into his pocket as a souvenir.

'It'll be poor old Britain blooming well last again,' he grunted. 'Well, I'll finish even supposing I keep 'em waiting till lighting-up time.'

There was time to spare and the bench was padded. Alf took off his boots and lay down for a rest.

Alf had his eyes closed when his name was called out. He blinked and saw that Commander Churcher was standing by the bench.

'I've been surprised to find your name among the competitors in the Ten Thousand Metres Race,' said Churcher. 'Surely your longest race has been the five thousand?'

Alf nodded.

'There's been a mix-up,' he replied.

'Now, for goodness' sake, don't take this personally, but I advise you to withdraw,' said Churcher. 'You haven't a chance, you know, against men like Clemmsen and Hemmal. A tremendous pace will be set and once you're out of the pack you'll be finished, for you'll never catch up. I'll be blunt. It will be bad from the international point of view for the crowd to see a Britisher hopelessly beaten.'

'I've got my number,' Alf said. 'I'm going to run.'

Churcher shook his head angrily, turned round and strode out. But, he had given Alf something to think about. His remark about staying with the pack had caught Alf's attention. He shut his eyes again and thought it over.

Big race thrills

Alf crouched behind the starting line and gazed down the track. The sun blazed down. The terraces were packed. While the long race was occupying the track, jumping events were to continue inside the arena.

Alf was between Clemmsen, who was a dark, hairy fellow, and Vestro, who was light-complexioned. Alf had mixed them up till he had seen their numbers. Clemmsen had run the distance in 32 minutes, and all the others within thirty-three.

Alf knew that the proper way to run a distance race was to rely on one's own pace-judgment and lap accordingly. But, as he had no experience over the 10,000 metres, he determined to have a pace-maker.

'I'll gum myself on to the second man,' he muttered. 'If I can hang on to him I'll be doing all right.'

At the gun, Alf made a good start.

It was Vestro who jumped into the lead. Clemmsen followed closely. Alf tacked himself on to the famous Swede. The others seemed all around him.

The styles differed. Vesto had a short, quick stride, Clemmsen a long, smoothly flowing step. Alf found that he could match his rhythm to that of the Swede.

The track was good but just a trifle looser than it might have been. Alf felt comfortable. He was starting to sweat, but he was fine and relaxed. He knew the pace was a cracker, but the men in front and around him were helping to take him along.

As yet there was no jockeying for positions, but coming round for the twelfth time, Jacques was seized with cramp in a leg and hopped off the track, his face contorted with pain.

A bell clanged to announce that half the race had been run. Alf perked up. He was not feeling done, not by any means.

The high jumping in the middle of the field ended and the loudspeakers boomed that Jack Cade, of Granton Hall, England, had beaten Lemair, France, in the final.

'That's one up for the swanks,' muttered Alf. 'Well, I'm not letting 'em laugh at me.'

Alf pounded along but he was beginning to feel the strain now. Trailing Clemmsen was like trying to keep pace with a steam engine. His legs moved as smoothly and as tirelessly as a pair of pistons.

Alf wondered if he dared ease off, if he could fall back a bit and seek a slight respite from the rapidly mounting strain.

'No, no, I mustn't,' his brain hammered. 'If I start falling back I'm out of the race.

He kept behind Clemmsen, two strides behind him. The crowd's attention was fixed on the race now. Other activities within the ring had ceased.

Alf had lost count of the laps. He did not know how many times he had circled the track. He made himself into a second shadow for Clemmsen and stayed there.

Alf's vest was sticking to him. A bit of grit had got into his right shoe and was grinding into his heel. It hurt him. Every time he went to put his right foot down, he was waiting for the little stab of pain.

He began to think he could not last out. He assured himself that the next lap must be the last, but still the bell did not ring. It would be the next

time then. No, it was not the next – or the next.

The stone in his shoe seemed to be growing bigger, its point sharper. He watched Clemmsen's calves expand and relax, expand and relax, watched them a hundred times, a thousand times it seemed.

Alf's mouth was wide open but he could not suck down enough air. His lungs felt tight. He could feel his heart thumping. He had a funny ringing in his head.

He saw a yellow shirt and it was misty and blurred. Then all he was able to see was Clemmsen's legs. He seemed to have been seeing them all his life.

A bell rang. Moments passed before its meaning reached Alf's brain. They were on the last lap, and it felt as if a knife were jabbing into his foot.

Alf stopped. He grabbed hold of his shoes and hurled them off. He felt the grit under his toes but his foot did not hurt any more. He ran and he hunted Clemmsen. The crowd yelled. The famous Swede was going to the front. He was neck and neck with Vestro, he was in front of Vestro and the runner with the wolf's head badge was on Clemmsen's heels, running in bare feet, running with an ashen face and a head that lolled from side to side like an apple on a twig.

Alf went into a kind of stupor. There was a hazy, ghostly figure in front of him that would not get out of the way. He swerved out, angry because the misty runner blocked his path. Then there was nobody in front of him.

The spectators were on their feet screeching. The runner with the wolf's head was in front, in front of Clemmsen. He was staggering towards the tape just ahead of the Swede.

Alf tottered. A yard from the line he fell on to his knees. On his knees he crawled over the line while above him Clemmsen broke the tape.

The pandemonium was such that a minute passed before the crowd heard the oft-repeated announcement that the race had ended in a tie between

[249]

Clemmsen, Sweden, and Tupper, Great Britain, in 32 minutes 30 seconds.

Alf lay stretched out on the grass. As he gulped for breath, a scowl appeared on his face.

'I was a daft idiot to go and fall over when I had the race in my pocket,' he panted, though experts knew that he just had not another stride left in him.

© D. C. Thomson & Co. Ltd.

At the side of the track, a message was handed to Captain Mercier, of the Brussels Police. It began 'You are to take into custody Alfred Tupper and return him under arrest to—'

With a flourish, Captain Mercier tore up the paper and threw the bits aside. He was not going to arrest a man who had just run the way Alf Tupper had run.

Notes

1 Television watching in Britain only became an everyday occurrence after the IBA charter was granted in 1954. This change was given added impetus by the massive popularization of television culture given by the televising of the Coronation in 1953.

2 They weren't like the visual, comic-strip format of today, but were densely written stories of two or three pages each, that tempted the reader into them through a quarter-page title-sequence.

3 D. W. Winnicott (1971) *Playing and Reality*, London, Tavistock; Penguin edn 1980.

4 See D. Riemer Jones (1987) 'Rereading American literature from a men's studies perspective: some implications', in H. Brod *et al. The Making of Masculinities*, London Allen & Unwin.

5 The whole of this chapter is deeply indebted to Chapter 11 'Gendered television: masculinity', in J. Fiske (1987) *Television Culture*, London, Methuen.

6 A 'centred' reading subject is one who has a fixed, unified positioning by the social framework, that she exists in. Any unsettling contradictions in the reading process are concealed within an imaginary state of unity.

7 C. Belsey (1980) *Critical Practice*, London, Methuen.

8 Fiske, op. cit.

9 L. Mulvey (1975) 'Visual pleasure and narrative cinema', *Screen*, vol. 16, no. 3.

10 G. Orwell (1939) 'Boys' weeklies', in *The Collected Essays, Journalism and Letters of George Orwell: Vol. 1*, Harmondsworth, Penguin.

11 See P. Hoggart (1984) 'Comics and magazines for schoolchildren', in Jane Miller (ed.) *Eccentric Propositions*, London, Routledge & Kegan Paul, 'I hope to show here that the success of popular literature resides at least in part, in the way it incorporates "authentic" elements of working class experience, in its ability to "swallow" the oppositional and the co-operative.'

12 ibid.

13 See A. Easthope (1986) 'Boys will be boys' (on 'Dennis the Menace'), in *What a Man's Gotta Do*, London, Paladin.

14 This is still a common feature of many masculine narratives in popular culture. See the television series, *The A-team* for a clear example of this.

15 For an interesting parallel observation about the culture of working-class girls see A. McRobbie (1987) 'Working-class girls and the culture of femininity', in *Women Take Issue*, London, Hutchinson/Centre for Contemporary Cultural Studies. 'They are both saved by and locked within the culture of femininity.'

16 P. Macherey (1978) *A Theory of Literary Production*, London, Routledge & Kegan Paul.

17 This section on 'Wilson' in the *Wizard* is very much influenced by my reading of Valerie Walkerdine's chapter, 'Some day my prince will come', in A. McRobbie and M. Nava (eds) (1984) *Gender and Generation*, London, Macmillan.

18 See J. Batsleer *et al.* (1985) *Rewriting English*, London, Methuen.

19 R. W. Connell (1985) 'A new man', in *The English Curriculum: Gender*, London, ILEA. English Centre.

20 R. W. Connell (1987) *Gender and Power*, Cambridge, Polity.

21 See Althusser's theory of ideology as interpreted in D. Macdonell (1986) *Theories of Discourse*, Oxford, Basil Blackwell. 'His argument is that we exist as subjects only in ideology. . . subjected and tied to an imaginary identity. That is to say, ideology installs each of us in an *imaginary relation to real relations*' (my emphasis).

22 J. Bruner 'Life as narrative, *Social Research*, vol. 54, no. 1.

CHAPTER 12

Widening the ripples: the value of critical life-history work for men

In this chapter I try and broaden out the implications of this kind of critical life-history approach (using my own autobiography as one possible example that we can all learn from) by exploring its potential relevance and value for other men.

I start by looking at the processes through which I became engrossed in this kind of critical relationship to myself, and how I began to appreciate its importance in my own life. Then I go on to investigate the value to other men in taking up this kind of approach, and the potential snags and blockages that prevent some men from doing this.

The third section shows what is meant by the phrase 'the social and historical construction of masculinity'. It tries to show how a historical awareness of gendered identity (and the importance of this way of thinking about ourselves) is built up through a critical understanding of the institutional, social practices and relations, psychological forces and cultural struggles that have shaped our sense of ourselves. I go on to show how such understandings, if they are linked to actions, can help to emancipate men from imprisoning notions of the unified, innate self that we are all stuck with.

The chapter ends by exploring how critical life-history work can play a valuable part in dismantling those walled-off dimensions in men's lives between public/private, reason/emotion, and masculinity/femininity – the means through which many men hang on to supremacy in their segregated public and political lives.

What critical life-history work has meant to me and how did I get to this present position?

I have been obsessively locked into a traumatizing sense of the past for as long as I can remember. Blockages about childhood, often too painful to really look at, have retained their power to push and pull me around, at an unconscious level. Bottling up my grief over my mother's death, having my 11-plus results doubted and checked out by my father, being reduced to worm-size by the seven years of going to an all-boys' boarding school – all of these childhood events have haunted me to such a degree that I felt a constant sense of being tyrannized by them.

Whenever I met my sisters we would bring out the family photograph albums and the evening would usually end with me wallowing in this treacly, unworked-through hurt, with my eyes often brimming over with tears. It seemed that I was either luxuriating in a compulsively sentimentalized version of the past, or burying that grief even deeper in my exclusions and silences. Paralysed, I seemed to be stuck with a fixed, unbearable past, and my wallowing sunk me, deeper and deeper, into the quagmire.

It's only now, after a long struggle of shifting relations and practices, increased domestic labour, therapy and this process of critical life-history work, that I can begin to say that I'm no longer trapped by that imprisoning past, although there are still blockages and avoidances. But those changes didn't come quickly or easily overnight.

Here, in this chapter, I'd like to focus on the potential value of critical life-history work and the relevance of this kind of activity for other men. What I mean by that term will become clearer, I hope, as the chapter develops. Possibly the best starting point is to explore the personal origins of this approach by sharing that complex process of learning and development that I went through to arrive at this present vantage point.

I've always been drawn to autobiographical, oral-history and documentary work. In my work as an English teacher and educationalist, and in my private life, I was constantly fascinated by personal accounts of growing up, probably because of my own shaky grip on my own sense of self.

[253]

Over the years I noted down and hoarded scraps and fragments of seemingly direct autobiographical moments, and vaguely promised myself that I would do something about them in the future. One list I made was modelled on the 'I remember' form of Joe Brainard:[1]

I remember 'coal mining' down under the sheets in my parents' bed on Saturday mornings and getting nearly suffocated.
I remember saying, 'HMS Vanguard firing a broadside', whenever I let rip a loud fart.
I remember being called 'Parachute pants' by my sisters when they caught me undressing.
I remember asking, 'Will it be dark when I come out of school? Will I have to stay for school dinners? Will I have to take my shoes off for PE?'

The recurring problem with these jottings was that they implied an uncritical acceptance of 'direct, honest experience' that actually prevented me from developing any critical grip on why I had so much emotional investment in certain moments and episodes from my childhood. All that seemed necessary, within the naïvety of an autobiography-as-individual-self-expression approach to experience, was to describe or narrate the truth of what I'd lived through, as strikingly as I could. At that time in my life, emotional fidelity to experience was everything. I seemed to be spontaneously driven towards certain events and happenings that exerted a powerful control over me.

What was missing in my compliance with these drives was any recognition that I was using language, implicitly, as a transparent medium, that I believed it was reflecting, rather than constituting, an innate sense of self which could be expressed through certain selected experiences. As a result, I could never take full charge of my own life, as an adult, because I lacked the alternative tools of critical analysis which might have shown how those apparently 'spontaneous' experiences had been constructed; and how those feelings and events were partly the products of social and historical forces, at a particular time and at a particular place.

Also conventional forms of literary autobiography, like Laurie Lee's *Cider with Rosie*,[2] influenced me to select life-history moments of exotic detail and heightened moments of self-affirmation rather than more awkward, self-critical times that I could learn from, such as the everyday repetitions of social interactions and routines and the daily complexities of intimate relationships. Literary autobiography suggested a narcissistic celebration (often in luscious, theatrical prose) of the frozen, innate workings of a personality, rather than an attempt to learn how to move towards inner and outer change through critical interrogation.

In my public work as a teacher there was a similar direction, but with a slightly different emphasis on 'authentic voice' and the empowering process of learning through talking, writing and publishing, and I was often engaged in oral history/autobiography/documentary work. For example, I worked with comprehensive-school pupils, then later with adults as a coordinator of a local publishing project, Your Own Stuff Press (Nottingham), which later became affiliated to the Federation of Worker Writers and Community Publishers, and was involved in occasional 'living memory' work in WEA groups, a psycho-geriatric day-care centre, a residential home for the blind and a joint community education project where adults participated in the same group as children.

Motivated by other community publishing like Ken Worpole's[3] initiatives in the Centerprise project at Hackney, East London, my public commitment to that kind of work started to have a defined sense of political purpose. It was there to challenge the systematic underrepresentation of working-class voices within the established literary canon, to validate the 'vigour, power and sheer quality of working-class vernacular speech' against 'bourgeois conventions and literary practices',[4] and to encourage working people and school students to involve themselves in the empowering process of controlling the techniques of publishing and printing.

But even this project still took a naive approach to language. Language was still being seen as an unmediated means of expressing an authentic voice or self; and what mattered was the 'communication of true experience'.[5] Yet again it implies an essentialist view of the self, with an authentic core of being just waiting to be truthfully expressed. These unworked-through assumptions about stable, coherent, unified identities prevented these life histories from being seen as shiftingly contradictory and fragmentary, and therefore open to political change.

Because of my own dislocated history of exclusion, displacement and lack of belonging (from being removed from my mother's bed

[255]

through to being a semi-evacuee, having a concealed history of immigration on my father's side, and being a working-class scholarship boy uprooted from his own class), I think I unconsciously tried to borrow some elements of a more 'solid' identity from my distorted representations of the 'authentic voices' of the industrial north of England. I envied and lusted after the rooted integrity and continuing sense of place of some of these working-class people who grew up in terraced streets in the industrial north in the 1920s and 1930s. Despite hardship and poverty, their life-history accounts of tin baths behind the door, mangles in the yard, the old brick copper in the corner of the scullery, the 'beer-off' on the street corner, offered me a compensatory sense of romanticized warmth and completeness[6] that seemed to fill up some of the gaps in me.

However this sense of being nourished was deceptive. Although I wouldn't want to doubt the political importance of the work in the ways that I've indicated above, for me it was a very contradictory experience. In some strange way I used the life-history work of other people to construct a substitute identity for myself. The correct appearance of 'giving voices to worker writers' seemed to lend the fragmentariness of my personal history a shoring-up wholeness and purpose. Perhaps, in some way, I was propping up the unbearable brokenness of my life history through imposing an illusion of rooted stability onto the lives of working-class people, a borrowed coherence that I had partly lost through my social mobility as a working-class scholarship boy.

Even though I frequently used my personal history as a quarry for precise examples for other students to engage with their own life histories, I was still very much the proselytizing teacher with a social mission, expecting the students to grapple with their awkward, emotional stuff rather than also being prepared to look at my own.

In the end, for me, this life-history work didn't become critical because it severed the personal, experiential details from the invisible social structures that partly shaped those details and surrounded them.

Slowly, my sense of personal dislocation and shifting social relations began to mesh with fresh, sometimes bewildering, critical perspectives coming from my reading. Post-structuralist ideas were begining to seep into English studies, and the dominant 'personal growth' model of that field of studies, with its uncritical acceptance of 'experience' and 'personal response', was starting to look a bit shaky. Also, perspectives from feminism, critical theory, history from below (seen in History Workshop's approach), the value of social forms of talking and writing in English studies etc. were creeping in and I was partly resisting them and partly struggling to make sense of them and apply them to my own practice.

The chain of events that really changed my thinking was being a part of a loosely gathered group of comprehensive schools heads of English (about five or six of us) calling ourselves the Nottingham Politics in English group. What really hooked me was a programme of INSET study we put on for ourselves and other teachers of English and cultural studies in the East Midland region investigating the ideological history of English studies.

Without going into specific detail here, the course was nothing less than a critical deconstruction of my personal and professional investment in a particular version of English studies – my commitment to a liberal-humanist/personal-growth model of the subject. Through the weeks of the programme it showed how that version had been historically shaped, and how my habitual practices in the classroom, which I had assumed were my personal invention, were in fact the semi-products of a social and historical construction. 'From the new vantage point of these critical perspectives I began to have a dawning recognition that my professional practice wasn't just the self-determined expression of one, unique, rational individual but was partly made up of common, collective features that I could share and dig deeper into through the help of others who had travelled some of the same routes.

Broadening out the implications of those insights, and gradually relating them to my personal history as well as the history of my working life, I began to develop a critique of an individualized, expressive approach to autobiography. Fleetingly, I saw that the reality of my lived experience couldn't just be accepted at face value. I also understood that the 'common sense' of that personal experience had to be opened up to an informed, critical analysis if I was to move from life-history work through to critical life-history work.

As an inner sense of contradiction deepened within my life between the rapidly crumbling identity of a thrusting, striving

'I', built up through work, and a more vulnerable and emotional 'I', I felt increasingly confused and bewildered as I tried to carry on living between these conflicted versions of myself. I felt precariously suspended, trying to prepare myself for the inevitable crack-up.

This deepening sense of personal crisis provoked a general state of self-reflective stocktaking in which these new methods of critical analysis (taken from the wide range of personal influences associated with a more thorough-going politicization after 1979, a range of critical reading[7] connected with the Politics in English group and undertaking a part-time diploma in an adult education group that was taught on Freirean[8] lines) began to be used by me to make sense of what was going on in my private life.

Slowly the inadequacy of my previous thinking about life-history work became clearer to me. If I was to stop being a willing prisoner of a destructive childhood, then I had to stop thinking in terms of 'unlocking the past', 'taking the lid off the past', or even 'unmasking', as in this book title. That approach implied a fixed, unified identity waiting to be disclosed or uncovered, and which left the circumstances of my life as statically given.

Instead, what mattered now was seeing autobiography as a part of a process of personal and social transformation, where my personal past had to be actively reconstructed, partly through my own active efforts, and also in collaboration with friends.

When the big drop came it convulsed my life. The compulsive pursuing of drives, achievements, targets, performances – all integral parts of straining towards a 'proper', heterosexual, masculine identity, ended up in me collapsing at work, being in hospital for 16 weeks, and having a replacement heart valve and pacemaker implanted in me. I don't want to repeat what I've already said in Chapter 3 but this physical and emotional breakdown gave an urgency to my developing interest in exploring issues about men and masculinity.

For the first time in my life I could feel more fully engaged emotionally in an area of politics. I had a desperate need to look back and try to understand what had happened to me, after a series of upheavals in most areas of my life that had left me all at sea with my old habits, social relations and images of myself as a man.

Previously, I had been thwarted by possessing inadequate methods for life-comprehension work.[9] Now it seemed that the time was right to bring together my new tools of critical analysis with my growing awareness of gender relations, and especially my interest in the construction of masculinity. This process also helped me to reintegrate my personal and public worlds so that I could act to change both. I was no longer using the public world to hide away in, but was able to bring my public face more into contact with my everyday living so that I could apply these new perspectives to a more complete range of social relations.

Through this long process, I had eventually found an adequate autobiographical form that was able to release me from wallowing in a fixed past, through a method of selective reconstruction. But this reconstructive process doesn't pretend to be neutral or value-free. Instead it deliberately sees itself as selective reworking of a personal history, in the light of certain social values. Through this book I have been trying to reconstruct my life history through the selective lens of an anti-patriarchal and anti-capitalist world-view. That's why I've concentrated my critical investigation on those episodes, relations and atmospheric contexts, and forgotten about others, where I have something to say about the shaping influence of the social construction of masculinity and social class (and ethnicity to a much lesser extent) in the complex making of my gendered identity.

The value of critical, oppositional autobiography for me has been the way it has helped me to move towards inner and outer change, along with changing relations and actions. I no longer feel I'm bogged down with a damaging personal history that I can't bear to look at, or paralysed by a crippling sense of individual, personal failings and weaknesses.

What I feel now is a much more charged, active grappling, along with other men, to overturn the taken-for-granted significance of those past events in our lives, so that we can move into a changed world of the future.

What value has this critical life-history process for other men?

During the process of talking about and writing this book, I shared what I was writing with many men. What they all seemed to be saying, in their different responses to what they read, was that the reading encouraged them to look back at their own boyhoods, and in doing so challenged them to break with a 'commonsense' view of their pasts.[10] As one reader wrote in a letter of response to the chapter on violence at school: 'It certainly. . . encouraged me to look back at my own school days in a critical light.'[11]

To my mind, the main value of this critical life-history process and other approaches like it is not found just in the personal stories or the critical commentary, but in the specific way the creative collision between the confessional and the theoretical invites other men, other readers, to interrogate their own pasts. The organization of those dissonant elements seems to unsettle the reader's conventional expectations so that they are provoked to relate what they are reading to their own lives; not in a spirit of celebrating or feasting off a fixed or given past, but in a critical light that invites a conscious break with common sense.

To explain this a bit further, it seems to me that a reader is made willing to reflect critically on her/his own life history because of the reconstructive framing within the book. These discontinuities between story and commentary create breaks, gaps, pondering spaces in the telling, often arising from an antagonistic clash between two totally different discursive anticipations in the reader – the framework of theoretical commentary and the framework of conventional, literary autobiography. A more engaged, questioning participation of the reader in this process is activated by the reader wanting to make sense of these unsettling breaks and gaps by entering a critical dialogue with the writer rather than remaining passively outside the book.

Therefore the reader isn't being offered the comfortable satisfaction of an already known form (conventional literary autobiography), but is being challenged into joining in on a creative collaboration with the writer in exploring a new, cross-over form. Through this collaboration readers are offered a different way of relating to their own over-familiar, habituated pasts.

The only snag with this is that men's willingness to look at themselves in this kind of way is much more uneven, scattered and diverse than I've been making out so far. At the moment I think I can distinguish four main male approaches to the possibility of looking back at the making of their boyhood/manhood in a critical light.

Life story as a resource to make sense of our experience
This is an approach to life-history reconstruction as an ordinary, tacit resource that all people do inside their heads, or share with other people, every day of their lives. Through the human necessity of narrativizing the chaotic flux of experience, we all tailor down the whirl of daily living to a personal size that fits our needs (that is, it obeys our currently dominant self-image and world-view). In doing this we carve out a personal place for ourselves in an already given social framework. We usually don't question the framework. We use life-history stories to find a way of feeling more at home within it.

For this approach to become radicalized would mean that we would have to bring into critical visibility the often bolstering, self-affirming life stories that we tell to each other in pub, workplace, sports ground, home. The process of becoming critical would entail some kind of investigation and remaking of the hidden links between personal experience and the given social framework that those experiences are shaped within, rather than literal, face-value description. A major part of this investigation would be to challenge traditional masculine identities that these stories often celebrate. In shifting the focus on to the construction of our masculinities, in the light of anti-patriarchal/anti-capitalist values, that might also mean a radical decentring of the 'centre-stage' assumptions of conventional masculine identities.

Men who defend themselves against life stories
A hostilely defensive approach to opening up and sharing personal, life stories is shown by those men who suggest, by their actions, that there is a great deal to lose (in terms of their established power and traditional identification) in taking up this kind of approach. So they often adopt a Max Miller[12] way of living, sealing off different parts of their lives in watertight compartments, and keeping their public and private lives cut off from each other.

But it's easy to be too negative here. It's important to recognize that all of these men, whether they want to hide it or not, are also engaged in the daily necessity of making sense of and ordering their lives through life-story narratives inside their heads. There are some crucial life stories, in repressed men's lives, that resolutely refuse to remain buried, surfacing in dreams or unlikely moments. (Think of the men who had been shattered by the experience of trench warfare in the 1914–18 war, and the way that nightmarish memories kept on haunting them in their lives, despite their efforts to keep silent about them.)

Troubling, repressed life stories do have a nasty habit of turning on the men who are trying to bury them for ever, in later life. They insist on being taken seriously when they threaten to crack open the well-protected frontiers between public and private lives. Then the force of internal contradiction can often activate a period of critical reflection. But unless it's supported by other vulnerable, loving men, who might have been through similar crises, it has a tendency to vanish rather than leading to long-term change.

Life stories of displacement as ways of understanding male life crisis

This is an approach to life stories by men who are trying to resolve life crises, sometimes popularly known as the male meno-pause. In some men, the experience of discontinuity and crisis (like separation/divorce, a time in hospital, moving house, becoming unemployed, the death of a loved parent), often in mid-life, can sometimes generate a critical consciousness about what they've lived through. There is often a more deliberate stocktaking, a more careful pondering of key points in their lives 'and, above all, the structuring and re-structuring of experience'.[13]

However it isn't just the experience of discontinuity that prompts men to start changing the way that they live. Indeed, I would suggest that they can go in two possible directions; either in the direction of a reaffirming disjuncture where the old patterns reassert themselves after an initial break, or in the direction of a more radical disjuncture.

Critical life-history work can play a useful part in this process of radical disjuncture in helping some men to deepen their conscious critical reflection on the underlying origins of a life crisis. Marcia's work on identity makes it clear that what really matters at that time is the conscious critical reflection on the 'discrepancy between experiences and expectations',[14] and how that is connected to the cause of the crisis.

As described in Chapter 6, my secret hunger for closeness (expectations) was always in sharp conflict with my predatory sexual approach that was linked to an ego-bolstering emphasis on performance and conquest (the bitter disappointment of the experience not living up to my expectations). That became a radical disjuncture at the point where, provoked by the continuing hollowness of the experience, I was able to apply an anti-sexist analysis to key personal-history stories involving compulsive heterosexual performance. But without the help of adequate methods of critical analysis (in terms of long-term social values and priorities) then the shock of disjuncture won't lead to deep-rooted change.

However, there are also other times when the pain of confronting the stuff we can't talk about is just too much. I can also remember a time when I've felt that no area of my life has been stable enough to offer the background reassurance needed for change. In that context I've defensively avoided learning from the unexpected breaks and shocks of those crisis periods, and no amount of critical life-history work is going to help me to stop clinging on to the safety of the old, familiar patterns.

Life stories as critical interrogation

Autobiography stops being seen as individual self-expression and starts to become a part of personal and social transformation in a critical-interrogation approach to life stories. This often happens at the point where personal experience stops being glorified as the narcissistic triumphs of a single individual and is linked to invisible social networks. Personal and social change start through the daily attempts to grapple with, question and contest assumptions about how men develop in the way that they do.

As a result, this approach doesn't just stop at celebrating men's humanity ('defending men's rights to be human too') through sharing life stories that dignify men's struggles, but, in Gary Kinsman's[15] words, 'deepens the challenge to an interlocked web of oppression: sexism, heterosexism, racism and class exploitation' through interrogating the unconscious assumptions of privilege, authority, confidence and strength embedded in men's stories of how they came to be men.

At the centre of this interrogative approach is a critical deconstruction of how we were historically and socially formed as masculine subjects in a patriarchal/capitalist society, at a particular time, and how that can lead on to conventional masculine relations and identities being changed and reconstructed. Both of these concerns are at the heart of the next section.

Critical life-history work as a way of building an awareness of gendered identity

Personality as a political site of struggle

> personality appears as one of the major sites of history and politics
>
> (Bob Connell)[16]

Ignored by the Left for far too long and trivialized by liberal humanism, personality is at last being recognized as a political arena worth struggling over.

The Left has been too locked into abstract debates to notice the significance of men's longings, anxieties, desires, problems, needs in their personal, everyday lives. Too many men on the Left have been constructing authoritative, correct identities rather than bothering to investigate their everyday behaviour as men critically or the reasons why that behaviour has come about.

On the other hand, liberal-humanist[17] approaches to personality have filled the vacuum left empty by the Left. In its distorting preoccupation with individual self-development and personal growth, liberal humanism has tended to insulate the subject of personality, walling it off from the messy world of history and politics. But questions like the development of personality can never be isolated from the historical and social structures that shape a specific development and within which it exists.

As a result, self, personality or character can no longer be thought of as an elusively slippery entity, mysteriously innate. A politics of identity becomes possible when personality is viewed as the product of a lifetime's relationship to a diverse spread of social practices and power relations within a variety of institutions. And the most accessible way of understanding and getting to grips with that socially produced personality is through the life history.

Therefore, masculine personality or identity isn't just an expression of an innate self but a social construction which we can approach through interrogating the social, psychological and cultural forces that have gone into the making of that identity.

Critical life-history work accepts that it has to start from men's immediate experiences of their life journeys or life maps because

[264]

that's where most men feel most deeply committed to the daily incidents, actions, feelings, relationships that affect their lives. But it doesn't just stay in the personal. It also wants to work critically on the personal details, see where they come from, ask how they are formed, attempt to change them.

'This is what men do, isn't it?'

The major value of critical life-history work is that it encourages men to view their lives without fatalism. The dawning awareness that our masculine identities aren't innate, biologically determined, or merely a result of individual weakness or failure but built up, systematically, through a lifetime's social relations, can energize some men to want to reconstruct their lives actively. It can even open up some men's cramping and guilt-ridden sense of themselves to political choice and possible change.

The problem is that our sense of ourselves has become so naturalized ('This is what men do, isn't it?') that the historical conditions of our own construction have become concealed. Critical life-history work can have a significant part to play in giving us back, layer by layer, a historical and critical genealogy of the precise social practices, relations, psychological and cultural forces that have masculinized us, week after week after week, in the way we are now.

Then later, perhaps, after such a critical deconstruction can come the long and tortuous movement towards reconstruction. The two movements happen more simultaneously than that, though, as, in a way, you can't deconstruct yourself if you have nowhere to go to. So, in practice, it feels like deconstruction within reconstruction.

Psychological forces

What we need is a critical investigation that explores the links between social relations and unconscious patterns of emotional attachment. It is not enough to prioritize the social structures or imply that the 'unconscious' exists outside the web of social power. If it's going to be really useful it has to be more dialectical.

In this book I've tried to explore the psychological foundations of my insecure gender identity. Indeed, without some attempt to connect my present sense of myself to those infantile, unconscious desires and passionate attachments, as well as the complex web of social forces, my account would be very thin and lopsided.

[265]

In the account I give of my close attachment to my mother in Chapter 6, for instance, I have tried to ground the production of my unconscious structures in the concrete wartime conditions of 1940–5. My continuing search for an imaginary intimacy and contact with another woman (worked through at long last) has traceable origins in my mother's wartime isolation, and my early relationship with her of such physical closeness and sensual oneness that I couldn't give her up completely.

Perhaps we now need more work in this area that is informed by feminist psychoanalysis, and particularly its emphasis on object relations theory. We need to acknowledge the importance of the pre-Oedipal mother/son relationship in the psycho-social construction of masculinities and to investigate the Oedipal triangle.

As an example of this from my life history, I was caught between the contradictory tensions of a desire for stability and closeness, on one hand, and a continuing need to go on asserting my independence (often as a way of compensating for my emotional dependence on a woman), on the other. I suspect that many other men are in something of the same position. That's why we need more men acknowledging, in public, the pull of those needs, admitting their contradictoriness, along with a curiosity about where those emotional needs come from.

Lynne Segal has recently drawn attention to these psychological problems associated with exclusive mothering in a sexist society, the 'terrors and pleasures of men's early relations to their mothers', as she puts it.[18] Her view is that an aggressive, masculine psychology, necessary for male domination within capitalism, is produced through the denial of weakness and dependency.

She puts her case like this:

'Developing "masculine" identities through the repression of their infantile dependence upon, and identification with, their mothers, boy children, in this view, grow into men who fear and devalue all they see as "feminine", while expecting permanent servicing from women.'

And again: 'the boy must repress and deny the intimacy, tenderness and dependence of the early symbiotic bond with the mother if he is to assume a "masculine" identity.'

Many more explorations of these issues are now urgently needed if we are to develop our critical understandings of why men act in the ways that they do. And why they go on repeating the same old damaging actions and routines in their everyday relations.

More risk-taking is now needed if, informed by the debate above, men are going to be able to learn something from our life-history accounts. We all need to share more about the psychological and social foundations of our hidden longings, pain, excitement and grief.

Cultural struggles

Masculine identities are produced through cultural and ideological struggles over meaning as well as through social practices and relations. Today, in 1990, it's clear that all those dominant discourses, images and cultural messages about men and masculinity are having a powerful effect on the construction of the way we see ourselves. Films like *Rambo*, television commercials advertising lager and jeans, the messages stuck on the backs of car windows, sporting disasters like Heysel and Hillsborough – all have some effect on the way some men imagine themselves.

My account, based on the period between 1948 and 1950, focuses on boys' comics and adverts like the ones for Shredded Wheat and Charles Atlas and their influence on me. Although I read in an occasional, distanced, ironic way, the comics played a small but significant part in securing my consent to a future gendered organization of labour, and prepared the way for my 'natural' acceptance of a thrusting, obsessive energy and a single-minded determination to win at all costs.

We now need cultural-studies investigations that explicitly address questions about masculinity, cultural practices and identities within specific and historical formations, and these are beginning to come through.

Institutional social practices and relations

Throughout the book I've tried to expose the geological layers of my own formation. Patriarchal power is produced and reproduced through the everyday, institutional practices and routines,[19] like those I experienced, day in, day out, in my primary school between 1945 and 1951. Being lined up separately as boys at the end of morning and afternoon playtimes for six years has an accumulative effect. It isn't dramatic or spectacular enough to be noticed very much but it has an important part to play in

[267]

the social construction of masculinities. Similarly, having separate boys' and girls' playgrounds at primary school, with the boys' one physically elevated over the girls' space, also had a shaping effect on me. And with those social routines went the implicit power relations between masculinity and femininity, each segregated into their own exclusive but unequal spheres.

This daily social shaping went on in the varied social institutions of the family, school, church, peer group, sports club, workplace. Quietly unobtrusive but significant, these practices and norm-enforcing mechanisms went on slowly building a masculine identity, and were reinforced by the joking, bantering, bullying, swearing routines of male bonding that I experienced at boarding school for seven years of my life.

What is now urgently needed are some concrete accounts from men (different in race, class, age, region, able-bodied and disabled), making more publicly visible the specific, institutional conditions and relations of their shaping.

Critical life-history work as a part of the politics of 'subjectivity'

The post-structuralist concept of 'subjectivity'[20] has a greater critical potential for provoking inner and outer change in men than the liberal humanist notion of the innate, essential self. This is because:

(a) It makes visible the social processes that go into the making of masculine identities and the ways men understand their relations to the world. It also helps us to bring under a more conscious control our most intense experiences of being who we are. It also shows how that construction of self informs and organizes our everyday actions and relations etc.

Our masculine sense of selves is historically produced in a series of social practices and power relations within different discursive frameworks. These frameworks offer us subject positions with invitations to take up or turn down and a mode of masculine identity that goes with them. The frameworks also offer certain categories and classificatory systems through which many men are invited and sometimes constrained to think about themselves as men. But all of this sounds overdetermined: in reality, conflict, contestation and contradiction are a part of the subject's relation to a discourse and the relations between different discourses are also open to those kind of struggles as well.

(b) It shows why so many men have so much emotionally invested in 'taking up positions in discourses which confer power and are supportive of our continuity, confirming ourselves as masculine'.[21]

(c) It's impossible in this sexist society to understand the social production of our sense of ourselves without reference to the importance of gender relations and the social meanings given to biological differences in this particular society. This is to stress the complementarity of the masculine/feminine binary system. Indeed, the relations of difference,[22] from the gendered Other, are always implicit in the construction of the gendered self. Therefore many men define themselves in opposition to or in relation to the feminine.

(d) It decentres the thrusting, dominating self of traditional masculinity, and replaces it with the possibility of multiple selves, much more fragmented and contradictory in make-up, being formed within changing conditions, practices, relations and frameworks.

(e) It shows the shaping influence of historical, material and power relations and frameworks of understanding and signification on the building of a masculine sense of identity.

The value of these features of gendered subjectivity, in helping other men to understand the construction of masculine identities critically, is that they open up men's personalities as no longer being strictly 'Private. Keep out!' areas but ones that are more accessible to political change.

In making ourselves politically visible in this way we also often move from a position of individual numbness, where we see our personal problems and dilemmas as the result of personal weakness and neurosis, through to a more political position where we can see that our previous personal failings are in fact socially shaped conflicts and struggles that can be investigated and shared by other men who themselves may be in roughly similar positions and perhaps can learn from them.

Gradually, a new form of politics is emerging around gender relations, sexual orientation and issues of men and masculinities, in particular. It is a politics of identity that grapples for both inner and outer change, at the same time, recognizing that desires and longings are just as important as webs of social power.

It starts by questioning the rationally coherent, humanist self with its illusions of a single, unified, innate form of masculinity. Instead it sees political change not just operating within the outer world but a much more complex and contradictory process, working at many different levels at once in challenging the historical construction of our subjectivities.

Radical psychoanalysis and discourse theory have been valuable in helping us to understand the multi-layered quality of this shaping of subjectivity. The origins of our selective, emotional investments in specific versions of the self within certain, dominant frameworks of meaning (like hierarchical, heterosexual masculinity) have to be looked for in our early patterns of desire, as long as the problems of normalizing those psychological roots of masculinity are acknowledged. That means that these patterns of desire will always be specifically individual, often contradictory and surprising, and always affected by particular, historical conditions.

The other main problem is to try and avoid the individual-society split, and hang on to the individual pattern of desire whilst acknowledging the force of the social at the same time. That's certainly not easy as there is always a tendency to imply a pre-social unconscious structure. The reality is much more linked and interactive.

The difficulty with discourse theory is that it's not very strong on political agency. We aren't always rigidly and statically positioned by dominant frameworks of meaning. Instead, there is a much more resilient interplay between agency and structure. We are offered social legitimacy and safety, as well as power and privilege, in taking up a particular identity, and lured into trimming ourselves down to the fixed slot within the controlling regime. But, in practice, we can, and often do, resist these locked in relations. We refuse to acquiesce through our parodies of heavy images of manliness, changing our everyday practices (like doing more of the childcare or domestic labour), or turning down the invitation to fit in.

Within this new politics, there would have to be a commitment to the varied levels of contestation (transforming institutional practices, challenging dominant frameworks of meaning and re-structuring habitual patterns of desire) by including radical coun-selling and therapy, alongside campaigning and social action, and consciousness-raising groups. What I mean by 'radical' here would be a critical approach to counselling that linked social analysis with clinical practice, so that as well as being enabled to unblock, emotionally, men who are being counselled might be encouraged to confront the naturalized myths of what it is to be a 'real man'.

To clarify all this through a particular example, the discourse of patriarchal power that I was partly positioned within, in the period between 1964 and 1968, in the north of England, offered me the comfortable and privileged position of breadwinner who could wield the law of the father.

I attempted to settle down within these power relations at the start of my relationship with my first wife. But as I describe in Chapter 5, that established web of relations felt like wearing the borrowed clothes of a middle-aged man's navy-blue cardigan. My much more contradictory and ambivalent sense of myself wouldn't allow me to slot easily into the allotted place. So I resisted and tried in a muddled way to turn away from the cosiness and traditional male power of that position. The muddle is still there, but things are gradually getting clearer, and I get the sense that many more men are looking up and wanting to join in the struggle.

Critical life-history work, forms of knowledge and the public arena

the identification of masculinity with rationality undermines the identity of men. The impersonal character of reason makes it hard for us to appropriate a history and culture of masculinity, especially in opposition to the dominant culture.

(Victor Seidler)[23]

One of the ways male supremacy has been able to sustain itself is through establishing a dominant definition of what counts as serious knowledge – a mode of knowing that is detached, rational and falsely objective. It's been able to do this historically

[271]

through segregation, exclusion, having the power to define its own territory, and gaining an official legitimacy for one version of knowing over others.

The public arena (the exclusive realm of rational knowing) has been drawn by men in opposition to the subordinated, private/home world of emotion and personal experience falsely associated with women. These limiting dualisms have contributed to male power in that they have helped men to hang on to privilege by identifying themselves solely with rational knowing within the public realm, at the expense of putting down the private sphere. As a result, the mutilating splits between public and private, masculinity and femininity, reason and emotion have played their part in perpetuating the unequal power relations between men and women.

Victor Seidler has shown how men frequently experience themselves through an inherited 'rationalistic culture of masculinity' that effectively hides their fears of losing power and identity. In public workplaces as diverse as board and committee meetings, trade union gatherings, staff meetings, interviews and conferences, men often protect their interests by keeping knowledge distanced, factual and remote from the emotional contradictoriness of their own personal histories.

Although some men also tell personal anecdotes, often with a great deal of hearty gusto, cynical reductiveness and mocking irony, the superficial appearance of tentativeness is often deceptive. Sometimes it's not a real attempt to make sense of personal experience, or to relate experience to theory in a new way, but often consists of rehearsed stories that don't break with a 'common sense' acceptance of the given social world. Indeed the established hierarchy of knowledge is confirmed by those anecdotes that prove the manhood of the teller or defensively shore up the shaky identity of the speaker. The way it seems to work is that the split between trivial and serious knowledges is reinforced by these sudden movements from the high seriousness of rationality to the light relief of the occasional anecdote.

Many men have a vested interest in maintaining a certain level of abstraction in the public sphere. Their power and privilege in the external world is achieved through detached rationality being accepted as the 'only source of valid, serious knowledge'.[24] This is done through normalizing rational knowing as universal knowledge, so that the equation (rational knowing = human knowing) becomes a popular consensus, organized at the expense of other ways of knowing and women's interests.

Some of the really destructive results of this are many men (and some women), who identify themselves through this patriarchal way of knowing, have the power to ignore and marginalize crucial aspects of our personal experience. Personal knowing, which costs the person something in the telling (in terms of feeling), is either seen as too trivial or self-indulgent and is usually squeezed out. But it's this excluded knowledge that we can often learn most from. Indeed in writing this autobiography it was moments of personal fear, uncertainty, weakness, failure that often provoked me into the most careful pondering: moments like the episode of sexual impotence described in Chapter 6, the moments of intensely personal investment like that describing the influence of my grammar school on my language (especially the moment of failing the 'O' level English Language paper in 1956), and the two bullying episodes in the dormitory described in Chapter 8. These scenes of direct personal experience had the force to unsettle stale habits and call into question the old certainties of my masculine identity.

Another of the negative spin-offs of this male domination of the public sphere, and related ways of knowing, is that it has estranging effects for men as well as women. A single-minded concentration on a rational way of knowing makes many men numb to the full range of their emotional lives. The overemphasis on disembedded, rational knowing, that severs the relationship between personal experience and abstraction, often means that we become used to living from the top of our heads. This is done at the cost of all those hidden longings, hurts, pleasures, desires, pains that make us all so much more complex and contradictory than our public presentations of selves suggest.

Critical life-history work can play a useful part in redefining what counts as valid knowledge in public and political life. It can help to break down the walls between public and private spheres, and the split between reason and emotion in our lives. The defensive impersonality of many men's bland, public faces can be shattered by the emotional urgency of the specific incidents, relations and details of 'learning how we have become the men that we are'.[25]

[273]

New forms of knowing (like men's emotional accounts of growing up into manhood being accepted as important sources of knowledge) are increasingly being recognized in institutional training contexts and in qualitative research projects. Critical life-history work, often referred to as 'life-story' research, offers a way for men to move beyond a safe, rational distancing into the particular emotional commitments of their personal histories. Staff-development training courses (often focused on equal opportunities issues) like the male-awareness training programmes[26] run by John Langford and Tom Richardson in Sheffield regularly use approaches that attempt to do just that:

> It's when they [men] start to look at themselves and how they were brought up that they get in touch with their emotions. Lots of men have lost the emotional, human side to themselves and when they talk about how it has disappeared, it comes as quite a shock.[27]

Similarly, educational courses exploring men and masculinity (often run by the WEA) have also used men's life stories as a preliminary way in to feeling, thinking about and questioning some of these issues. Dave Cooke, in his description[28] of four WEA courses for men on issues of sexism, organized and run through Manchester WEA, says: 'Within each course there was a session which could broadly be called, "Learning to be men". In this we explored formative experiences, our conditioning and what we remembered feeling about this.'

As a way of understanding the emotional realities of men's lives within more academic research projects, and also as a way of getting away from the 'patriarchy of disinterested positivism',[29] life stories are increasingly being used as a method of qualitative investigation. Bob Connell, Norm Radican and Pip Martin have started to use life-story methods in their research project on masculinity in Australia. They write:

> The making of masculinity cannot be understood without taking close account of the patterns of social power, and yet power, in turn, cannot be understood abstractly. It is about relationships, and can only be understood by looking at how men live their lives on a practical day-to-day basis.

Our research has used the collection of personal histories as its basic tool. This approach gives abundant evidence of the social pressures operating in childhood. A boy growing up encounters rules, rituals and symbols that define 'masculinity' in its dominant form. Conforming may not be easy. Adam, now an architect, offers an early memory: 'How a man throws a ball is different to how a woman throws a ball. I didn't want to throw a ball in front of my Dad because I wouldn't look right. It wouldn't be the way a good strong boy would throw it. And once, I remember, I was brave enough to throw it. And he made for me and said I threw it like a girl.'[30]

Some of the same contrasts can be seen in one example from my own experience in the political arena. At the Socialist Conference at Sheffield in June 1989 there was a campaigning-priorities meeting that I attended on health issues. There was a great deal of heated discussion about technical strategies for challenging the recent government White Paper on health, 'Working for Patients'. But we all seemed to be holding our ideas in a detached way, cut off from our daily experiences of going to the doctor and being a patient. Indeed our politics seemed, at some deep level, disconnected from our personal day-to-day needs, experiences and relationships.

I wanted to involve myself actively in the health campaign, not just because of an abstract commitment (although there was certainly a socialist commitment to defending and improving the NHS), but also because of what I felt about my recent experiences in hospital and what I had observed of the social relationships in there. I felt that my feelings, as well as 'correct' political theory, were engaged in this campaign.

About halfway through the meeting the group was acknowledging that, although we had to go on fighting against the introduction of market forces into the running of the health service, the fight had to be broader than that because there were many things wrong with the NHS in its existing form. There was also a need to struggle for long-term socialist priorities in health care. Instead of joining in the political debate at the level of critical overview or practical strategy, I felt that I wanted to share my experience of being a patient in the regional specialist heart hospital.

[275]

I started to talk about my experience of the daily routine and organization of the hospital ward that I was in. As a patient I was surrounded by women workers. But the ironic thing was the worst-paid women (the cleaners and the auxiliary and student nurses) gave me more of their time, speaking in a relaxed way and making me feel more at home, than any of their senior colleagues. In fact, the higher they climbed the seniority ladder the less time they had for you as a person with specific feelings and needs. Instead the ward routine seemed to be organized around the demands of the male consultants, preparing the patients in readiness for their daily rounds.

The consultants' visits were always fussed over by the sisters and the senior nurses, who seemed more concerned with displaying the smooth running of the ward to the consultant than attending to the needs of the patients. There were exceptions to this but generally it seemed to be true.

One particular episode I remember is being asked by one of the senior nurses to get up from the chair where I was reading, put on my dressing gown and lie on the top of my neatly made bed, in readiness for the consultant's visit. The first time she asked me to do this I silently complied, and then had to wait 45 minutes or an hour for him to arrive, half sitting, half lying on my bed.

So the next time she asked me I refused, saying I would go on sitting in my chair and if the consultant wanted to examine me then I could easily get back on to the bed when necessary. After a short wrangle she left me where I was. I refused, not out of heroic defiance, but because I was fed up with being used as a passive dummy to fit in to the men-on-top, pyramidal, social organization of the ward.

After I had spoken up in the health group in the Socialist Conference it seemed to alter, in some minor way, the habitual relations of some members of the group to what constituted political argument. Perhaps it made it more possible to relate these general ideas more closely to personal experience, so that both elements were changed.

Here I'm not arguing that there is no place for discussions solely about political strategy, or that you always have to build theory out of personal experience. What I am saying is that gradually we can learn that the influence of the new social movements (gender, race, disability, the environment, old age, sexual orientation etc.)

on the old Left is not just in terms of its programme, content or agenda, but through the new forms of its political organization, its new forms of knowing, its changing ways of talking to each other, and its fresh relationship between critical argument and personal histories. In this example there is a hint that critical life-history work can play a part in changing the ways we talk to each other in the political arena, and challenging an impersonal approach to politics that goes on implying that it's mainly about a series of removed ideas which pretend that they don't have people inside them.[31]

Critical life-history work starts from this hidden 'knowledge in use',[32] like my hospital experiences, that is often ignored, trivialized or kept buried in men's lives. It argues that there is an urgent need for men's feelings and personal experiences to be the original source from which later theorizing about masculinity can emerge. It views all that threatening, emotional stuff, which we try to deny in ourselves, in a constructive way; it recognizes that the suppressed, emotional contradictoriness can activate the really difficult, awkward questions about our construction that can lead us on to engaging ourselves in personal and social change.

Initially there has to be a period of validating men's personal experiences as a legitimate source of knowledge. Rather than prematurely running for cover within safe generalisations, a preliminary time is needed for building confidence in what men have actually lived through, and learning to trust in whatever feelings those recalled experiences bring up, however dangerous and uncomfortable these may be.

At a later state, the personal experience needs to be placed within a wider network of social power so that those experiences can be critically investigated, rather than accepted, too easily, at face value. It's only then that a continuingly reciprocal movement can be set up between feelings/personal experience and abstraction. But not before we've done justice to the haunting power that personal experience can have in our lives. We need to find time to linger in the odd details of our personal experience (mainly through sharing our life stories), to dwell in them and ponder them together before we are ready to move on to a later stage, a period of critical probing and reflection.

In this way knowledge stops being a disembedded abstraction and becomes a series of more passionate, critical ideas that have had the chance to develop out of the direct experience of our lifetimes. Through this more dialectical and interlocking growth of ideas, men begin to change their relationship to traditional, rational modes of knowing. Admittedly many men need support to stay with the hurt and panic of some of this rediscovered emotion, but if they hang on for long enough they can begin to question knowledge as an external structure that often alienates them in the process of coming to know. As Sheila Rowbotham says: 'I think that each effort of abstraction must be constantly re-examined, criticised, dipped back into experience, merge and be born again.'[33] It's the constant 'dipping back into experience' that helps to prevent our catch-phrases and rhetorical rituals from becoming empty, parrot words.

A clear example of critical ideas developing out of emotional experience is given in Chapter 5. It was from the gradual owning up to sadness as the primary emotion that I felt towards my father, rather than from the rational pressure upon me that I ought to be feeling anger, that made me want to dwell on certain selected experiences from my life history that seemed to sum up some of the lost opportunities for closeness and contact between my father and me.

The experiences of the toy fort, the memory of my father's death and the Christmas party at the fire station all made me want to linger and quietly tease out what these moments had meant to me. The feelings associated with these life-story episodes – loss, rejection, misunderstanding, sadness – puzzled me but eventually led me on to investigate where they came from.

The later critical probing of these feelings of sadness and loss has provoked me into understanding the common features of our insecurities and sense of being half-misfits in a world of conventional masculinity. It has also moved me on to acknowledge our differences as well as trying to make sense of our similar straining to achieve a state of illusory manliness.

These preliminary inquiries have broadened into a more critical awareness of how we've both overcompensated, in our different ways, for fear of unmanliness by playing up our brave faces and stoical strength. So I can now recognize, through the coming together and merging of strong feelings and critical thinking, where that 'strange, sad sense of mutuality' with my father came from. That explicit recognition has helped me to gain some kind

[278]

of critical purchase on my own personal history of denial (the disowning of the emotional and vulnerable parts of my character) and to notice the overlappings and differences between my father's life and my own. The original feeling of sadness has motivated me to follow my father into the most murky crevices and to acknowledge my lost relationship with him. Now I think I can recognize, a little more clearly, that my sadness comes from the undeclared mutuality that I have vaguely sensed about him and that springs from the way we both tried to deny the emotional principle in our lives.

So we see that the critical arguments about men and masculinities, in public and political life, can grow from the personal incidents, relationships and episodes of our life histories. Theory and abstraction are never above those personal histories, but rather an integral part of them.[34] If we are to stand a chance of reconstructing our given masculinities, and changing the social inequalities between men and women, we have to keep on expanding our critical relationship to our contradictory experiences and be more prepared to learn from them in the unlikely contexts of workplace, academic and political worlds. Within this actively self-critical commitment to remake ourselves, and the often oppressive circumstances we exist within, we might be able to break through the protective defences of a rational form of knowing to re-examine what we thought we knew by being dipped and redipped in the felt complexities of our personal histories. Perhaps it's through this kind of personal and political reconstruction that oppositional histories of men's lives will begin to emerge?

Notes

1 See his prose poem collection, *I Remember*, New York, Full Court Press (1975), in which he has captured a great number of snapshot, autobiographical moments all starting with the repeated two words, 'I remember. . .'. (The address of Full Court Press is 249 Bleecker Street, New York, NY 10014, USA.)
2 L. Lee (1959) *Cider with Rosie*, London, Hogarth Press
3 As an example see the collection he co-edited. K. Worpole and D. Morley (1982) *The Republic of Letters*, London, Comedia.
4 G. Gregory (1980) 'Working-class writing: breaking the long silence', *English Magazine*, May/June.

[279]

5 J. Mace (1980) 'Giving voices to worker writers', *Arts Alert*, June.

6 For an example of this see K. Price (1980) *Looking Back: A Nottingham Woman Remembers*, Nottingham, Your Own Stuff Press.

7 Books like T. Eagleton (1983) *Literary Theory: An Introduction*, Oxford Basil Blackwell; C. Belsey (1980) *Critical Practice*, London, Methuen; P. Widdowson (ed.) (1982) *Re-Reading English*, London, Methuen; F. Mulhern (1979) *The Moment of 'Scrutiny'*, London, Verso, S. Hall *et al.* (eds) (1980) *Culture, Media, Language*, London, Hutchinson/Centre for Contemporary Cultural Studies.

8 See P. Freire (1972) *Pedagogy of the Oppressed*, Harmondsworth, Penguin.

9 'And the will, the measureless store of belief in oneself to be able to come to, cleave to, find the form for one's own life comprehensions'. From T. Olsen (1978) *Silences*, London, Virago.

10 'every person must move within his own subjectivity and break with the common sense world he usually takes for granted'. W. Pinar (1975) 'Currere: towards reconceptualisation', in G. McCutcheon (ed.) *Curriculum Theorising*, London, Macmillan.

11 Personal correspondence from David Morgan.

12 Max Miller's wife only discovered that her husband had been dividing his time between her and his mistress when, at his death and the reading of the will, it was revealed that he had left the other woman a considerable amount of money. Max Miller was a famous comedian.

13 'We are impressed, too, with the heightened importance of intro-spection in the mental life of middle-aged persons: the stock-taking, the increased reflection, and above all, the structuring and re-structuring of experience.' From B. Neugarten (1979) 'Adult personality: towards a psychology of the life-cycle', in L. R. Allman and D. T. Jaffe (eds) *Readings in Adult Psychology: Contemporary Perspectives*, New York, Harper & Row.

14 J. E. Marcia (1966) 'Development and validation of ego-identity status', Journal of *Personality and Social Psychology*, no. 3.

15 'The men's movement has reached a turning point. It has to choose whether it is simply a movement for men's rights – defending men's rights to be human too – or whether it will deepen the challenge to an interlocked web of oppression: sexism, heterosexualism, racism and class exploitation.' From G. Kinsman (1987) 'Men loving men: the challenge of gay liberation', in M. Kaufman (ed.) *Beyond Patriarchy*, Toronto, OUP.

16 R. W. Connell (1987) *Gender and Power*, Cambridge, Polity.

17 The contrast I'm trying to make between liberal-humanist approaches and a social-constructionist approach can be made clearer by examining the differences between kinds of life-history workshop used in men's groups and other consciousness-raising activities. The first approach is often called 'life journey' or 'road map'. Here's an example of what I mean, taken from D. Brandes and H. Phillips (1977) *Gamesters' Handbook*, London, Hutchinson:

Road map

Materials   Large sheet of paper per person and pencil or felt tip.

Aims   Self-validation.

Procedure   Each person is asked to make a road map of their life so far, beginning with birth and extending to the present. Each map should somehow show the good places (scenic or open road etc.) or the bad places (bumpy spots etc.), hospital (road works etc.), and barriers, detours and the general direction of their present course. Compare life's past course with your imagined future, i.e. goals etc. How will they be achieved? What has made the good spots?

The other approach calls itself, 'The making of masculinities: life-history work as a way of understanding the personal/political foundations of our masculinities'. Its way of working is as follows: 'For the first half an hour we'll be working in pairs sharing our life histories, and then move back together as a whole group to explore and challenge some of the common features within the making of our masculinities'. Taken from Nottingham Men for Change conference, October 1988.

The difference between the two approaches is really that between a description and an interrogation: the liberal approach, 'Road map' doesn't offer any tools of critical analysis that might later challenge the 'commonsense' assumptions of individual experience; whereas the social-constructionist approach starts from the emotional engagement of people's life-history incidents but, later, attempts to 'view these life history stories from a critical, anti-patriarchal perspective' by introducing 'a social/historical analysis of these narratives and a psycho-analytical account'.

Clearly this social constructionist approach needs time to develop trust in the participants so that they can gradually move into the critical perspectives, where the interaction between personal experience and interrogation is kept up. So we're really talking about a year's course rather than a single session of two hours, within which very little can be achieved.

18   L. Segal (1990) *Slow motion: Changing masculinities, Changing men*, London, Virago.

19   '[The formation of masculinity] comes from an enormously diverse array of social practices. Masculinity, like femininity, is systematically produced throughout a whole lifetime, and for boys, connects with the physical strength built up through competitive sport, the skills acquired through education and the use of tools and other technology, the ideologies of sexual performance, the segregation of the workforce, the experience of family life, and the inescapable weight of cultural image and definitions that ubiquitously enclose us.' L. Segal (1987) *Is the Future Female?*, London, Virago. See also J. Hearn (1987) *The Gender of Oppression*, Brighton, Wheatsheaf, pp. 145–6.

[281]

20 The post-structuralist concept of 'subjectivity' redefines the fixed and essential self of liberal humanism. In this process of reconstruction personal identity is now seen as culturally and socially shaped, constantly shifting according to changing historical conditions and the dominant frameworks of understanding and interpretation it is formed within (like class and gender). See pp. 00–00.

21 See J. Henriques *et al.* (1984) *Changing the Subject*, London, Methuen, especially the introduction to the third section, 'Theorizing subjectivity'.

22 This idea derives from Saussure's theory of the 'sign'. Chris Weedon's interpretation of it is as follows: 'The meaning of signs is not intrinsic but relational. Each sign derives its meaning from its difference from all the other signs in the language chain. It is not anything intrinsic to the signifier 'whore', for example, that gives it its meaning, but rather its difference from other signifiers of womanhood such as 'virgin' and 'mother'. See C. Weedon (1987) *Feminist Practice and Poststructuralist Theory*, Oxford, Basil Blackwell.

23 The whole of this section is deeply indebted to the arguments about men's rational modes of knowing found in V. Seidler (1989) *Rediscovering Masculinity: Reason, Language and Sexuality*, London, Routledge.

24 ibid.

25 ibid.

26 See John Langford and Gary Abraham (1986) 'Male awareness training', *Women and Training News*, no. 24 (autumn).

27 From 'Men on the mat', an article by Maggy Meade-King on male awareness training, *Guardian*, 1 October 1986.

28 D. Cook (1985) *Thinking About Men*, Manchester, WEA North Western District.

29 'Men doing research, learning, teaching, study, theorising and academic discourse about men and masculinity need to subject our own practices to scrutiny. The relationship of researcher to researched, learner to learned, teacher to taught are problematic and need repractising (not just rethinking) in ways that do not reproduce the patriarchy of disinterested positivism.' From D. Ford and J. Hearn (1988) *Studying Men and Masculinity: A Sourcebook of Literature and Materials*, Bradford, Department of Applied Social Studies, University of Bradford.

30 B. Connell, N. Radican and P. Martin (1987) 'The evolving man', *New Internationalist*, September.

31 A good deal of the argument here leans upon S. Rowbotham, L. Segal and H. Wainwright (1979) *Beyond the Fragments: Feminism and the Making of Socialism*, London, Merlin.

32 Sylvia Harvey contrasts official knowledge with knowledge in use in her article (1984) 'Who wants to know and why? Some problems for Documentary in the 80's', from *Ten.8* (60 Holt Street, Aston, Birmingham B7 4BA). She defines knowledge in use as 'knowledge that we use on a daily basis. . . to inform our action and interaction,

our love and hate; it affects our chances of happiness and may determine our chances of survival'.

33 See S. Rowbotham (1979) 'The women's movement and organising for socialism', in Rowbotham, Segal and Wainwright, op. cit.

34 ibid.

Index